Corporate Power and Responsible Capitalism?

For all my colleagues and students at the University of Bath: 1976–2015, who contributed directly and indirectly to the knowledge and ideas that lie behind this book.

Corporate Power and Responsible Capitalism?

Towards Social Accountability

Bryn Jones

Senior Fellow, Department of Social and Policy Sciences, University of Bath, UK

 Edward Elgar
PUBLISHING

Cheltenham, UK • Northampton, MA, USA

Published by
Edward Elgar Publishing Limited
The Lypiatts
15 Lansdown Road
Cheltenham
Glos GL50 2JA
UK

Edward Elgar Publishing, Inc.
William Pratt House
9 Dewey Court
Northampton
Massachusetts 01060
USA

Paperback edition 2016

A catalogue record for this book
is available from the British Library

Library of Congress Control Number: 2014959493

This book is available electronically in the **Elgar**online
Business subject collection
DOI 10.4337/9781784717285

ISBN 978 1 84844 970 1 (cased)
ISBN 978 1 78471 728 5 (eBook)
ISBN 978 1 78643 092 2 (paperback)

Typeset by Columns Design XML Ltd, Reading
Printed in Great Britain by Clays Ltd, St Ives plc

Contents

Acknowledgements

I am grateful to Alex Pettifer and his colleagues at Edward Elgar for their patience in the gestation of this work and for help with its completion. Gratitude also to Dong Hoang and Will Whitefield for sharing their data with me. I must also thank all of the following, who gave valuable advice and criticisms on various drafts of parts of the text: Phil DeSouza, Asa Desouza-Jones, Leah Desouza-Jones, Andrew McCulloch, Rod Morgan, Andrew Pendleton, Andy Rowell, Anthony Waterhouse. Of course I, and the rest of society are responsible for any errors and inaccuracies which remain.

Abbreviations

AES	Alternative Economic Strategy
AGM	Annual General Meeting
BITC	Business in the Community
CEO	Chief Executive Officer
CERES	Coalition for Environmentally Responsible Economies
CME	Coordinated Market Economy
CoC	Codes of Conduct
CORE	Corporate Responsibility Coalition
CSO	Civil society organisation
CSR	Corporate social responsibility
D&D	Downsize and disinvest
EDF	Environmental Defense Fund (USA)
EMO	Environmental movement organisation
EPA	Environmental Protection Agency (USA)
ETI	Ethical Trade Initiative
EU	European Union
FT	Financial Times
FTSE	Financial Times Stock Exchange (plc list)
HMRC	Her Majesty's Revenue and Customs
ID	Industrial district
IFS	Institute for Fiscal Studies
IGO	International governmental organisation
IRI	Istituto per la Ricostruzione Industriale
LME	Liberal Market Economy
LSE	London Stock Exchange
MCC	Mondragon Cooperative Corporation
MNC	Multi-national corporation
MSI	Multi-stakeholder initiative
NAO	National Audit Office
NGO	Non-governmental organisation
NHS	National Health Service (UK)
NWF	National Wildlife Federation
OECD	Organisation for Economic Cooperation and Development
Ofcom	Office of Communications

OFGEM	Office for Gas and Electricity Market
OFWAT	Water Services Regulatory Authority
ONS	Office of National Statistics
PLC	Public Limited Company
PPPs	Public Private Partnerships
R&D	Research and development
R&R	Retain and re-invest
RC	(corporate) remuneration committee
S&P	Standard and Poor's (credit rating agency)
SME	Small and medium-sized enterprise
SMO	Social movement organisation
ST/EM	Share traded/executive managed corporation
SV	Shareholder value
TCA	Transaction cost analysis
TGWU	Transport and General Workers' Union
TNC	Trans-national corporation
TUC	Trades Union Congress
TVA	Tennessee Valley Authority
WTO	World Trade Organization

Prologue

On a tiny planetary speck, in a vast and otherwise lifeless universe, a chance combination of chemical and geo-physical conditions allowed the evolution of creatures which increasingly relied on social organisation as their means of survival. This 'genus' of homo anthropoids continued to perish arbitrarily, sometimes in great numbers. Between one million and half a million years ago, one species in this genus – homo sapiens – developed social institutions to organise the community to control the natural environment for sustenance and against external threats. This social organisation has, so far, enabled homo sapiens, unlike its homo relatives, to transcend biological and environmental threats and protect its infant and physically weaker members. Yet, from time to time, these social institutions seem to over-evolve, becoming divorced from their primary functions of both binding their community's members together and integrating with the natural environment. The excessively intensified powers and autonomous goals of these institutions drove the societies that they originally evolved to serve, into disaster or extinction. Such communities became socially 'top-heavy' and collapsed.

On Rapa Nui (Easter Island) in the Pacific, in the tropical woodlands of Central America and, more diffusely, in the centres of the Roman Empire, castes of warrior and priests brought their societies to economic, social or environmental collapse. To use a concept elaborated throughout this book, in these societies the dominant organisations of the power holders became 'dis-embedded' from the social relationships on which the way of life was founded; and also from the natural environments on which the populations depended. In the past two or three centuries another pattern of dis-integrated power and socio-institutional imbalance has been developing and expanding from its homelands on the Atlantic rim. Age-old cooperative and reciprocal relationships for meeting cultural and economic needs have been replaced by, or converted into, systems of indirect and unequal trade through commodities exchanged for money. During the last century or so, one commodity-mediating organisation has come to predominate.

This business corporation has come to resemble, in its functions and consequences, the environmentally and socially destructive powers of the priestly/kingship castes of the failed civilisations of the past. Like them, the corporation exercises almost unassailable powers. It drives out, or absorbs alternatives. As Naomi Klein has recently warned, in her book *This Changes Everything*, corporate business – through the systems of production and consumption which it propagates and defends – threatens, this time on a planetary scale, to destroy much of the environment on which humanity and other life forms depend. By pursuing their goals and advancing their powers, corporate business institutions may succeed in precipitating the end of this galactically unique phenomenon of sentient life. Depleted and impoverished life might persist in the face of cataclysmic climatic and bio-chemical change. Or planet Earth might even return to the lifeless uniformity of the rest of the universe. Such awesome prospects are neither imminent nor inevitable. However, like the more immediate and human desecration already ensuing, these enormous threats provide compelling reasons for understanding the corporate nemesis better, and for exploring ways to challenge and displace its current dominance. It is with these implications in mind that this book was written and should be read.

Introduction: business – beyond social control?

Plus ça change? The name of Lorenzo the Magnificent, head of the great Medici banking dynasty of Renaissance Italy, still resonates for his artistic patronage and political role in Italian history. His 'magnificence' and munificence came from his family's business innovations. These created a multi-national banking, trading and textile empire which prefigured the subsequent 'modern' corporations of the Atlantic seaboard economies. The Medici enterprise pioneered such business practices as: limited liability ('accomondati') for investing partners; specialist managers for five European regional branches, including London; and managers' remuneration based on their profits. Lorenzo left business dealings to confidantes and those managers in order to further his dynasty's penchant for political power and cultural patronage in Florentine and Italian society.

Alas, then as now, such delegation distorted the whole enterprise. As *de facto* head of an unelected Florentine oligarchy, Lorenzo's response to the inevitable business crisis was to raid state finances. In vain: in 1494, two years after his death, the banking empire was dissolved. The Medici were expelled from Florence and Savonarola's anti-elite revolt, symbolised by the Bonfire of the Vanities, liquidated or sequestered the businesses. The following chapters argue that contemporary society is afflicted by similar over-reach of corporations into political and social aggrandisement. Like the Medici they have broken the social ties which assisted and legitimated their rise. This time, however, the disjunction of investors and stakeholder interests from the executive managers who control business resources, has enabled the managers to wield excess power and influence. Even so, as the rest of this book recounts, today's executives bear a suspicious resemblance to Niccolo Machiavelli's contemporary description of Medici's managers, as behaving more like 'princes' than private individuals (de Roover 1946, p. 79).

In the twenty-first century, business scandals proliferate and business-driven economic crises persist. Corporate power and its abuses pervade political, academic and wider public debates. The topical issue is: how can big business be made more 'responsible'? Across the spectrum,

politicians talk about creating 'responsible capitalism'. A more fundamental, but less voiced question is: what is the source of irresponsible
corporate power? Academics, activists and pundits have written about the
economic power and irresponsibility of large businesses, especially
multinational corporations (MNCs), for nearly a century. However, the
current phenomenon involves a much wider range of corporate influence,
ranging from an expansion of corporations' traditional base in the market
economy, and into politics and the wider society. Concerns about big
business activities span both their immediate economic domains of
competition, customer relations, employment and executive pay, but also
new business roles in politics, the environment, civil rights and social
welfare. Commentators have been right to emphasise the disproportionate, even illegitimate, political power involved here. But this aggrandisement is but one, albeit crucial, aspect of the more general over-reach of
the corporate role.

This book has two main aims: (1) to identify the economic and
socio-political roots of this multi-dimensional escalation, and (2) to
provide a critical analysis of contemporary recipes for containing or
curbing some of this over-reach; particularly those focussing on corporate
responsibility or accountability. Although this case is developed sequen-
tially the chapters are arranged into three more general parts: I, Context
and History; II, Social Embedding and Disembedding of Business
Systems; and III, The Pursuit of Responsible Capitalism: Campaigns and
Recipes. Students and researchers may read these separately or in
appropriate combinations and with the separate Conclusion – which
re-caps the arguments and evidence from each part.

To re-use a popular metaphor, corporate economic power and socio-
political influence is now the 'elephant in the room' of political debate in
Anglophone societies – particularly the UK. Controversies over corporate
tax evasion, pricing of resource essentials such as oil and gas, as well as
outrage at the colossal salaries and bonuses which executives seem to pay
themselves, are mirroring academics' and campaigners' longer-standing
critiques of corporations' institutional powers and prerogatives. The
entire economic miasma besetting Western nations is mired in the
seeming irresponsible autonomy of the banking sector. But banks in
English-speaking, and some other countries, share with many counterparts in manufacturing and service sectors the key feature of critics'
analysis: they are organised as share-financed firms controlled by a
separate category of executive managers and directors, that is, they are
share-traded/executive managed (ST/EM) corporations.

The following analysis culminates in the final two chapters which
assess the policies of the UK's leading political actors for achieving a

responsible capitalism and propose solutions which go beyond politicians' nostrums. This account shows how contemporary mainstream politics recognises the corporate elephant's unpleasant excrescences but averts its eyes from the problem of its outsized presence. The three main political parties do not address the corporate role as a structural problem. Instead they cherry-pick electorally significant cases of malpractice or excess and inter-weave these with prescriptions from two main intellectual paradigms: neo-liberalism and communitarian social responsibility. Chapters 4, 5 and 10 explain and dissect these paradigms and the complementary practices of corporate social responsibility (CSR). All the main parties' solutions are based on different mixes of corporate responsibility methods with accountability through market competition; although Labour and the Liberal Democrats include selective and limited borrowings, from more radical campaigns, to offer more 'transparency'.

Building on other commentators' critiques, the analysis in this book traces the mounting crescendo of business scandals and economic crises in corporatised societies back to the corporations' expedient organisational forms. Chapter 2 describes the basic financial and structural traits which have evolved to become the pillars supporting corporate power. These pillars of the ST/EM form are identified as: its legal personality; limited liability; separation of notional (share) ownership from executive control; multi-divisional organisation; mass production-mass consumption/mass financing complex with its global scale of operations; and, finally, a financialisation ethos aimed at maximising shareholder value. Key aspects of these traits, several of which were originally designed to distribute responsibility and minimise financial risk, have over-expanded the scale and scope of business power. As a result the ST/EM corporation dominates in economic areas of questionable relevance to its legitimate remit; but also socio-politically. It now shapes political governance and is taking over or re-shaping the functions of social institutions such as families and communities. The basis of this over-reach phenomenon derives from the delegated powers and a-social autonomy which corporate structures have bestowed on corporate leaders.

The scale and nature of this intermeshing of corporate interests and political institutions are reviewed in Chapter 1. This conjunction mushroomed first in the USA, where presidents and congressional representatives are now beholden to corporations for election funding and policy legitimation. Reprising the old saying, that what America does today Britain does tomorrow, corporate political influence now also penetrates the governance of the UK (Wilks 2013, pp. 95–146). The present focus is mainly on the evolution of business-society relationships in the United Kingdom; but not only because of the size or significance of the UK's corporate sector. It is the UK's commitment to the neo-liberal privileging of markets and business institutions which makes it a kind of test case of the liberation and promotion of the most obtrusive corporate form: the share financed and executive controlled company. The origins and predominance of this institution in the English-speaking world have led to its designation as the 'Anglo-Saxon model'. This book prefers the less archaic and more precise shorthand label of the share-traded/executive-managed (ST/EM) firm, to differentiate this most typical Anglophone type of big business from other forms which are analysed in Chapter 7.

Seemingly irresponsible social behaviour amongst corporations has been intensified by their increasing emphasis on financial results and mechanisms as measures of success. This 'financialisation' of big business purports particularly to dedicate the corporation to the enhancement of returns to the corporations' investors. Yet this notional primacy of shareholder value has given rise to the paradox of apparently greater power and autonomy of the executive managers, vis-à-vis the investor shareholders (cf Goldstein 2012). This paradox in the dominant trend of the past 30 years is given close scrutiny in several of the succeeding chapters, notably chapters 4, 5 and 10. Financialisation has been carried to such extremes that it has even threatened to displace the conventional ST/EM model itself. Taking corporations into the ownership of private investor groups involves their de-listing from stock exchanges and abandonment of the rules of governance required by the listing authorities. It could be argued that this activity is the logical extreme of the financialisation trend and one which has more salience as an object of analysis for corporate irresponsibility. However this deviant corporate form is beyond the scope of the present analysis. Detailed accounts of the businesses owned by the private equity, sovereign wealth funds and hedge funds involved in this trend are available; see Gospel et al. (2014). In fact, such financially controlled firms still represent a minority type of large business organisation, and the private investors involved often aim to return the purchased firms to stock exchange status after extracting profits and raising the firm's marketable value. Moreover, in terms of potential for reversal of corporate autonomy and over-reach, the conventional ST/EM form, for all its limitations, still provides a basis for improving social accountability.

ST/EM corporations are closely controlled by their executives – supplemented by advisory non-executive or 'outside' directors. In theory the executives are monitored and sanctioned by their shareholders. It is this relationship which, in one form another, is at the heart of the corporate over-reach problem and its mooted solutions. Are shareholder-investors the legal 'owners' of the corporation? Are they the social 'principals' to whom executives act as 'agents', as some economic theories claim? This book follows Wilks (2013, p. 219–21), in taking this system of corporate governance as akin to a political constitution, in which there is an absentee, 'owner' monarch and a permanent regency of executive directors (cf also Gomez and Korine, 2008). Chapter 11 and the Conclusion develop these constitutional analogies but refute the sovereign shareowner thesis: because shareholders, as investors, are merely one category of creditor. Shareholders have financial claims on the value of the corporation but not substantive ownership of all its tangible and intangible properties. The opposite idea is the principal-agent relationship, which is popular with neo-liberal advocates of 'free' markets. Such proponents use this legal-economics thesis to claim managers are financially accountable, as agents, and also to justify top managers' legitimacy and relative autonomy from the corporations' stockholders and wider range of stakeholders. Chapters 4 and 5 pinpoint empirical limitations of this theory, and its neglect of the wider social and historical conditions which produced and sustain the contradictory investor-executive relationship; along with the ways in which it privileges investors. The alternative assumption used here, is that society rather than the shareholder/investor, should be regarded as the 'principal' – the absent monarch. For it was society, in the form of the sovereign state, which originally ceded corporations' and managers' rights.

For readers who have not been monitoring reports of corporate crises, controversies and current affairs scandals, Chapter 1 provides an indicative review of the scale and nature of the problems stemming from corporate power and over-reach. That chapter classifies and updates a raft of illustrative cases and commentaries like those described in several publications in the rising tide of corporate-critical literature (Bakan 2004; Hertz 2001; Klein 2000; Korten 1995; May 2006; Mayer 2013; Monbiot 2000; Monks 2007; Sklair 2002; Wilks 2013). Although this stream of critiques began with 'outsider' polemicists and civil society activists, its theme of excessive corporate power has now become a central concern of mainstream academics and even business 'insiders'. Chapter 2, and the historical account in Chapter 3, show how corporations became too big for their institutional boots.

Following Karl Polanyi, I argue that ST/EM firms have outgrown and threaten to dominate, envelop and even undermine, some of the social and political institutions on which a sustainable market economy depends. Any rebalancing of the relationship between corporations and the rest of society must therefore interrogate the nature of the relationship between market organisations, such as firms, and the social institutions to which they are linked. These issues require consideration of theoretical perspectives, particularly as the business-society relationship, and its stability and conflicts, have been central to the sociological canon, encompassing Marxian, Weberian and Durkheimian schools. More recently, analysts of corporate globalisation and business power have drawn inspiration from a revival of Karl Polanyi's theory of 'economic embeddedness', which has given these classical ideas a fresh perspective (Block and Polanyi 2003; Cutler 2006; Dhir 2012; Haufler 2006; Jessop 2001; Munck 2002; Wilks 2013, pp. 15, 172). The Polanyian perspective has become popular amongst academics because it stresses the negative social and economic consequences of detaching market institutions from their social and cultural roots. Its appeal is enhanced by the 'social embedding' it proposes for a return to a more sustainable market economy. Thus social embeddedness theory can be used to identify how corporate structures and roles might be reformed to reduce excessive powers and increase their social accountability. Chapter 6 explains and explores this significance of Polanyi's ideas.

Polanyi identified the last great re-embedding with the social democratic period arising from the Depression and Second World War conjuncture. Because social democratic regimes sought state control of corporations as nationalised or publicly owned enterprises, these approaches are often regarded as the most appropriate form of social embeddedness. Chapter 3 describes and evaluates this approach to business accountability by re-examining the successes and limitations of collective ownership through 'nationalised' businesses in twentieth century Britain. However, as various authors have pointed out, Polanyi himself considered a variety of socialistic forms of re-embedding as desirable and was not necessarily wedded to the social democratic model (Block 2003, p. 298; Jessop 2001, p. 222; Skonicki 2008). Accordingly, Chapter 7 assesses business systems that are more embedded, through different institutional structures, in their respective societies than the Anglo, neo-liberalised corporation has been.

Neo-Polanyian analysis tends to see currently dominant neo-liberal economic orthodoxy as being the driving force for, and synonymous with, the disembedding of economic institutions from the wider society. However, it can be argued that neo-liberalism has indirectly spawned two sets of institutions which could be regarded as forms of re-embedding. One complex is the regulatory systems which, at least in the UK, have been set up to protect market participants – customers, investors and the public purse – from the potentially monopolistic powers of big corporations. Chapter 4 subjects this kind of claim to critical analysis, examining the recent scope and efficacy of the neo-liberal business order which, from the 1980s onwards, replaced social democracy's regime of state-owned and controlled industries. The second candidate for a new social re-embedding of corporations' enlarged and dominating power comes from diverse campaigns and advocacy for corporate 'social responsibility'. Some of these movements – ranging from intra-business pressure groups to oppositional NGOs and social movement campaigns – still oppose corporations' wider powers. However, many of these also have, as a common thread, a claim that big business is being, or can be, 're-moralised' (cf Holzer 2010).

The scope and impact of this variegated movement, variously described as communitarianism, corporate social responsibility (CSR), corporate citizenship, or stakeholder engagement, is analysed in chapters 8, 9 and 10. These chapters examine the broad sweep and logic of the movement and then a number of critical cases which reveal the narrow limits of any such re-moralisation: despite some particular benefits for communities and the wider civil society, CSR is ultimately limited by the political-economic context. These limits are mainly the financialised markets of the neo-liberal world order and the corporation's current institutional and legal structures. It is these conditions which narrow and prevent opportunities for wider accountability.

What then of those business systems beyond the Anglo-Saxon world? Do these more socially embedded institutions constitute alternatives to, or reform paths for the ST/EM corporate system? Neo-liberal perspectives often claim that the ST/EM corporate model dominates world trade and international stock exchanges. They can also claim that it is the business form most respected by international economic authorities such as the WTO and IMF. However, equally effective forms of business organisation have succeeded, in other parts of the world. The Japanese industrial corporation mounted a severe competitive challenge to western industrial corporations in the last decades of the twentieth century. Macro-economic developments, together with defects in Japan's domestic economy, have partly diminished this threat. However, Chapter 7 shows that the spread of free market policies has not converted the Japanese corporation, or the equally distinctive German (or 'Rhenish') business system, into variants of the ST/EM model. More striking is the continued success of the German system since the onset of the current recession, which seems to have caused more damage to firms in the Anglo-Saxon neo-liberal sphere. As that chapter explains, Germany can still be touted as proof of the stabilising effect on corporate economic practices of socially embedded governance. Other relevant and possible alternatives to ST/EM dominance considered in that chapter are the state-coordinated East Asian (for example Chinese) forms, the industrial district model –

still particularly pronounced in Italy – and the intriguing complex of cooperatives, known as Mondragon, in Spain. The latter type of alternatives to the corporate system – 'self-organization among mutually interdependent actors' – were also identified as possible forms of social embedding by Polanyi (Jessop 2001, p. 218).

These counter-examples of business organisation suggest social embeddedness can take forms which are far removed from, and even antipathetic to, the emphasis on social-democratic controls which some of his followers associate with Polanyi. The key question is whether the ST/EM corporation can be re-embedded in more socially accountable ways than the unfashionable social democratic and dysfunctional neoliberal systems. In the final chapters the various attempts and prescriptions for achieving such conditions in the UK are brought together and analysed in relation to both historical and contemporary alternatives. That analysis contrasts the limited reforms currently advocated by the main political parties with those of more radical reformers, especially in relation to accountability and ways to democratise corporate power. The final two chapters assess which traits are most critical for maintaining corporate power and which reforms or transformations might remove or disarm them. Polanyi's thesis, that social democracy/socialism is the most viable form of re-embedding, derives from his belief in 'the tendency inherent in an industrial civilisation to transcend the self-regulating market by consciously subordinating it to a democratic society' (Polanyi 1944, p. 234). Re-appraising this claim, these chapters assess which forms of democratic accountability might re-embed corporate autonomy for a post-socialist and, perhaps, a post-neoliberal age.

This final focus on the ownership-control separation and its governance, as the key institutional element for reform concludes by considering ways to remove disruptive investors from the ownership and control of the business. It draws on the examples of relative success of some mutual and 'para-mutual' enterprises, like the re-organised Welsh Water plc. For the majority of stock exchange companies, however, it recommends a variant of the Swedish system of executive accountability. This approach could adapt more easily to the UK than some other overseas models allowing both non-speculative shareholders and 'stakeholder' groups, such as unions, local government, community groups and NGOs, some control over executive managers' appointments and remuneration processes. Such processes would be independent of the executive directors who manage the operations of the business as a whole. Over time the character of the company boards could reflect more accurately the interests and values of long-term shareholders and stakeholder groups. Because these groups would be drawn from wider social spheres than the corporate-financial, but would still be linked to them, accountable forms of social embedding could be achieved. By such reforms we could embark on the road to demoting the managerial regents and restoring society's sovereignty over the corporation.

PART I

Context and history

1. A climacteric of corporate crisis and over-reach

INTRODUCTION

In 1983 the directors of a middling English, top-tier football club, Tottenham Hotspur, scented the wind of market forces stirred by Thatcherite economics. They converted the club's status into a public limited company (plc). By the attendant listing on the London Stock Exchange (LSE) they aimed to bring in millions of pounds from a share issue. This income could be used to 'buy' expensive, quality players to give the team a competitive edge in fighting for trophies. The scheme succeeded in attracting some new capital, but not for winning many trophies. By 1999 twenty top clubs in professional English football had become plcs. The collapse of the international investment bubble in 2000, and clubs' inability to convert massive TV incomes into consistent share dividends, diminished the attractiveness of corporate status. Most clubs subsequently 'de-listed' but their removal into the sphere of big business was irreversible. Many became private businesses bought and owned by rich benefactors, speculators or overseas corporations. Some, like Manchester United, continued listing to exploit their international brand recognition and tap more overseas investors. As of 2014 Manchester United was listed on the New York stock exchange (NYSE) had an income of £420 million, operating costs of £373 million and debts of £350 million. Directors were exultant about selling the brand to mass audiences in North America and more shares to investors on the NYSE (*Guardian* 2014).

Yet in the opinion of business professor (and Everton FC supporter) Tom Cannon, formerly of Manchester Business School and the City of London's Gresham College, the corporate model is totally unsuited to the running of football clubs. Many United and other fans no doubt share this opinion as they have witnessed profits accumulate but match ticket prices escalate and, in many cases, playing fortunes deteriorate. Football and sports are not alone in being taken over by the corporate model and its ethos. Plcs or their executive management systems have taken over swathes of public and social activities throughout Britain. In the terminology of the German sociologist Jurgen Habermas, they have colonised the lifeworld. The significance of this penetration was recognised by a former French economy minister. Arnaud Montebourg alleged that internet giants such as Facebook and Amazon had made databases usable for almost tax-free commercial gain and exploitation by US intelligence experts. A German minister, Sigmar Gabriel, wrote:

> Every ... 'search' for something on Google ... captures information about ourselves which can not only be sold for targeted personalised advertising, but is, essentially, also available to our bank, our health insurance company, our car or life insurance company, or – if the need arises – to the secret service. (Garside 2014)

Even allowing for some political hyperbole, such dominance indicates corporate over-reach; an excess manifested in the increased frequency and range of big business scandals and crises.

The tide of corporate over-reach actually intensified after 2007, with the wider economic depression – which can itself be attributed to the irresponsibility of the corporate sector's financial wing. The tsunami of corporate crisis spans its own economic domain, as well as environmental, political, civil rights and social welfare spheres. Irresponsibility and financial mendacity on corporations' own turf are a glaring aspect of broader corporate over-reach: the power to exploit position for advantage. It is chiefly this economic aspect that has provoked various segments of the political class into prescriptive critiques and even business representatives themselves to call for more integrity and responsibility. Thus, John Cridland, the Director-General of the Confederation of British Industry, identifies a public rejection of corporate 'poor performance and perceived excess'. Yet he recommends as solutions only 'more transparency' by each firm ('produce an A4 page of narrative to explain exactly what [tax] it's paying', Heath and Fournier 2013), plus competition and closer identification with 'the customer' (*Guardian* 2013b). Financial editor and policy adviser Martin Wolf is more specific. He assesses the corporation as 'the core institution of contemporary capitalism ... a brilliant social invention', but with 'inherent failings':

> the most important of which are that companies are not effectively owned. That makes them vulnerable to looting. Incentives allegedly provided to align the interests of top employees with those of shareholders, such as share options, create incentives to manipulate corporate earnings ... Shareholder control is too often an illusion and shareholder value maximisation a snare, or worse. (Wolf 2012)

For remedies, Wolf alludes to: 'other forms of ownership, including partnerships and mutual … genuinely independent, diverse and well-informed boards', 'pay packages [that] are transparent' and removal of 'destructive forms of remuneration'. But he concludes that 'governments should not intervene directly'. The political parties are more dramatic in their diagnoses, but hardly more radical in their prescriptions. Wolf's ownership flaw is a conundrum that has been at the centre of much academic research in corporate power and societal subordination. It is outlined in broad terms in chapter 2 and probed for its relevance to corporate reform in the final two chapters.

The present work links this and other key pillars of corporate power to critical areas of corporate over-reach beyond their market remits and beyond the economic domain altogether, into the spheres of politics and social relationships. However, a preliminary idea of the scale of the problem can be gleaned from considering just the environmental, international social and financial problems created by corporate over-reach. Repeated environmental disasters are particularly notorious hallmarks of corporate over-reach. This history includes emblematic flashpoints such as: the Union Carbide (now Dow Chemicals) explosion at Bhopal, India in 1985; the BP oil-rig explosion in the Gulf of Mexico in 2012; and persistent abuse in, often illegal, deforestation of tropical rainforests – driven by logging for hardwoods, and major western food corporations' demand for cattle pasture and palm oil plantations.

Persistent social and political controversies have included a saga from the 1980s over Nestlé's infant milk substitute in developing societies; continuing fallout from the persecution of Ogoni protestors against Shell's Nigerian oilfields since 1987 (Rowell et al. 2005, p. 83–84); and exploitation and human rights abuses amongst Western multinationals' supply chains in the global South. Long-standing supply chain scandals culminated horrifically in the inadequate monitoring, by brands such as Primark, Matalan and Benetton, of the Dhaka factory which collapsed in Bangladesh (with 1,100 deaths) in April 2013. The more insidious financial crises have ranged from fraud and collapse in multinational banks, the 2001–02 accounting frauds at Enron, Tyco and WorldComm in the USA; through bribery cases involving UK weapons and aerospace contractors BAe (2006/7) and Rolls Royce (2013); plus allegations of price-fixing by energy companies such as Shell and BP in 2012. Banking corporations' malpractices have become major political crises: price-fixing of the LIBOR inter-bank lending rates in 2012, illicit lending and investment practices since the millennium precipitating bank collapses, the crash of the global financial system and international economic recession from 2008. Yet executives continue to receive exorbitant salaries and bonuses, even in unprofitable corporations. More fundamentally, the fiscal crisis resulting from the financial crash has generated swingeing welfare cuts in developed economies. Yet excess public debt is caused, at least partly, by tax avoidance by a host of multi-national corporations (MNCs), including Amazon, Boots, Google, Starbucks, Topshop, and Vodafone in 2013.

Space constraints prevent a more comprehensive account of corporate misdemeanours but bear in mind also the cases of: illegal information gathering by news corporations (see the 2012 UK Leveson Inquiry), mis-sold financial products, and illegal meat foods and so on. Since this book went to press others will certainly have occurred. Twenty years ago such patterns might be attributed to a 'few rotten apples', or a rash of 'swindlers', 'looters', or 'predators' deviating from normal standards to take advantage of relatively free markets and lenient regulation (Bakan 2004, p. 1). Now it seems more plausible to see wayward power and autonomy as a systemic problem, which stems from the nature of the corporate institution itself. Concentrations of power and massive finances are, of course, always likely to generate frauds, misdemeanours and catastrophes. However, the frequency and range of scandals, executive self-interest and abuse, seem more consistent with inherent faults. The grand scale of malfeasance can be traced back to a common source: the expanded scale of corporate activity tantamount to a monopoly of power, not just in the economy but throughout society. Scholars describe this capacity as: instrumental power – ability to realise a specific interest or advantage, structural power – limitation of politicians' capabilities by dependence on business consent or agendas, and, finally, discursive power – ability to define the ideas and terms in which issues are addressed and debated (cf Fuchs 2007, pp. 56–63). The rest of this chapter maps the contours of these powers through their economic and political dimensions, firstly in general terms and then with reference to the specifics of the UK polity and society.

1. ECONOMIC AND SOCIO-POLITICAL HEGEMONY

I begin my Corporate Power course at the University of Bath by asking students to log the corporate products and services they have used or encountered in the past 24 hours. The usual lists amount to between 30 and 60 competing or complementary products and brands, from toiletries through foods to phones and financial services, ending with entertainment, such as sports and television. Three or four giant corporations usually figure in each consumption category, from Starbucks to

Sainsburys, Levis to Lynx, or Microsoft to Manchester United. It only takes students a few minutes to recollect about 16 aspects of their daily lives that depend upon corporate products and brands; and these are relatively low spending students. In higher spending demographics corporate penetration of daily life, with dependence on their products and services, is probably much greater. From that first sip of corporate water in the morning to switching off the energy-oligopoly lighting before sleep, corporate products and services permeate and structure our daily lives. This 'colonisation of the lifeworld' in Habermas's apt metaphor (Habermas 1981), is the visible tip of an iceberg of socio-economic dominance and political hegemony spanning social institutions and civic life. Corporate dominance stems from economic power over social life and its institutions; but, in turn, these businesses' exceptional legal and political privileges extend and consolidate that supremacy.

1.1 Economic Scale

MNCs make up 70 per cent of the world's foreign trade total of US \$7 trillion (UNCTAD). In the USA the top 500 industrial corporations control 'over two-thirds of the business resources … and collect over 70 per cent of all US profits (Share the World's Resources 2007; OECD 2013a). The internet was originally a publicly organised but semi-spontaneous, even anarchic, realm of individual self-expression. But it has since become a vivid illustration of the expanded scope of the corporate world. The migration of commerce, personal communications, entertainment, information gathering and sharing to the internet represents a major slice of the corporate colonisation of social and personal life. In the past couple of decades, both the operation of web services and their content have become more closely guarded spheres of corporate influence, control and market exploitation (Consalvo 2003; Dahlberg 2004).

It has been claimed that online, social media offer considerable scope for civil society actors and protesters to mobilise, organise and campaign against political overlords and corporate power itself. However, this argument tends to overlook the fact that these online arenas are now provided and facilitated by the giant internet corporations. They can limit and, in conforming to governmental diktats, have limited the scope of popular dissent and protest. Moreover, in pursuit of other commercial gains, big businesses have begun to shape social media participation to their own ends, as the allegations against Google, Amazon and Facebook in the Introduction indicate. Marketing advisers have gleaned from the most active business users of online communications that:

... social media-based conversations occurring between consumers are outside managers' direct control. This stands in contrast to the traditional integrated marketing communications paradigm whereby a high degree of control is present. Therefore, managers must learn to shape consumer discussions in a manner that is consistent with the organization's mission and performance goals. (Mangold and Faulds 2009, p. 357)

These and other corporate practices have been induced by the increasing dominance of the mega corporations, such as Microsoft and Google, as the industry has become more concentrated (Shah 2009). More general corporate levels of concentration are reflected in international trade. By 2007 there were 43,060 transnational corporations, as compared to 7,000 in 1969 when concern at their growth was first expressed (cf Vernon 1971, 1977; Tugenhadt 1973). But even within the multinational domain there has since been concentration. In 2009 20 per cent of global revenues were owned by just 1,318 of those 43,060 MNCs, and through shareholdings they owned most of a further 60 per cent of global revenues. A mere 147 companies form a 'super entity' controlling 40 per cent of the wealth of this elite group of 1,318. All own part or all of one another (Vitali et al. 2011). To illustrate their financial power, critiques of corporate status usually make invidious comparisons of their wealth and incomes with those of sovereign nation states, as in Table 1.1.

Admittedly, statistical comparisons of corporate and state economies, based on their sales revenues and GDPs respectively, risk conflating two different measures: essentially the (lower) value added in national economies with the (higher) transactions incomes of businesses. Grahame Thompson has shown that this conflation artificially magnifies the relative size of the corporate economies vis-à-vis the national ones (Thompson 2003, p. 407). Perhaps what matters more is the capacity to use such resources and the scope of their use. In other words: the freedom to spend their gains on things which achieve major outcomes. States seem to have substantial freedom of choice in their spending: on welfare, warfare or widgets. Corporations' priorities, on the other hand, are relatively fixed: wage bills, production, creditors and shareholders. Contrarily, some states are highly constrained by their constitutions, electoral protocols or – increasingly – their own indebtedness. Yet some firms have achieved such economic hegemony that their fiscal autonomy is restricted only by the limited concerns of their shareholders. In the end this is an empirical question for different states and companies, beyond the present study. However, even if caveats such as Thompson's are accepted, the relative potency of corporate resources is still formidable.

Table 1.1   Comparison of nations' GDP with corporate revenues, 2010

Company/Country	Revenues/GDP ($ billions)
Norway	414
Wal-Mart Stores	408
South Africa	364
Greece	305
Exxon Mobil	285
Chevron	164
Romania	162
General Electric	157
Peru	154
Bank of America Corp	150
ConocoPhilips	140
Ukraine	138
AT&T	123
Ford Motor	118
J.P. Morgan Chase & Co	116
Hewlett-Packard	115
Berkshire Hathaway	112
Bangladesh	112
Citigroup	109
Verizon Communications	108
McKesson	107
General Motors	105
Vietnam	104
Tesco (2011)	60
Sri Lanka	59

Source: www.globalpolicy.org/images/pdfs/Comparison_of_Corporations_with_GDP_of_Countries_table.pdf

At the peaks of these corporate Himalayas the really big corporations, such as Apple, Walmart and Exxon-Mobil in the USA, or the UK based Tesco, Shell or HSBC, have both size and the financial clout to exert major influence not only in their market sectors, but also in civil society and public spheres. Apple's financial wealth of $76.4bn in 2011, as measured by cash balances, was greater than that of the entire US government (Investment Week 2011). Although this was a temporary situation, Apple still has enormous cash reserves for diverse investments. It 'shelters' its profits overseas, beyond the reach of US tax authorities, and these can then be invested worldwide. Ironically, 'it holds $21bn of US government debt – a vast sum for a single private investor' (*Guardian* 2012b). This holding is more than Malaysia's $19bn and only $4bn less than Spain's entire investment in US debt. The US's Walmart retailer and the UK's Tesco have sales revenues of $444 billion and $113 billion respectively (Institute for Global Labour and Human Rights, 2012).These sums compare favourably with the UK government's total income tax revenue of £152/$246 billion (National Statistics dataset – HM Revenue and Customs receipts) in the same year.

Masses of individuals depend on such firms for employment. Numbers vary by the products and services sold, but the biggest MNCs command vast armies of workers. Walmart's 2.2 million labour force is exceeded only by the numbers serving the US Defence Department (3.2 million) and the Chinese Red Army (2.3 million). Not far behind is McDonalds 1.7 million (*Economist* 2011) with the UK-based G4S marshalling 620,000 worldwide. A different type of corporate entity, Foxconn (also known as Hon Hai Precision Industry Co Ltd) has been estimated to employ around 1.2 million. Intriguingly, this Taiwanese firm has no significant public face in the West. It concentrates on manufacturing about 40 per cent of the content of the world's popular electronic consumer goods, like smart phones and portable computing devices. The lack of visibility of this concealed hinterland of Western brand corporations is reflected in the fact that Foxconn's employment figures are also estimates. Yet many of these workers are a kind of surrogate labour force for western MNCs as their labour is devoted mainly to the manufacture of Apple products. Indeed campaigners have forced the US corporation to take some tacit responsibility for exploitative working conditions (Guglielmo 2013). The sales and marketing reach of MNCs is now becoming almost global, extending to some of the most remote communities on the plant. By a clever alliance with NGOs and rural self-help groups, Unilever, the world's largest producer-supplier of hygiene and personal care goods, has extended its sales into the 70 per cent of India's one billion people who reside in rural villages accessible only by dirt roads, motorcycles or bullock cart (Rangan and Rajan 2007).

1.2 Political Influence

Such market power justifies widespread concern about competition, consumer dependence and labour rights. But international, often global, economic strength also seems to translate into – and partly derive from – power or influence in the political sphere. The international spread of a neo-liberal market system, following the so-called Washington Consensus and based on the Plaza Accords of 1985, strengthened the influence of corporations, especially financial ones, within international economic governance. The establishment of the open-market World Trade Organization (WTO) in 1994 through 'the twin drives of managing the trade rivalry among the leading industrial countries and containing the threat posed by the South to the prevailing global economic structure', effectively enshrined openness to MNC trade (Bello, n.d.). By pressuring the national governments which make up the WTO membership, MNCs were able to help shape its overall framework of 'equal' trade treatment and were given opportunities for lobbying for specific measures and cases (Jones 2004; Sell 1999).

Following this Washington Consensus on open markets and tariff reductions, plus the rise of neo-liberal ideology and policy, the current international trade system secured special advantages for corporations in governance institutions such as the WTO. By increasingly 'offshoring' operations to countries with weak or indifferent regulatory powers, MNCs have effectively insulated themselves from the potentially tougher rules of the states in which they originate (Cutler 2006, p. 207). On wider concerns, such as environmental policies, coalitions of MNCs have proven effective adversaries in forums such as the United Nations (Newell and Levy 2006, p. 160). MNCs have found a particularly congenial political environment in the governance structures of regional economic blocs such as the European Union and North American Free Trade Association. In the latter body, business groups managed to secure a constitution which grants 'foreign companies more rights than domestic citizens' (Colgan 2005, p. 109; Lewis 1993).

Summarising a diverse literature, Fuchs (2007) notes the disproportionate participation of MNCs and their representatives in international regulatory forums for technology (warfare technologies/bio-technologies), intellectual property, and environmental policy, as well as the bodies through which national governments try to exercise global economic governance: the IMF, WTO and the United Nations. Cautioning that mere presence does not necessarily translate into achievement of goals, Fuchs nevertheless points out that MNCs have superior resources for information and expertise generation and can outbid the punier claims of labour, NGOs and even (inter)governmental organisations (Fuchs 2007, pp. 84–91). The evolution of the European Community into the European Union has meanwhile created a cornucopia for corporate lobbying and advantage-seeking. Between 20,000 and 30,000 (mostly business oriented) lobbyists work on about 20,000 EU officials, spending €60 billion to €90 billion a year within the EU, mainly in Brussels (Coen 2009). The 'public relations industry' is itself, of course, organised in large corporations. At one point, four such businesses controlled 50 per cent of the world's market for PR (Miller and Dinan 2003).

These and other operators have been increasingly influential in shaping the interface between policy and scientific agendas. For example, the authoritative sounding International Life Science Institute (ILSI) is a lobby group funded by 'hundreds of the biggest food, pharma and chemical companies', such as Coca Cola. It became part of the World Health Organization's investigation of dietary sugars 'by covertly funding some of the scientists involved' (Miller 2008). Particularly striking evidence of corporate influence comes from the tobacco industry where big tobacco firms persuaded other sector leaders to form an alliance to change the basis of EU policy making. From 1995 onwards British American Tobacco led an alliance of corporations which 'altered the way in which all EU policy is made, by making a business-oriented form of Impact Assessment mandatory', Thereby tilting EU policy making towards the interests of major corporations, including firms whose products involve health risks (Smith et al. 2010, p. 1).

These product-related and market-specific interventions have a tenuous legitimacy as intrinsically business concerns. But as their economic influence and operating scope has increased, corporations' 'discursive power' (Fuchs 2007, p. 149) has been heightened. Domhoff (1990) associated institutional networks of corporate executives and professionals not only with upper class concentrations of wealth but with policy-shaping networks of business-friendly foundations and think tanks. With the added discursive power of these networks, corporations have sought to shape wider policy areas and political agendas – particularly environmental and social ones. Inter- and trans-governmental action on climate change is probably the broadest of these environmental concerns. As Jacques et al. (2008, p. 362) observe, 'the strategy has shifted from defence of single companies or industries (such as tobacco or pesticides) to using sceptics to challenge environmental science in general'.

The means of achieving such strategies may be indirect. In the USA corporate financing of parties or individual politicians is a favoured channel. But at least as important is the complementary discursive impact which energy corporations have gained by seeking 'to undermine climate science via lobbying and participation in the now inactive Global Climate Coalition (GCC) as well as by directly funding CTTs (Conservative Think Tanks) and sceptical scientists' (Kolk and Pinkse 2007, p. 206). Such interventions have penetrated and influenced a swathe of mass and specialist media communications as well as legislatures (Levy and Egan 1998, p. 147–8; Layzer 2007). Significantly, however, business finds it difficult to speak with one voice on climate change. Some MNCs calculate more influence derives from eschewing outright opposition in favour of more responsive approaches involving 'market' solutions that ameliorate carbon emissions in profit-friendly ways (Kolk and Pinske 2007). Nevertheless in international policy making, Farnsworth and Holden (2006, p. 482) argue that discursive power is overwhelming.

> International business has helped to establish a consensus ... that has shifted policy agendas, including those of the major IGOs, towards a more pro-business one. As a result, the EU's competitiveness agenda is almost identical to the key demands made by international business and, where policies to control the negative aspects of corporate activities have been proposed ... strong lobbying from business has ensured that only voluntary codes of conduct have so far been introduced.

The United States, plus the UK, still acts as policy model for neo-liberalising societies elsewhere; and, in that country, business lobbying and political influence have become all-embracing. By the late 1990s the number of individual corporations with lobbying bases in Washington had risen from the 165 in 1968 to over 600; with these and others also represented through trade and industry associations.

Marshalling these separate forces is the Business Roundtable, representing 200 CEOs of large and giant corporations and credited with reversing the spate of social and environmental reforms of the Kennedy, Johnson and Nixon eras, and channelling neo-liberal, de-regulatory pressures. This free-marketism led, inter alia, to the Washington Consensus through the business-friendly administrations of Regan, Clinton and the Bush family. Following successive favourable Supreme Court verdicts, big business was also able to outbid other organisations in the funding of Political Action Committees which sponsor individual politicians, including presidential candidates. Corporations were the next highest donors to these 'super' PACs, after rich individuals – themselves probably having corporate wealth (Fuchs 2007, pp. 74–83; Barnes 2012; Demos 2012).

One of the most signal indicators of corporate influence over political actors is the benevolent lassitude with which governments and their fiscal apparatus have tolerated corporate tax avoidance. Multinationals have been able to use and/or misapply those rules. Even the 'capitalist club' of developed market economies, the OECD, warned these arrangements have allowed MNCs:

> to separate income from the economic activities that produce that income and to shift it into low-tax environments ... from transfers of intangibles and other mobile assets for less than full value, the over-capitalisation of lowly taxed group companies and from contractual allocations of risk to low-tax environments in transactions that would be unlikely to occur between unrelated parties. (OECD 2013a, pp. 19–20)

States' tax administrations, the OECD observes: 'have little capability of developing a "big picture" view of a taxpayer's global value chain' p. 22). Even while presenting a business-friendly tax reduction philosophy, US President Obama acknowledged that 'empirical evidence suggests that income-shifting behaviour by multinational corporations is a significant concern' (US Treasury 2012, p. 7). UK politicians have been more forthright. Parliament's Public Accounts Committee stated,

'Multinational companies appear to be using transfer pricing, payment of royalties for intellectual property or franchise payments to other group companies to artificially reduce their profits in the UK or to remove them to lower tax jurisdictions.'

This Committee's Report added, archly, 'We were not convinced that HMRC has the determination to robustly challenge the practices of these companies' (UK Parliament 2012, para 1.6). Such official reports indicate governmental tolerance of systemic corporate tax evasion. More partisan accounts allege extensive cooperation verging on collusion between tax authorities, politicians and corporate representatives like accountancy firms (Corporate Watch, 2010; Hodge/Public Accounts Committee, 2013). Even though fiscal capacity is a central pillar of nation states' functions, it seems that its workings, as in other areas of corporate over-reach, have been damagingly penetrated by the culture and political influence of big business.

2. SCALE AND HEGEMONY IN THE UK

Measured by output and value-added, five or fewer firms dominated, with at least 70 per cent of the UK market, for: sugar, tobacco products, gas distribution, oils and fats, confectionery, man-made fibres, coal extraction, soft drinks and mineral waters, pesticides, weapons and ammunition. Similar concentration levels applied in airlines, banking, and accountancy (ONS 2006, pp. 26–7). Strong reasons for associating this dominance with the growth of ST/EM corporations comes from the calculation that the proportion of the capital market (total shareholdings of publicly quoted companies) of the top 100 FTSE firms rose from 68.36 per cent in 1988, to 87.77 per cent in 2008 (Leone and Philp 2010, p. 16).[1] Around half of UK GDP in the 1980s and 1990s was attributable to business corporations and at least 80 per cent of that value came from bigger stock market quoted companies (Froud et al. 2000b, pp. 773–4).

Of course, UK residents shouldn't need such esoteric indicators to recognise the dominance of MNCs. Personal finance is dominated by four banks. Barclays, HSBC, Lloyds Group and RBS hold 77 per cent of all personal bank accounts (as well as 85 per cent of small business ones – *International New York Times* 21 July 2014). Alternatively consumers can stroll down high streets dominated by the likes of Vodafone, Everything-Everywhere (Orange/T-Mobile), '3' and O2 for mobile phone networks, and McDonalds, Burger King, Pizza Hut and KFC for fast foods. They probably buy from one of the big three grocery retailers: Tesco, Sainsbury, Asda/Walmart (totalling 65 per cent of grocery retailing), and choose online between Google, Yahoo, Bing (totalling 97.5 per cent), to buy from Ebay and Amazon; having selected internet service provision from the four internet service providers (BT, Virgin Media, Talk-Talk, Sky) that supply 87 per cent of UK internet connections (*Guardian*, 2011). Big businesses tend to get bigger by taking over other businesses. Since the 1980s, however, and especially in the UK, they have also grown by taking over and financing state activities and public services. This expansion constitutes over-reach in the sense that it has not been merely – some would argue not at all – a rational process of economic and democratic policy making. As the following account shows, expansion into public services is a crucial manifestation of corporations' acquisition of political power and influence.

2.1 The Capture of Public Services

Starting with the Thatcher governments of the 1980s and accelerating through the New Labour and Coalition governments, firms have taken over the provision of what used to be state-sector services such as health and education. Corporate giants such as Capita – 16,936 employees, £1.08 billion sales in 2012 – mushroomed in a few decades throughout the expanding outsourcing of internal and public service functions. These were added to contracts for ancillary services such as cleaning and catering and the longer-standing supply of private-sector goods, such as pharmaceuticals and medical equipment for the operation of public sector services. Neo-liberal international economic consensus on limiting state borrowings has led governments to look to the business sector to help finance their own capital expenditures. So construction for health, education and infrastructure has been paid for by long-term debt schemes such as the Private Finance Initiative (PFI), which leases hospitals, schools and other buildings to the public sector. At local levels, councils have been required to contract out the management and service delivery, a process reinforced by local public–private partnerships and central government financing conditional on projects involving partnerships with the private sector (Coulson, 1997, p. 34; Coates et al. 2000).

Long-term care is now predominantly provided by the private sector. Private companies have also been taking over some NHS services: some hospital trusts and general practice surgeries. The 2012 'reform' of the NHS by the Conservative-Liberal Democrat Coalition opened up further tracts of its services to medical and health care businesses. On one estimate, 70 per cent of NHS contracts awarded since the reforms were won by private firms (*Health Service Journal* 2014). Some of these businesses, such as United Health (paying out $820 million dividends) are multinational or, like Beresford Health (a division of HCPro Inc.), owned by MNCs like Halyard Investments. With contracting out of parts of local educational services to private firms, and with the spread of state licensed school academies and 'free schools', business ownership is being promoted for basic education (Groves 2014; *Independent* 2014). Under New Labour (1997–2008) local employment services were taken on by private firms such as Reed in Haringey, Newham and Liverpool, and Pertemps in Birmingham (Farnsworth and Holden 2006). Under the controversial 'Work' programmes all (re)employment services were contracted out to 18 'prime providers' corresponding to English and Welsh regions. Of these, some were small national or regional businesses. But four firms had more than three contracts and five were MNCs, like SERCO, Igneus and mega-employer G4S (UK Government 2013). On one estimate one third of all government services are now outsourced (Julius 2008).

The case for this increasing spread of corporate business provision through public services and welfare entitlements is that the status of the providing organisation is irrelevant to the quality of the provision. If private business can give a service that is equal to, or more effective than a public organisation, then business should have that opportunity (Whitfield 2001). The corporate case is enhanced by the presumption that business is usually more efficient than public 'bureaucracies': its managers more proactive and skilled, its workforces more responsive and flexible and its cost consciousness usually higher. But the real political trump card is that outsourcing and privatisation reduce public expenditure and the size of the state's budget deficit: an over-riding political criterion for the international fiscal system and its neo-liberal watchmen. The case against rests on the inappropriateness of applying business logic to services founded on ethical and civic values of care, equality or social solidarity. Businesses, this counter-case points out, have an over-riding aim of profit making and, if organised as corporations, a duty to privilege the interests of their shareholders. Consequently, in areas of uncertainty, financial ends will displace humanitarian ones.

More generally, carers lack the autonomy from commercial-managerial pressures to privilege the needs of patients, welfare recipients, or other dependants. Staffing itself will be subject to rigorous controls reducing the ratio of carers per recipient, minimising their training and hiring on the basis of wage costs rather than professional expertise. On one recent estimate 70 per cent of care home staff are effectively casual workers – employed on so-called 'zero-hours' contracts (*Guardian* 2013b). A string of scandals involving inadequate staffing and care levels in residential homes, disability assessments, medical help lines, prison services and control of asylum seekers, lend weight to these charges. Legal judgements also mean that recipients of privatised services do not have the same rights as those where the provider is a public body: for example Human Rights legislation or access to corporate records under the Freedom of Information Act for care home residents (McFadyean and Rowland, 2002; Reporters Committee for Freedom of the Press, 2007).

As other cases illustrate (see chapters 9 and 10), businesses' commercial priorities can over-ride the need for reliability and stability in public facilities and services. Crises of investment, overly frugal employment policies, and managerial turnover are all more likely in the private sector. Some of the giant oligopolies which have inflated to take on a range of public service contracts – firms like Capita, Compass, Interserve, Serco, and Sodexo – have been associated with such disruptions. The stability of Four Seasons Health Care, 'Britain's largest health care chain', has been twice shaken by the kind of financial turmoil which can beset the financial border zones of the corporate sector, experiencing debt crises and take-overs (*Guardian* 2012b). Major service failings have also been attributed to a customer-contract ethos which is incompatible with the carer mentality required for many sensitive public services. Operating with reduced staffing in order to lower costs, so as to win contracts and make profits, has also been cited as a source of poor services. The Southern Cross company was censured for neglect associated with mismanagement and understaffing in its Orchid View care homes after its descent into bankruptcy in 2011 (Wachman 2011). On the business side such public service contractors have defied even the logic of shareholder value by proliferating their range of businesses, thus becoming the kind of 'unfocussed conglomerates' alleged to be anathema to investment analysts. As in other sectors, critical questions have also been raised about the size of executive remuneration paid for managing what are near-monopolies. But, perhaps most significantly, corporate operation of public services has made the latter more remote from the levels of transparency and accountability expected of the public sphere (cf Harris 2013).

2.2 Shaping the Policies which Determine Public Services

Welfare reforms, like those to Disability Allowance, controversially carried through by private sector operators, have been linked back to the influence of commercial insurance companies during the New Labour governments of 1997–2010 (Black Triangle Campaign 2011). Corporate leverage on public service policy has become particularly pronounced in the continuous capture of the National Health Service by commercial firms. The new Conservative ministers in the 2010 coalition government soon announced a restructuring to allow more private sector 'competition' into NHS service provision. But it was corporate health businesses which influenced both the policy perspectives behind the new model and also the negotiations on the details of the actual legislation (Leys and Player 2011). It seems unlikely to have been coincidental that some executives of Monitor, the NHS regulator, were former employees of McKinsey, the all-encompassing consultancy and advocacy business. McKinsey's influence in the UK goes back as far as the firm's almost single-handed conversion of the internal structure of UK corporations into the US multi-divisional model during the 1960s and 1970s (see chapter 3). More recently McKinsey personnel had a role in writing sections of the eventual Parliamentary bill for the NHS restructuring – even though the firm has business links to some of the very commercial providers likely to secure contracts from the 'new' NHS. Despite usually being a staunch pro-Conservative newspaper, the *Daily Mail* reported that:

> many of the Bill's proposals were drawn up by McKinsey and included in the legislation wholesale ... the firm has used its privileged access to 'share information' with its corporate clients – which include the world's biggest private hospital firms – who are now set to bid for health service work. (*Daily Mail* 2012)

The Mail also reported that McKinsey executives attended and even hosted meetings of the 'Extraordinary NHS Management Board which implements the legislation. Yet McKinsey's receives "millions" of pounds from advising GPs on the reform Bill's implications ... and earned at least £13.8 million from Government health policy since the Coalition took office.' Lord Carter of Coles, head of the NHS regulator, the Co-operation and Competition Panel, also had extensive health business interests, including chairing American healthcare firm McKesson, according to the Mail.

Care UK, a division of a US MNC, made significant donations to the Conservative party, including £21,000 to the personal office of Andrew Lansley – the Minister who designed the details of the legislation (Huitson 2012). More egregious still was the UK Coalition government's recruitment of former New Labour adviser Simon Stevens from US MNC United Health where, as its 'president of global health', he worked to intensify market contracting of medical professionals (Forbes 2013).

In other public policy sectors, such as energy and foodstuffs, multinational corporations do not quite decide government policies. Yet it is certainly a big help to them that the unofficial Multinationals Chairmen's Group – reputedly representing firms like BP, British American Tobacco, Diageo, GlaxoSmithKline, Shell, Unilever and Vodafone – frequently meet the Prime Minister on matters of joint concern (Cave and Rowell 2104, p. 59). Their advice may not always be taken, but their representatives staff the advisory and policy bodies in which policy approaches and criteria are established. A recent investigation found, for example, that scientists funded by food multinationals staff the advisory bodies for health guidelines for sugar intake associated with the escalating obesity epidemic (Boseley 2013). More disturbingly, for expectations of a healthy, pluralistic policy environment, corporate interests have infiltrated the processes of debate and research. The campaigner George Monbiot has claimed corporations, such as the health-to-foodstuffs MNC Unilever, may use their ethical and CSR credentials to influence policy formation on development, environment and health issues through representation on national and international governmental forums: from Scientific Advisory Committees, through G8 bodies, to the UN's 'High Level Panel on global development' (Monbiot 2014a). As Cave and Rowell have documented, this trend is one which now encompasses the lobbying forces of corporations across the food, drink and energy sectors (Cave and Rowell 2014, pp. 75–77). The dynamics of these sectors will be examined in chapters 4 and 10 respectively.

The expansion of government outsourcing and privatisation of services in the past two decades has been shaped by business involvement in policy bodies such as the Institute for Public Policy Research. This notionally left-of-centre think tank was originally established as a counter to the powerful influence of neo-liberal bodies such as the Adam Smith Institute and the Centre for Policy Studies. By 1999, however, its 'Commission on Public Private Partnerships' was being funded by the global accountancy and consulting firm KPMG, BT plc, Serco, Nomura Bank (owner of Hyder Business Services), Norwich Union Mill Group (Norwich Union PLC), and Group 4 (Whitfield 2001, p. 34). These businesses were already involved in advising, contracting for, or participating in public spending and PFI projects and local authority strategic partnerships. Coincidentally, the Commission defined its aim as setting out 'a reform programme aimed at ensuring that in the future PPPs are used at the right times and to maximum effect.' It claimed to be 'open minded about the contribution that partnerships could make to public services', but to distance itself from: 'a perspective which holds that as a matter of principle public services should always and everywhere be provided by the public sector' (IPPR 2001).

Further privatisation-oriented policy output included 'private spending on healthcare' (sponsored by Norwich Union Healthcare and Genus Pharmaceuticals – Gosling 2008, p. 25). The influential New Local Government Network ('frequently called on to advise government on everything from city deals to neighbourhood community budgets') also receives funds from Serco, Jarvis, BT, KPMG, as well as Carillion, Nord Anglia Education plc, Amey, Sodexho, Capita, Arthur Andersen (Whitfield 2001, p. 37), and 'partners' with BT and Vertex, Serco, Amey, Kier, PricewaterhouseCoopers and PA Consulting (Gosling 2008, p. 25); all commercially involved in outsourcing and contracting. In 2008 the New Labour Government set up a Public Services Industry Review chaired by DeAnne Julius – fortuitously a senior non-executive director of the giant contracting firm SERCO – one of the 50 per cent of the review body members who were 'senior managers or business representatives (Wilks 2013, p. 139).

Other research policy organisations range from virtual in-house think tanks such as the Aldridge Foundation (ex-Capita) and the SERCO Institute, through PricewaterhouseCoopers' 'Public Sector Research Centre' (sponsor of the Demos think tank on 'public service codesign') , the Social Market Foundation on 'the death of deference' in health and education services, another IPPR project ('Public Services at the Crossroads'), and the New Local Government Network's 'incentives for councils to build major infrastructure projects'. By 2008 the UNISON report on the Public Services Industry could list 17 former ministers, MPs, and civil servants who had taken up paid posts with businesses involved in the PFI, health and public services contracting 'industries' (Gosling 2008, p. 28–9). There is a growing inequality of political influence between all of these modes of corporate interest promotion and the political system's declining responsiveness to public and civil society voices.

This inequality confirms that the problem of corporate power affects the very heart of liberal democracy. Big business does not just have the power to influence politics: corporations are themselves political actors. Moreover: 'Not only are corporations political actors, their political power is exerted on an everyday basis as part of our political system' (Wilks 2013, p. 41). The legitimacy of such roles must have been boosted by the 2014 appointment of John Manzoni, former oil executive and non-executive director of the giant multi-national brewer SABMiller, as the government's first ever chief executive of the civil service. Manzoni's former boss at the controversial petrochemicals giant BP, John Browne, had already been appointed as 'lead non-executive' director on the Cabinet Office board, as part of a plan to install 'non-executive directors', most likely business or ex-corporate leaders, onto the boards of all government departments (BBC News 2010, 2014). The reality of notions of pluralist democracy has always been highly debatable, but in the wake of so much corporate over-reach, its plausibility verges on fantasy.

3. PENETRATION OF CIVIL SOCIETY: CORPORATIONS AS PATRONS

Corporate colonisation of the public realm extends beyond the take-over of public services. Through their recent adoption of Corporate Social Responsibility (CSR) programmes, explored in chapters 8 to 10, corporations are starting to dominate the charity and voluntary organisation networks, analogous to the patron-client regimes of allegedly 'backward' or pre-modern societies (see Jones 2007). Moreover, the wider sponsorship of artistic and sporting events and programmes gives corporations influence over the character of these activities. As described in the introduction to this chapter, in sports such as football, the direct annexation of clubs occurred via conversions into share-traded plcs and the adoption of the commercial traits – financial dealings, marketing, management structures – of more mainstream corporations (Political Economy of Football n.d.).

Barclays Bank has a typically panoptic use of sponsorship to promote its business identity. The aforementioned English football Premier League is branded as the Barclays Premier League and the bank is also the official sponsor of key football bodies in the UK, including the Football Writers' Association, the League Managers' Association and – just to square off the football circle – the Professional Footballers' Association. These affiliations form part of a worldwide stable of sponsorships including Barclays' Absa subsidiary in South Africa, which sponsors South Africa's national football team, and the country's Absa Premiership domestic football competition. Other sports 'captured' include tennis (the Barclays ATP World Tour Finals at London's 02 Arena), golf (the Fed-Ex Cup on the PGA Tour in the United States) and the South African Springboks national rugby team. These, essentially brand marketing, tentacles spread down into local communities through 200 Barclays 'community sports sites' for over 40 different sports in China, Hong Kong, India, South Africa, Spain, the UK, the USA, Zambia and Zimbabwe.

In the wider art and entertainment world, Barclays sponsors includes the Barclaycard Mercury Prize for UK (pop music) Albums of the Year and, to spread its profile into high-culture middle class consumers, the avant-garde Donmar Warehouse theatre, exhibitions at the British Museum and the Victoria and Albert Museum, plus the main venue for the Hay-on-Wye Festival, 'the world's pre-eminent literary and arts festival'. More prosaically, an astute sponsorship of the Mayor of London's Cycle Hire scheme ensures that the bank's name and logo circulate throughout the capital's streets. Barclays also claims to be a 'partner' of the Metropolitan (London) Police, hosting community policing events at its local branches (Barclays Entertainment Sponsorships 2014). All of this sporting and community presence no doubt helps to compensate in the public mind for a series of regulatory and taxation penalties against Barclays for attempting to manipulate: the US electricity market, for which it was fined £299m by the US Federal Energy Regulatory Commission, the London Interbank Offered Rate (Libor) – £59.5 million fine – and the Euro Interbank Offered Rate (Euribor); as well as UK tax avoidance repaid at a cost of £500 million (Wilson 2012, 2013; Treanor 2012). Moreover, as we shall see in chapters 8 to 10, this nakedly commercial sponsorship blends seamlessly into apparently 'ethical' programmes of CSR.

4. SOME STRUCTURAL OUTCOMES

As both corporate advocates and some grudging critics accept, their organisational capacities have made MNCs, as Commonwealth Secretary-General Don McKinnon put it, the 'most powerful force for global technology transfer, skills development and international invest-ment flows' (UK Parliament 2002a). Its financial advantages are patent.

> The company is one of the West's great competitive advantages ... Companies increase the pool of capital available for productive investment. They allow investors to spread their risks by purchasing small and easily marketable shares in several enterprises. And they provide a way of imposing effective management structures on large organizations. (Mickelthwait and Wooldridge 2003, p. xxi).

Short of revolutionary transformation, governments, families, com-munities and many civil society organisations could not function without corporate products and services. Such dependence makes corporations' imminent removal, or transformation of their economic roles, highly unlikely. This immense capacity for meeting contemporary needs – at least amongst the developed world's institutions and populations – stems from the mobility of capital both between financial corporations and cognate businesses and internally within MNCs. They can increasingly move freely around the globe in search of both market opportunities and the least restrictive operating and profit-making conditions. But there are serious and growing consequences of the exercise of these powers on employment standards and governments' capacity to pursue social wel-fare programmes, or policies on the environment and culture (CAFOD in UK Parliament 2002b). Disproportionate corporate power is also making it increasingly difficult for the economically advanced societies to fulfil their official ideology of liberal democracy, and for newer capitalist and market societies to realise these democratic institutions. As indicated above, the democratic deficit from the power of TNCs to influence policy makers at national and international levels is widening alarmingly.

Corporations have also been decisive for the coalescence of a new ruling elite, which, on several accounts, constitutes the disproportionate wealth and influence intensifying inequality in societies like the USA and UK. The present analysis does not explore this social divide itself. The financialised elite's nature and power has already been documented with elan by Savage and Williams (2008, pp. 1–24) and in its corporate manifestations by Wilks (2013, pp. 64–94). My main concern is with the organisational structures which gestate and sustain these elites. Just as the medieval theocratic and aristocratic elites depended on their religious orders and manorial estates for their power, so today's financial and business elites would be stranded weaklings if dismounted from their corporate steeds.

These broader social considerations stem from an observation by management guru Peter Drucker, that the corporation is 'the first autonomous institution in hundreds of years, the first to create a power centre that was within society yet independent of the ... government ... of the state' (Drucker 2002, p. 156). Insofar as the state represents the wider society, we can deduce therefore that corporations are *in* society but not *of* society. The various forms of corporate excess and malfeasance indicate a common problem of 'corporate over-reach', which can be summarised as follows.

- Not following markets but neutralising market processes (mergers and acquisitions, inter-corporate collusion etc).
- Extending their power into shaping political and government policy making.
- Taking over public services via privatisations and outsourcing (e.g. Capita and G4S).
- 'Colonising' civil society by, e.g., expanding charitable and sponsorship relations (often justified as CSR).

CONCLUSION

In other words, business corporations have been taking on roles and powers for which they were neither designed nor originally authorised. As a result there is widespread concern, not confined to radical critics of capitalism, that ST/EM corporations' activities now constitute a threat, not just to economic stability and wealth distribution, but to the integrity of the societies they dominate and, as chapter 9 describes, to the environmental conditions on which humans and other life-systems depend (Mayer 2013, p. 161; Wilks 2013, pp. 267–8). The question to which we now turn is what are the historical structures which have facilitated this rise to malign dominance?

NOTE

1. The volatility of share prices on the stock exchange means that quoted share capital is not a reliable measure of the underlying economic value of corporate assets. But then again, all price-based figures are relative to a specific time and situation.

2. The 'Anglo-Saxon' business corporation: anatomy and evolution

Corporations are many lesser commonwealths in the bowels of a greater, like worms in the entrails of a natural man. (Thomas Hobbes, *Leviathan,* p. 218)

INTRODUCTION

Critics often liken corporations to grotesque life forms: 'monsters', 'predators', 'behemoths' – dinosaurs even. Such analogies suggest key evolutionary phases when their distinctive features mutated. So, what specific traits have corporations developed that assured their alien separation from most of the rest of society? More particularly how did these features help make corporations seemingly so 'disembedded' from, yet also dominant over, society?

To survive and function all social institutions require an element of autonomy. Yet most, if not all, are intimately enmeshed in, and subject to other social relationships. The one institution widely regarded as towering over and separated from the rest of society is the autonomous state. Otherwise, as with the structure and functioning of the contemporary family for example, institutions are subjected to pressure and change from cultural, economic and political forces. Even if its critics are only partially correct, the typical contemporary business corporation has acquired both economic dominance and substantial independence from social forces. As Polanyi's thesis, described in the Introduction, holds, released from its social bonds the disembedded enterprise has the potential to devour the institutions to which it was originally tied. Radical perspectives, such as Marxism, proffer automatic answers to this question: equating corporate supremacy with the necessary dominance and hegemony of capitalist interests. But this equation doesn't, by itself, explain why one particular form of business organisation comes to dominate all others.

This distinctiveness has been well defined by Peter Drucker's description of the North American species as: 'The first autonomous institution in hundreds of years, the first to create a power centre that was within society yet independent of the central government of the national state' (Drucker 1993, p. 156). In the case of the British form of the corporation different political and social contexts, such as the period of state intervention described below in chapter 3, might once have made this autonomy seem exaggerated. But the last thirty years of neo-liberal politics and economic globalisation have brought corporate emancipation and its economic expansion. So Drucker's US description seems applicable to the UK, and some other English-speaking countries. Moreover, Drucker is not a radical critic but a respected and erudite scholar and partisan for business efficiency.

The analysis in this chapter offers little new empirical evidence. Rather it synthesises the findings of organisational specialists, business analysts and historians who have now, for some years, mapped and publicised key features of the 'Anglo-Saxon' corporation and its origins. However, most of these experts have tended to focus on a particular aspect or development, such as legal privileges, or organisational dynamics, as being the keys to its growth, or autonomy and independence (Chandler 1990, 1977; Channon 1973; Fligstein 1990; Hannah 1983). Elsewhere, amongst 'neo-institutionalist' theorists (for example Hall and Soskice 2001; Jacoby 2007) or, less abstractly, in Perrow's more nuanced analysis, the corporate species is depicted as shaped by, and interacting with, the particular cultures, politics and historical conjunctures of specific societies, usually those of the USA. The Anglo-Saxon, or ST/EM corporation does have generic features common to both North America and the UK, as well as other Anglophone societies. However, because the focus of this book is on the UK variant, this chapter describes both the emergence of the universal traits and features specific to the UK.

The aim here is to grasp the weaknesses of the corporation as well as its scale, scope and strengths. Perrow's otherwise comprehensive account of the sociological significance of the giant corporation in the USA ends in 1900, without considering the full dynamics of mass production/mass consumption and the mutation of the nineteenth-century model into the multi-divisional structure which dominated in the next 100 years. Similarly Cassis's overview of 'big business' from the industrial revolution to the digital age presents recent developments as refinements of the multi-divisional frameworks which evolved in the early twentieth century (Cassis 2007). A more anatomical rather than historical approach indicates six key aspects of corporate strength and autonomy.

- Financing: the life blood of the large business; how do corporations acquire and maintain capital investment, mainly through share issues?

- Autonomous control: by what legal and institutional means do corporate actors achieve and maintain effective autonomy from other actors and agencies with legal powers over their existence?
- Size and scale: despite recent exceptions, corporations, especially industrial types, have huge dimensions; how and why have they acquired thousands of employees and massive operations to make and deliver their products?
- Expansion, reproduction and competition: like animal species, firms compete with each other and other economic actors; by what processes and activities do they survive and repulse competitors' challenges?
- Internal structure: what is distinctive about the organisational forms of corporations that allow them to control, operate, and reproduce?
- Ontology and status: beliefs about legitimacy, privileges and rights both structure and maintain corporations' social environments – which of these institutions support corporate autonomy?

The rest of this chapter analyses each of these features in turn. What it does not do is examine the popular emphasis on the multi-national, transnational or, indeed 'global' character of many of today's corporations.

As should become clear from the following analysis, despite their empirical importance these recent dimensional changes are mainly quantitative extensions of the ST/EM's basic features. However this chapter will also introduce a contemporary adaptation of the financing and competition functions, a process which academics have dubbed 'financialisation' for the optimisation of 'shareholder value'. For all of the above traits we need to ask how much they have contributed to the creation and persistence of corporations, not only as successful market-economy actors, but as quasi-political, *sovereign* entities, beyond easy control by other economic and social institutions. We cannot judge the recipes for corporate transformation or lesser reforms, discussed in the final chapter, until we know the key conditions for corporate autonomy and hegemony. Prior even to this analysis, we need to clarify the theoretical perspective used in the analysis.

1. INTERPRETIVE FRAMEWORKS: A CLARIFICATION

A business firm is a needs-satisfying machine; it is an entity invented and employed by society to better satisfy the society's interests. A society is better off when properly regulated business firms are allowed to carry the bulk of

economic activity than when they are not allowed to exist or are severely
regulated by the state. (Kantarelis 2010, p. 3)

The approach developed below rejects and departs from such a neo-
classically-inspired functionalist view. It also contrasts with the ascendant
explanation of the success of big business forms in the Anglo-Saxon
world. That view is based on the more anarchic, transaction costs
approach in so-called 'institutional' economics. Economics' dominant
paradigm usually treats corporations as empirical forms of various
idealised constructs that compose the 'theory of the firm' (cf Coase,
1937; Demsetz, 1988; Hart, 1995).This common theoretical focus is on
the dynamics of financial magnitudes – costs, prices, profits etc. As a
result, the success of corporations as 'firms' has mainly been investigated
in terms of cost and price-forming functions. Thus one of the founding
theories, that of Coase, proposes that the firm – and by extension its
corporate form – emerged and flourished because of its superior control
of 'transaction costs' (Coase 1937). Essentially, transaction cost analysis
(TCA) has attributed the corporation's success to its capacity for carrying
out some key business transactions by means of internalised (and
'institutional') controls within a firm's own organisation rather than by a
series of external contracts (cf. Coase 1937, more recent 'institutional'
economists, Williamson 1981, Mueller 2003, Bjuggren and Mueller
2009; and, in more synoptic fashion, North 1990).

Empirically, such transactional calculations are one powerful economic
factor in the rise and fall of business systems. They feature in various
chapters in this book. However transaction cost is, at best, one motiva-
tional cause that describes a broader process. Fligstein's research on US
corporations has shown its historical specificity as a dominant motive of
executives' policies (Fligstein 1990). Moreover, the capacity to internalise
transaction costs cannot also establish their institutional conditions of
existence, nor the sources of the power that enables some actors to
enforce price levels and transaction arrangements. In other words other
forces must have established the appropriate corporate organisational
model. At worst, transaction costs analysis (TCA) risks being a teleo-
logical explanation: the desired end becomes regarded as the source and
cause of a development. Like other 'rational actor' interpretations, such
perspectives risk reducing processes of business formation and evolution
to the calculative powers and volitions of unconstrained, rational individuals.

Sociologists, on the other hand, ask what social and cultural conditions
make it possible for individuals, or collective actors, such as corporations, to think in such rational ways and to have available the powers

and resources to realise their calculations in successful (trans)actions (Hindess 1984). Business people can only have opted for organised internal transactions if the institutional features were available and viable. Analysis of these and other pillars of corporate autonomy therefore has to relate them to social and political factors. Corroboration of this consideration comes from knowledge that the Anglo-Saxon corporate form is far from universal. As chapter 7 explains, there are other types of large business organisation, for example in Germany and Japan, where societal conditions have been different. Business in these latter societies lacks the forms of autonomy enjoyed by its Anglo-American counterparts. So the ways in which business enterprises become more or less socially 'embedded', in other social and political institutions, is decisive for their capacity to adopt one form of transaction costs rather than another.

2. CORPORATE ANATOMY: FINANCE

Markets for financial capital are critical for the establishment and growth of corporate businesses. Single-minded accumulation is also, increasingly, the *raison d' être* of the contemporary ST/EM corporation (Peetz and Murray 2012, pp. 50–1). Indeed some Marxist analysis defines corporations reductively, as agencies for the calculation of local applications of the 'laws' of capital accumulation (cf Cutler et al. 1978, pp. 128–201). Dependence on and access to external finance was an initial cause of the adoption of early forms of a separate corporate organisation. The legal term 'corporation' derives from the Latin 'corpus corporatum' – literally a 'body of bodies' – by which courts could deal collectively with the participants of a venture, whether commercial or not (Oliver 1850). All corporations including the urban civic authorities and universities, were legal creations of the Crown; existing on its sufferance. Medieval trade guilds were associated with these categories. But early commercial corporations originated in the medieval Italian city states, as simple expressions of the combined finances of groups of investors.

In later centuries these businesses clubbed together to finance the maritime ventures by which European traders began to exploit the resources and goods of the Americas, Africa and 'the Indies'. In sixteenth and seventeenth-century Holland, Britain, and the British American colonies, trading companies were formed to acquire the required capital and to defray the risks of loss to any single investor. The biggest enterprises were given the status of companies licensed, or 'chartered': in Britain, by the Crown and Parliament. From these arrangements rose the politico-economic behemoth known as the East India Company and, with neat historical destiny, the Massachusetts Company and Virginia Company which set up the first North American colonies. How appropriate that the eventual heartland of the Anglo-Saxon corporation should owe its own existence to an early ancestor of that model. Or, as the closing line of the film *Killing Me Softly* expressed it: 'America is not a community. It's a business'.

In these early ventures, investors paid for 'shares' equivalent to the size of their contribution to the venture's total capital, with each share giving a right to a proportionate return in the profits of the venture. Consistent with the culture of commercial inventiveness, which characterised post-feudal, seventeenth-century western Europe, it was soon possible to buy and sell the titles to these shares in the nascent 'stock exchanges' of London and Amsterdam. With this latter development began the later, critical and much debated 'separation' of shareowners' interests from direct concern with the operation or management of the company. With the open trading of shares' ownership came the prospect of a more remote relationship linked only to the relative financial values of different investment opportunities. But unlike the early merchants' ventures, or corporations with time-limited State charters, the privately traded corporation began to assume an eternal quality – not tied to a particular project or time scale. Meanwhile the ownership became transient and opportunistic: transient but not powerless. The possibility, and later the obligation, for stock-financed companies to 'list' their shares on the exchanges allowed investors, or groups of investors, to buy into existing firms. Thus by purchasing sufficient shares to outvote other stockholders they could, in theory, become the dominant controllers by acquiring the legal rights over the direction of the enterprise.

As chapter 7 will show, the nature of its share distribution and ownership differentiate the 'Anglo-Saxon' corporation from its counterparts in, for example, continental Europe and Japan. Although both Anglophone and continental corporations utilise fixed interest loans (often from banks), the latter firms make more use of these than the former. The ST/EM corporation label applies because the Anglophone firms place more emphasis on shareholder financing.

3. AUTONOMY AND CONTROL: LEGAL AND INSTITUTIONAL CONDITIONS

Stock exchange mediation intensified and institutionalised the potential division between those operating the activities of a company and, on the other hand, its investors. But the separation of roles was accelerated by the legalisation of the 'limited liability' principle. Until then the law held any investor ultimately responsible for all the debts and other financial liabilities of a company, unless there was specific provision to the contrary in their articles of association, or individual business contracts. Mid-nineteenth century legislation officially authorised a growing practice of narrowing the extent of shareowners' liabilities to the amount invested (Anderson and Tollison 1983). British acts of Parliament in 1844, 1856, and 1862, meant that when a company failed, shareholders now only had to pay for that part of any debts proportionate to the amount of the shares they held. Freed from a concern with the company's total debt, shareholders could and did restrict their interest in the business to the returns its managers paid, and, relatedly, to the price being offered for its shares on the exchanges. This 'limited liability' encouraged speculative, but wider investment and reduced investors' interest in controlling the detail of company activities. By the nineteenth century share-ownership could reduce to a few days, or even hours, as 'short-selling' – temporarily borrowing shares from the legal owners to sell and buy them back at a cheaper price (and hence a potential profit) – became established practice (Markham 2002, p. 161).

Two other changes in corporate legal status further distanced the corporate entity from the social and economic ties from which it began. The first was the erosion of the charters by which society, in the form of the state, authorised corporations' scope and purposes. The second was the designation of the corporation itself as a legal subject, distinct from both the investors who owned its capital, and also the managers who ran it. Politically, charters meant that the first commercial corporations were variations on the arrangement by which medieval states – normally by the office of the monarch – ceded towns and guilds varying degrees of independence. Continuing into the early modern period, the monarch/state gave charters to business corporations. These licences specified corporations' privileges to act independently in buying, selling, building and employing, and in collecting revenues.

In return the corporations would normally acknowledge taxation liabilities to the Crown. But this monopoly was challenged as alternative legal forms such as trusts and partnerships became popular for business ventures. Their *de facto* proliferation began to undermine the supremacy of the royal charters gained via Parliamentary approval. In addition, even though the latter did give firmer legal safeguards to investments and *de facto*, or virtual monopolies, chartered commercial corporations could only operate within specified time, commercial and geographic limits (Anderson and Tollison 1983, pp. 112–13). For example, the overseas trading companies were, at least in theory, restricted to certain overseas territories and activities (Fleischer et al. 2002, pp. 49–50). TCA writers claim that limited liability arrangements were growing spontaneously as a result of market trends. However, there is clear evidence that the 1844 Act clinched limited liability because of investors' concerns about irresponsible company directors and the influence the financial lobby was able to exert on Parliament (Aranya, 2014, pp. 265–6).

With independence from the British Crown, the fledgling United States gave their legislatures even more control of the scope of corporate charters (Democracy Unlimited 2014). As Bakan (2004), Korten (1995) and others have pointedly observed, such restrictions limited the power of corporation because they received only restricted sovereignty. Misdemeanours, infringements of charter provisions, or changes in political and economic sentiment or policy might end their existence through withdrawal of their charters. With the historic US Supreme Court judgement which rejected local political constraints on Dartmouth College in 1819 and the UK's Joint Stock Companies Act of 1856, began the relaxation of these limits in Britain and the independent USA. This process ended in the late 1800s with accountability no longer being directly held to the state (Shannon 1933; Perrow 2002).[1] Instead, accountability was refocussed, into the obligations of commercial law and thus to corporations' financial peers – their creditors and shareholders. The decline of time-limited charters, combined with the transferability of share holdings, also gave corporations potentially eternal life – far beyond that of their flesh and blood creators and 'owners'. This notional eternality was substantiated by the second nineteenth-century juridical development which confirmed the status of corporations as *legal subjects* in their own right. The logic and ramifications of this change warrant separate treatment and are explained in more detail below.

4.   STRUCTURE AND SCALE

4.1   Segregation of Control

Thus, by the middle to late nineteenth century, corporations in Britain and the USA already had legal, and substantial political, independence. What they lacked, to continue the biological analogy, was a fully autonomous brain to control the equivalent of their nervous system. Autonomous control of the corporation as a distinct organisation required the rise of its executive managers. In its early days the people who ran the daily operations of the share-owned business would be hired-hands and technical specialists, such as craftworkers, or ships' captains. Alternatively, those in charge were capital-owning entrepreneurs whose limited capital was augmented by additional partners and investors. As Pollard's pioneering work showed, there was no separate social category of managers during the early 'industrial revolution' (Pollard 1965). Interestingly, it was the anomalous chartered trading corporations, such as the East India, Hudson's Bay or Royal Africa companies, which required and developed cadres of managers to administer their wide-ranging and complex sets of monopolistic operations. Gradually however, the operations of industrial firms – the key developers of the next stage of corporate power – increased in scale and complexity. During the nineteenth century, the technological, logistic and financial functions required their own specialised managers. With the further expansion into the mass-manufacturing or 'Fordist' system of the twentieth century, the overall management of these separate functions developed into a specialism in its own right.

First in the USA and then in Europe, these top managers acquired the status of executives, often – and more recently and controversially – with partial remuneration through the allocation of shares. Interestingly, at least in the UK, this development was obscured by the legal requirement that in their legal role as directors of the company, these executives hold at least a token amount of the share capital. In 1930 a hugely influential book by the US academics Adolf Berle and Gardner Means crystallised mounting concern about, and attention to, the power dimensions of this rise of top managers (Berle and Means 1932/68). Executive managers, argued Berle and Means, were now socially and organisationally distinct from the investors to whom they once deferred and served. Before long other commentators were describing this 'separation of ownership' from control as embodying the rise of a new, possibly dominant class (Burnham, 1941; Bell, 1961). Anticipating political power analogies, to which we return in this book's concluding chapter, Berle and Means described the ascendant executives as 'princes of property', a term which might be better regarded as referring to Machiavelli's despots who seized power in Italy's medieval city states, than to the offspring of monarchic dynasties (Berle and Means 1932/1973, p. 58).

Two processes determined and still determine the expansion of corporations: 'organic' and acquisitive growth. By the latter decades of the nineteenth century both of these patterns of expansion were posing administrative problems for the top managers trying to control and promote their operations. Organic growth meant that firms expanded the scale of their production or sales operations by increasing the size of their markets, or by adding new and/or related products to their original products. As a consequence, factories, offices, distribution, sales and accountancy functions also grew in scale and scope. Acquisitive growth was a parallel expansion by which firms purchased controlling shares in supplier or distributor firms to achieve what became known as vertical integration. Alternatively, they bought out competitors to gain 'horizontal integration'. Significantly the administrative burdens and constraints placed on top managers by these expansions of scale concerned North American corporations well before they were seen as problems by the expanding British firms.

4.2 Internal Control Systems and External Markets

In the USA, pressure for change led to the adoption of a crucial piece of today's corporate organisational jigsaw, which has become known as the 'multi-divisional' or M-form of organisation. From this point onwards, the British and other Anglo-Saxon corporate types were induced by competition or business norms to follow the forms and practices established by the North American giants. Chandler's account remains the basic perspective for understanding the internal dynamics that led to this distinctive mutation. Of particular relevance is his depiction of the significance and development of the multi-divisional, or 'M-form' of organisational structure in US firms. However, these structures developed in conjunction with the underlying developments of mass-production operations, which thus require a preliminary brief explanation.

Britain had led the world in the promotion of manufactured goods for consumer essentials and for the technologies of their production. The British model was based upon complexes of workshops in factories, skill divisions between craftworkers and semi-skilled or unskilled 'operatives', and, of course, ownership through joint-stock companies. The financial and technological innovations involved in these highly adaptive and increasingly independent institutions enabled Britain to steal a march on erstwhile competitors and soon establish a near-global ascendancy in the export of metal goods, textiles, and machinery. But the logistic, technical and labour elements of this British system were, in retrospect, remarkably narrow and particularistic. Even in the notionally mass-production sectors, such as cotton, there was high dependence on the role of skilled specialists in the production process (Lazonick 1990, chapter 4). Technical standards for manufactured goods were arbitrary or specialised rather than generalised. Up to and beyond the end of the nineteenth century, the 'workshop of the world', as British industry, rather self-importantly, liked to be described, was in reality the workshop for a variety of different local, regional and international customers. This diversity meant corresponding variations in product specifications and, as a result, limited standardisation of production processes (Jones 1997, pp. 27–36).

By contrast in North America, state-military and more homogenous and expanding domestic markets, favoured early emphasis upon more standardised products and processes. The rise of the self-consciously styled 'American System of Manufacture' involved standardised dimensions for large batches of components – and hence products – machined and assembled by special-purpose machines, often operated by semi-skilled workers. Under this system, as the US population and market-demand grew, the same processes could be expanded in scale. For Piore and Sabel, 'the modern corporation was created for this purpose' – to form mass markets (Piore and Sabel 1984, p. 49). By contrast, a more limited domestic market and a propensity to cater for diverse tastes and preferences meant that British production could only be increased by adding new cadres of specialist craftworkers, workshops or firms. There were some specialised manufacturers in the USA and some relatively large, mass production firms of consumer-goods in Britain. But the early adoption of the ASM in the USA encouraged its manufacturers of new products to seek standardised systems for their design and production.

However, a more appropriate label for the dominant mass-production/mass-consumption sectors in Western economies from the middle decades of the twentieth century is 'Fordist'. The eponymous car manufacturer and his contemporaneous imitators and competitors took the ASM even further in search of economies of scale and mass profits. By standardising all components and their assembly into a uniform product, Ford was able to sell his single automobile model by the million. In a relentless search for ever-greater, cost-cutting scale-economies, in the space of a few years Ford had centralised his car manufacturing at the gigantic River Rouge plant where steel, parts and complete assemblies were integrated into a multi-process plant with its own power-station and railroad termini. Other car manufacturers did not follow Ford into such extremes of operational integration. Competitors such as General Motors did not imitate the levels of concentration of Ford's Detroit operations. However, they shared comparable complexities in the management of volume manufacturing. General Motors also overtook Ford in the other dimension of his growth strategy. Where Ford bought out and merged his suppliers, GM's acquisitions also included other car assembly firms. As its name implies, General Motors sought market strength from selling a wide range of car models, which were developed not from start-up operations but from taking over other firms making similar or even distinctively different types of models: from utilitarian family cars to luxury-level vehicles. With his limited-model, integrated-production, business strategy Ford battled on combatively for several decades using a centrally controlled, virtually autocratic management system, which mirrored its centralised production processes (cf Jones 1997, pp. 41–44).

However, GM, like giant manufacturers in other sectors such as DuPont in chemicals, led a search for more decentralised management systems. For not only was the expansion of operations through mass-production creating chains of complex management responsibilities to plan, coordinate and supply manufacturing processes, it was also creating administrative overloads amongst top managers. These were struggling to oversee and develop complexes of essentially separate business at the level of the corporation as a whole. Through trial and error, executives such as Alfred Sloan at General Motors, and Alfred DuPont at his family's chemicals corporation pioneered new management structures which had far-reaching implications (Chandler 1990, pp. 130–162).

Essentially, what became known as the 'M-form' of corporate structure, consisted of grouping business operations into largely self-sufficient organisations dedicated to: product development, manufacturing, logistics, and, in some instances, marketing and operational finances. These groups, or divisions, could consist of product-types, for example luxury cars, market segments, or specialised functions such as research and development. Each division had its own microcosmic management structure and hierarchies, but was set financial targets and allocated working and investment capital by the overall corporate management. This ingenious system freed corporate-level executives from the burdens of managing the detailed affairs and problems of the operating divisions. It also gave top executives more freedom to specialise in planning the overall strategies of the corporation: its relations to competitors, investors, and governments, and to plan new acquisitions to add to the existing divisions.

The M-form took a while to cross the Atlantic owing, in part, to British business attachment to the looser forms of corporate structure consistent with the piecemeal and specialist character of manufacturing that persisted from the 'workshop of the world' era (Elbaum and Lazonick 1986; Hannah 1984, p. 13). As British firms grew larger through acquisitions, they tended to maintain almost intact the local management structures and operations rather than, as with the Americans, integrating these into the rest of the business. Thus the 'holding company' model which favoured *de facto* financial levies to extract profits from a range of disparate operating businesses became a dominant mode of expansion in Britain (Loveridge 1981, 1983). One 1968 survey found that 66 per cent of the top 120 British firms had a central hierarchy limited to the chairman and managing director (Channon 1973, p. 212). It was not until the 1960s and 1970s, through the agency of international consultants, particularly McKinsey, that the American M-form system was adopted in Britain and then other Western economies (Hannah 1976, p. 173). Larger firms in more advanced sectors succeeded with M-form re-organisations but others struggled to make the transition. In the 1960s and 1970s these strugglers became prone to state-promoted rationalisations of their activities. These latter events both accelerated the decline of indigenous localised industrial business networks, discussed in chapter 7, and contributed to the climacteric of public ownership policies described next in chapter 3. But those businesses which had achieved a measure of organisational convergence through divisionalisation were then well placed to move to the next stage of evolution with the neo-liberal promotion of globalised markets.

5. EXPANSION, REPRODUCTION AND COMPETITION

The establishment of divisionalised businesses accelerated and crystallised into what Chandler has called a 'market for control'. With their eyes now fixed on broader national and international strategies, M-form corporations could focus more effectively on take-overs and mergers with other divisionalised firms. Western economies have since experienced various waves of merger activity when propitious financial conditions prompt corporate aggressors to enlarge their capital and status in their industry through raids on competitors and additions to their range of businesses. As in the board game 'Monopoly', the existence of semi-independent divisions made it easier for corporations to trade between themselves parts of their empires which were less profitable or more difficult to manage. But even more significantly, the expanded 'market for corporate control' also made it easier for 'predator' corporations to take over and absorb in their entirety other divisionalised firms. Compatible divisions can be slotted alongside existing ones in the predator firm's structure and the less compatible operations sold off as job-lots to other corporations. Like the praying mantis which completes the sex act by devouring its mate, unions of mega-corporations end with the sacrifice of the taken-over firm's management and, often, swathes of its workforce.

Thus by the middle decades of the twentieth century the essential structures and traits of today's corporate creatures were evolved and functioning. These attributes, which make possible autonomy from, and influence over, other social institutions can thus be summarised as follows:

- Separation of financial ownership from the practical control of the organisation;
- Operational scale geared to matching production of thousands, sometimes millions of identical products to far-flung markets consisting of similar numbers of customers;
- Competitive struggles for survival and control of resources by take-overs and mergers.

6. ONTOLOGY AND STATUS

6.1 Commercial Status

For some critics the most distinctive feature of such firms in the Anglo-Saxon societies derives from their legal status as independent, corporate subjects (cf Bakan 2004). There is of course a social class of human executives with its own interests and distinctive types of behaviour. At times the pursuit of these interests may damage and even disable their corporate hosts. However, such managers can only pursue their separate interests through, and on behalf of, the collective entity. Financial decline, failure, or take-over of 'their' company casts managers into a sea of potential oblivion unless they can gain control of another corporate vessel. Managers are therefore constrained to act for, and in the name of their firm. The limited liability principle further encourages the promotion and aggrandisement of the corporate entity rather than the individual executives themselves. In law corporations can enter into contracts. They can pay – and avoid paying – taxes and sue and be sued. In recent decades this legal entity has blurred into a cultural identity.

In the popular, anti-corporate film/video *The Corporation*, members of the public were invited to describe the personality of well-known corporations. The passers-by had no trouble in attributing human characteristics such as 'young', 'energetic', 'outgoing', 'enthusiastic', or even 'aggressive' and 'deceptive', to various prominent, international firms. Since the nineteenth century owners and managers have used the names of their firms as generic publicity for their products. In recent decades, however, this 'brand identity' has gone several steps further.

As the radical critic Naomi Klein has shown, sophisticated marketing and public relations management has been used to blend product characteristics and corporate personas into independent identities within popular culture (Klein 2000). These identities go beyond the utilitarian qualities of the purchasable article. In what Marxists would interpret as hyper-reification, the popular consciousness now perceives corporations as semi-mythic yet real actors to whom they must relate commercially, emotionally and even politically. Much as some media celebrities exist for their publics only as the character or on-stage persona which made them famous, so corporations have come to be identified principally for their cultural identity. Brand value may constitute more of the pricing and costs for taken-over firms than it does of the purchased firm's material assets and revenues; .as with the tobacco giant Philip Morris's purchase of the Kraft foods firm, (*Chicago Tribune*1988).

These corporate identities are thus more than glossy, or controversial, images which haunt the market place and advertising media. In employment relations and human resource management, they have taken on the guise of quasi-spiritual entities with which employees are expected to identify. Much as the role of the football supporter involves sacrificing personal time and commitments for the good of 'the team', so the employee is urged and encouraged to act for the benefit of the employing organisation. In the mid-twentieth century US corporations like IBM, sought – with some success – to inculcate a distinctive corporate mentality ('the IBM way'). Today's corporations expect employees to subscribe to their firms' elaborately publicised 'principles', 'values' and mission statements; credos which all emphasise the distinctiveness of 'their' corporation's personality. Such personalisation of a commercial undertaking – separate from the values or personality of a dominant or founding entrepreneur-owner – would not be possible unless the corporation had achieved separate legal and social status, on a par with, but in some respects exceeding that of human subjects. What the marketing revolution of 'branding' added was another socio-cultural dimension to the corporation's legal personality.

6.2   Some Social Functions of the Modern Corporate Form

There is, however, a danger of these cultural expressions of corporate status obscuring and legitimating the underlying structural essentials. As Perrow has persuasively argued of US corporate developments, the beauty of the share-financed/managerial corporation for its beneficiaries and principal 'agents' is twofold.

1.   It minimises external accountability to its non-financial stakeholders, civil society and the state.

2.   It maximises the opportunities for the business elites to compete amongst each other for financial advantage.

Having the corporation itself as the juridical subject, acts as a kind of legal shield, or masking device, which minimises risks and accountability to the controllers of the firm's critical business decisions. If and when things go wrong – and unless individual executive managers have patently broken laws – it is the non-human subject of the corporation which has to be sanctioned. The business media, and much academic analysis since Berle and Means, tend to identify the executive management as the crucial set of actors in business melodramas. But, as Perrow points out, in the formative years of the US joint-stock corporations there was actually a boardroom troika, composed of the operations managers, wealthy independent shareholders, and representatives of finance houses (Perrow 2002, p. 206). In more recent times, 'venture capitalists', 'corporate raiders' and other forms of independent financial actor sometimes manage to obtain roles within corporate boards. (To appreciate the range of these ventures see Gospel et al. 2014.)

These financial elites thus form the final and critical feature in the anatomy of the contemporary corporation. It is their vested interest in its peculiar independent status which drives them to maintain that independence from political and legal interference and the incursions of other social actors. When new unincorporated businesses appear and flourish pressure and control of expertise and financial resources by these elites constrains the newcomers to convert to the share-financed/managerial model: to 'go public' in the contradictory argot of the business culture. The adroitness and institutionalised behaviours in working the corporate model to its, and their advantage leads financial and executive controllers' to spin off new corporate entities for particular business and financial purposes. Their fondness for its carapacious security is like the snail and its shell: without the corporate framework business executives find it difficult to function. The shell is an organic feature of the snail's anatomy and has to be maintained by it. Likewise the business elites who manage the Anglo-Saxon corporations can only survive and flourish by nourishing and defending, or getting control of, the complex organisations they inhabit and direct: investing capital, optimising income, and paying its various creditors.

CONCLUSION

The key organisational and economic features in the development of the ST/EM or Anglo-Saxon corporate model can therefore be summarised as follows.

- Restricted accountability: to the 'limited liability' of shareholders, together with separation of capital ownership from operational control; creating managerial interests, identities and powers, leaving share owners with only restricted financial claims on these managers.
- A need for vast amounts of capital and shareholdings because widespread adoption of the Fordist model and 'mass commodification' endow corporations with the capability to meet and exploit any human need with a product or service, provided a mass market can be created and sustained.
- Containing operating businesses as divisions of the M-form organisation enables controls over operational complexity and simultaneously creates entities which are both self-sustaining 'communities' and commodities which can be bought and sold amongst corporations as circumstances require.
- Corporate survival and autonomy is secured by the juridical status of corporations as perpetual and independent legal subjects; precluding their re-absorption into society unless the state changes or over-rides this status.

These features constitute the pillars on which the corporation's institutional autonomy rests. In different ways each has contributed to its 'disembedding' from accountability to other social institutions. It is difficult, in the abstract, to single out just one development responsible for the corporation's accumulated power and autonomy. The final chapter explores the question of which is most important for maintaining autonomy from contemporary UK society and which might be changed in order to achieve significant social re-integration.

The next two chapters update the corporation's evolution to its twenty-first century status. These focus particularly on the rise of neo-liberal economic and social policies from the *Sturm* and *Drang* of socialist-collectivist challenges which tried to re-embed the ST/EM model in the 1970s. These last gasp efforts of social democratic and socialist politics were finally headed off by neo-liberal political and ideological programmes. This restoration not only placed corporate roles at the centre of pro-market policies but, through the resulting liberalising of 'global' markets, induced additional adaptations of the basic model. The explosion of deregulated financial markets diversified corporate investors and, together with neo-liberal policies, made financial returns rather than sales, investment or growth, the standard for managerial performance. Externalised supply chains were added to the Fordist logic, resulting in a neo- or even post-Fordism according to some analysts.

As Piore and Sabel have demonstrated (Piore and Sabel 1984), slightly different conjunctions of decisions and politico-economic struggles could have minimised the dominance of Fordist ST/EM firms. Had legal developments and juridical decisions in the UK and USA been less one-directional and more attentive to wider civil society concerns many of the above developments might have been less conducive to corporate autonomy. At present, it would take some kind of revolution in the principles of jurisprudence to reform the legalities on which contemporary business sovereignty rests.

The limited liability principle does, in some respects, minimise corporate obligations to any wider public. But this would not have become so important if investment capital had not become a separate economic interest through the development of stock markets for shorter-term investments. Limited liability did intensify these market relationships. So, in turn, it further limited investor-owners' concerns for the substantive character and actions of the firms. None of that might have mattered so much if corporations had not been able to expand their powers by cracking the operational obstacles which limited their scale, markets and technological capacities. Except for the temporary challenge from organised labour in the 1960s and 1970s, disposal of such enormous economic and organisational resources has meant that only state authorities have any comparable powers with which to challenge or curtail corporate sovereignty.

The inevitability of the Fordist mass-production, mass consumption, mass financing dimensions will be evaluated in chapter 7, through contrasts with alternatives which have had some success outside the English-speaking sphere. Here we will encounter business systems in which some of these corporate features, such as Fordism and separated and remote investor participation, are less crucial. This comparison helps us to assess whether modifying them in the British context could reduce corporate autonomy from society. In chapters 11 and 12 we return to corporate governance aspects such as restricted legal accountability and absentee shareholding, to see whether and how reforms to these might overcome social disembeddedness.

It is possible that private financial funds – hedge funds, sovereign wealth funds etc – might replace much of the shareholder form of corporate governance. This financialised mutation would be even more resistant to increased social re-embedding. Such a 'financialised' economic world – dominated by private-equity owned firms fuelled by speculative and equally autonomous global financial capital – was strengthening prior to the 2007 financial crash. The impact of the financialisation achieved before the crash is examined in chapters 5 and 10. But the survival of a reformed ST/EM model with its mutual advantages for investment funds and executive managements, make its continuation more plausible than replacement by a private equity regime. Other alternatives include mutual and cooperative forms of financing and ownership, whose advantages are examined in chapters 7 and 11. However, because of its identity as a subject, the ST/EM firm needs public-facing corporate cultures and responsiveness. It also possesses the rudiments of shareholder democracy and legal liabilities. All of which, as the final chapters show, have endowed the Anglo-Saxon model with some potential for progressive reform towards greater social integration and accountability. Of all the pillars of corporate autonomy, it is these *governance* aspects which seem most amenable for reducing that autonomous power.

From sociological perspectives, the preceding evolutionary account is, of course, highly selective. There are many empirical and historical nuances to these features. By the mid-1960s the ST/EM corporate system seemed to be perfectly formed. In some respects the financialisation and deregulation changes after 1980 only intensified the potential inherent in its basic traits (Toms and Wilson 2003, pp. 15–16). Yet the Anglo-Saxon model actually encountered severe economic and political stress-tests in the 1970s, some of which threatened to lead to other alternatives. It was only by surviving this turmoil that the current, revitalised, financialised and globally oriented version prospered. Before examining this latter development in chapter 4, we need to review the failure, in the UK, of 1970s programmes for greater social accountability. For these failures, ironically, helped create the political space and popularity for today's financialised and more disembedded forms of the basic ST/EM model.

NOTE

1. For a dissenting interpretation of the significance of the Dartmouth College judgement for corporate personhood, see Hessen 1989.

3. Social challenges for corporate accountability: the rise and fall of state collectivism

> Left thinking on ... public ownership ... in the context of globalization and contemporary economic conditions has scarcely advanced since the early 1980s and the heated debates ... around the alternative economic strategy (AES) and movement for workers' control. (Cumbers and McMaster 2012, p. 359)

INTRODUCTION

These days, calls for (re) nationalisation become louder when there are corporate failings and outrages, such as those by energy or rail companies. But these appeals are usually ignored within mainstream politics. Collective ownership and control within a statutory framework now appears as 'the road that cannot be travelled': an approach seen as having failed and therefore being discredited. This demise helps to explain both why contemporary corporations are now largely free from such challenges and why collectivist forms of accountability and control are difficult to advocate. The previous chapter's story of the share-owned, executive-managed (ST/EM), 'Anglo-Saxon' corporation has been an international one. We have examined the growth of similar appropriate legal forms and common, cross-national organisational structures. This chapter, however, concentrates on the United Kingdom between 1945 and 1979. This narrower focus is adopted because it was the failure of collectivist attempts at greater social control in the UK which contributed to the broader international resurgence and dominance of the ST/EM corporation.

Over a few decades, 1945–2000, the UK has been a test bed for contrasting and conflicting ideas, experiments and business models. From a system dominated by independent investor capital and businesses and stock-market financed corporations it moved to an economy based on 'nationalised industries'. Then, after experiments with combinations of industrial democracy and strategic state investments, privatised and weakly regulated stock-financed businesses have become dominant. The

54

UK's geo-political position, as a cultural half-way house between Europe and the USA, has also created examples of public policy approaches to business that have influenced many other countries. In some respects the UK has represented a battle-ground of ideas about economics and business between the differing North American and European traditions: the one biased more to lightly regulated, market-based coordination of business, the other articulated to state and public institutions. Both traditions have alternated as the dominant influence on the British system.

In these and other respects the UK usefully illustrates the importance of politics and ideas on the apparently pragmatic and objective field of market institutions. This chapter therefore examines the logic and aims of the mid-century nationalisation programmes in the UK, their complications and also the attempted solutions to the impasses of the model. Nationalisation sought to 'socialise' corporations by explicit changes to the autonomous control, financing and competitive dimensions described in the previous chapter. Implicitly, the nationalisation programmes also aimed at changing the social status and legitimacy of big business from a private, profit-oriented enterprise to one based on contributions to the collective social welfare of the whole society. Crudely, more success was experienced with the explicit aims than the implicit discursive ones. We need to consider not only the structural changes and policies, but the ideas behind the rise of the collectively owned, public corporation, the dominance of the 'nationalised' industrial model and the 1970s conflicts to establish alternatives.

One key alternative attempt in these conflicts, which has contemporary relevance, was a democratisation of corporate governance. In the 70s this project was aimed at the internal hierarchical dimension of the corporate model discussed in chapter 2: a feature which the mid-century nationalisation programmes had largely ignored. Analysis of this climactic episode shows not only why that democratisation movement failed, but also how the related decline of all public ownership and control programmes facilitated the demise of collective control and the rise of its diametric opposite. That is, neo-liberal privatisation and deregulation were enabled as the only credible alternative to what was once a near-consensus on the merits of state-controlled collectivism. Yet this eclipse did not occur because of intrinsic economic (in)efficiencies, nor even because of public costs – as capitalist folk-lore claims. A resurgent ST/EM model triumphed because the dynamics of economic and business development became concentrated within the narrow but intensive conflicts of political calculation and schism.

1. BUSINESS ACCOUNTABILITY AS COMMON OWNERSHIP

On 3 August 1945, Labour's Minister for Fuel and Power, Emmanuel 'Manny' Shinwell convened his first meeting of advisers and civil servants to plan the public ownership and integration of coal mining firms as the election manifesto of his victorious incoming government had promised. As his story has it, Shinwell was disappointed to find that there was 'no blueprint' for the new form of public-sector corporation. Ironically, for a government dedicated to economic planning, and whether through civil service machinations or Labour Party incompetence, a detailed and common legal and organisational form for the new entities had not been prepared (McKendrick and Outhwaite 1986, p. 229; Greenleaf 2003, p. 386). Instead, Shinwell and other Labour ministers rapidly adopted the existing public corporation model of state-owned and governmentally controlled public corporations. Why did common ownership, and this particular organisational model, become the default paradigm for focussing business operations onto wider social objectives?

The answer lies in the 'mixture of socialist theory, liberal expediency and political empiricism' (Beacham 1950) which dominated during the middle decades of the twentieth century. The staccato strengthening of trade unionism after the 1920s and then during World War II gave it more influence on corporate management. But to union leaders and reform-minded observers it was clear that, whatever the benefits of trade unionism, it could not influence the numbers of jobs created and the location and type of investment and employment. World War I had also involved panoplies of controls and direction of industry, but these were not continued in peacetime. Then governments' influence was limited to taxation, subsidies and other inducements and penalties such as encouragement of mergers in 'declining' industrial sectors (Eichengreen 1994, p. 34), or the regulation of working conditions, safety and hours. Apart from mild subsidies and soft loans, like social infrastructure improvements under the Special Areas Commissions (Garside 2002, pp. 255–65), there was little or no public or state control over what was to be produced, where and by whom. A range of centre and left-wing opinion interpreted 1920s turmoil and the 1930s Depression as showing that orthodox market competition between firms was economically and socially wasteful and potentially ruinous, while the alternative of exploitative private monopolies was economically inefficient (Jackson 2012).

State control of industry and business 'may be supervisory, regulatory or proprietary' (Schmitoff 1951, p. 564). In Britain, unlike the USA, state control became synonymous with proprietary control; albeit mediated via organisation as state-owned but separately managed public corporations. In the USA however, Franklin Roosevelt's Democratic administrations of 1933 to 1945 deliberately chose different non-proprietary controls. As Hawley describes it, the 1933 National Industrial Recovery Act authorised: 'self-governing trade associations that would write their own codes and enforce them through public power with a minimum of government supervision' with planning by industrial councils of the associations. The state was only to be involved as a kind of ringmaster for collectivist democracy and purposive national planning, through the 'concentration, cooperation and control' of business, farmers, labour and the state (Hawley 1995, p. 44). Such types of political coordination are usually identified as 'corporatism'.

The relative failure of some of these New Deal initiatives swayed the British Labour movement towards alternative, more direct forms of control and accountability; as it refocussed its strategies during 14 years out of office between 1931 and 1945. Roosevelt's first, and subsequently abandoned, National Industrial Recovery Act involved agreed price-setting and regulation; plus output and capacity targets amongst industry and trade associations of firms coordinated by government representatives. But the schemes produced only limited benefits and were, in any case, struck down by a Supreme Court decision in 1935 only two years after their inception (Hawley 1995). The New Deal did set up some enduring non-industrial public corporations (Federal National Mortgage Association, Federal Deposit Insurance Corporation, Federal Crop Insurance Corporation) but only one *de novo* state-owned industrial corporation was established. This was the multi-functional, and still functioning, Tennessee Valley Authority. TVA was the exception that proved the rule that, in general, the New Deal administration preferred working with oligopolistic cartel-oriented business groups, rather than replacing these with publicly controlled and accountable alternatives. Industrial planning and coordination through the National Recovery Administration's corporatist trade groups was initially favoured by some in the British Labour movement. However the NIRA's failure persuaded Labour's more influential sections against corporatist supervision for the UK, while the isolated success of a 'nationalised' TVA re-affirmed the longer standing support for nationalisation by bodies such as the Trades Union Congress (Malament 1978). There was no consensus on the exact forms within which publicly or collectively owned and controlled undertakings would be organised.

2. THE IDEA OF A NATIONALISED INDUSTRY

Although a common model did appear *post hoc*, this was via a process of separate nationalisation acts which each relevant minister, such as Shinwell, had to introduce. The reasons for this vagueness and the pragmatic solutions that the erstwhile collectivist Labour governments adopted are worth analysing in light of the subsequent consequences of their eventual 'nationalisation' model. In Beacham's contemporary diagnosis the various nationalisation acts were 'compounded of a mixture of socialist theory, liberal expediency and political empiricism' (Beacham 1950). The eventual model adopted can be explored through each of these three influences.

2.1 Socialist Theory

The roots of the socialist theory of collectivism go back to the nineteenth-century ideological origins of socialist economic philosophy and the early twentieth-century birth of the British Labour Party. A decisive intellectual version of the centuries-old socialist dream of the replacement of private by common ownership was that based on schematic definitions in the writings of Marx and Engels (Tomlinson 2002, p. 14, n. 31).This had direct and a more important indirect subsequent influence via its inspiration of the Russian Marxists and the path-breaking practices of economic organisation in the Soviet Union. Despite the centrality of collective public ownership of business to their version of socialism, Marx and Engels provided no detailed prescription for the organisation and control of socialised capital. All that they did was to set out highly precise criteria and functions for common ownership. Marx's *Critique of the Gotha Programme* (1875/1970) – a tract targeted at the formative German Social Democratic Party – set out succinct definitions and rationale.

> If the elements of production are so distributed, then the present-day distribution of the means of consumption results automatically. If the material conditions of production are the co-operative property of the workers themselves, then there likewise results a distribution of the means of consumption different from the present one. (Marx 1875, Section I, 3)

In the much earlier, but more widely known, *Manifesto of the Communist Party*, Marx and Engels explained the logic for 'socialising' the capital locked up in private firms.

> Capital is a collective product, and only by the united action of many members, nay, in the last resort, only by the united action of all members of society, can it be set in motion. Capital is therefore not only personal; it is a social power. When, therefore, capital is converted into common property, into the property of all members of society, personal property is not thereby transformed into social property. It is only the social character of the property that is changed. It loses its class character. (Marx and Engels 1848, Chapter 2)

The purposes of common and collective ownership are therefore not necessarily the intrinsic economic ones of, say, greater efficiency or optimising the allocation of resources. It is rather to serve social ends to contribute to the erosion of class divisions and inequalities. The *Critique* also explained another Marxist trope: the necessary logic of associating common ownership with large-scale industry.

> On the other hand, the proletariat is revolutionary relative to the bourgeoisie because, having itself grown up on the basis of large-scale industry, it strives to strip off from production the capitalist character that the bourgeoisie seeks to perpetuate. (Marx 1875, Section 1, 4)

This vision had little time for other forms of common ownership, despite their obvious localised and partial successes. Thus Marx contrasts transformation of capitalist firms with cooperative forms of business ownership:

> … working to revolutionize the present conditions of production … has nothing in common with the foundation of co-operative societies with state aid … as far as the present co-operative societies are concerned, they are of value only insofar as they are the independent creations of the workers and not protégés either of the governments or of the bourgeois. (Marx 1875, Section 3)

2.2   Political Empiricism

The relevance of these distinctions to Manny Shinwell's dilemma lies in their influence on the definition of common ownership in the founding constitution of his Labour Party. Despite the relatively early formation of industrial capitalism in Britain and its massive working class, it lagged behind others in the formation of a socialist political party. It was not until 1900 that a loose consortium of trade union and socialist MPs formed a parliamentary Labour Party. The formal formation of a national body which federated existing socialist, cooperative and trade union organisations was delayed until 1918. At that point the Fabian Society representative, Sidney Webb, was delegated to write the new Party's

constitution. On the thorny issue of collective ownership Webb's diffi-
culty was devising a formula that would satisfy the contrasting expectations and philosophies of the Party's different constituent sections: trade
unions, radical and 'guild' socialists, the cooperative movement and
State-centric reformers such as the Fabians themselves. Webb's formulation, subsequently agreed by all of the constituent groups, was a
masterpiece of compromise and abstraction.[1]

Its subsequent impact and connotations, for national politics in the UK,
make the eventual Clause IV, section 4 of the 1918 Labour Party
constitution worth considering in full.

> To secure for the workers by hand or by brain the full fruits of their industry
> and the most equitable distribution thereof that may be possible upon the
> basis of the common ownership of the means of production, distribution, and
> exchange, and the best obtainable system of popular administration and
> control of each industry or service.

Karl Marx would have turned in his grave at this denial of his Gotha
Programme critique of the notion that collective ownership could return
'the full fruits' of workers' labour.

However, the two critical, substantive features of the Clause IV
declaration are: (1) the idea that common ownership functions to serve
distributive ends, and (2) there should be no fixed means for controlling
and holding collectively owned business to account. 'Administration' and
'control' were to be 'popular' – in the sense of accountable to the British
people. However, they were also pragmatically defined: 'the best obtain-
able system', but variable and relative to the 'industry or service'
concerned: Webb's logic was impeccable and effective. These phrases
allowed each of the Party's ideological constituencies to believe that their
preferred form of ownership and control – cooperatives, state enterprises,
worker-managed – could still be achieved when the powers of government office would enable them. A summary verdict would be that the
British Labour Party adopted common ownership as a branding device to
distinguish itself from other political parties – Liberal Party leaders were
already proponents and prompters of state intervention in industry – and
as a compromise formula to unite its different political factions.

After the adoption of common ownership as the differentiating concept
for the fledgling Labour Party in 1918, the role of publicly controlled
businesses was seen as a, possibly *the*, major means for promoting
equality and economic welfare. As the influential1934 Party document
For Socialism and Peace argued, capitalist ownership created an inherent
restriction on the economic potential of industry and services:

the public ownership and control of the primary industries and services is an essential foundation step, and on no other terms, as their previous history and present situation make manifest, can these industries and services be freed from the fatal restrictions placed upon them by vested interests and chaotic conditions. (Labour Party 1934, p. 19)

For Labour, at this time, reorganisation of industries through public ownership would also entail 'their increased productive capacity [to] secure the higher wages, the shorter hours of labour and the economic security' (Labour Party 1934, p. 20). 'Common Ownership of the Means of Production' and of '... systems and methods of administration and control to promote not profiteering, but the public interest' (Labour Party 1918, p. 12) would realise this greater efficiency. This was an argument for nationalisation that can be traced back to Sidney Webb's treatise for the Party.

2.3 Liberal Expediency and the Rise of the 'Nationalisation' Model

But Sidney Webb's subtleties and the bold visions of *For Socialism and Peace* were of little help to Manny Shinwell sitting in his office at the Ministry of Fuel and Power in 1945, bemoaning the absence of a 'blueprint'. In the absence of any conceptual model and categorical guidelines, Shinwell and other cabinet colleagues fell back on politically acceptable and practically effective existing arrangements for the 'best available system of popular administration and control'. Under the influence of powerful figures in the Labour movement's leaderships, they turned to the public corporation form pioneered in the inter-war years in organisations such as the British Broadcasting Corporation (BBC) and London Transport. In this public corporation model the relevant government department appoints the top executives. Its authority is defined by a charter with capital and spending and revenue plans approved by the government department which decides the proportion of revenues or state subsidies for a set period.

The relative efficacy of this model can be gauged by the longevity of its prototypes. The BBC model was established in 1927 and London Transport (as the London Passenger Transport Board), effectively a regional nationalised industry, in 1933. Despite crises and modifications, especially to London Transport, in the volatile politico-economic period of privatisations during the 1970s and 1980s, their basic organisational principles have remained unchanged for around 80 years. The common principles are that the prices set for the corporations' basic services – for the BBC this is the fee which licenses use of television and radio receivers – have to be approved by the government department, or London local government authority in the case of London Transport. Out of this revenue capital expenditure is funded.

The post-WWII corporations, however, differed from these earlier forms in being directly accountable to the relevant minister in terms of policies and appointments and, thereby, indirectly accountable to Parliament for policies adopted (Schmitoff 1951, p. 568). These dedicated services were not expected to serve as wider-ranging social contributions and political functions. Yet, as in other countries (Clifton et al., 2004, p. 8) the inherent contradiction in the nationalised industries set up by the post-war Labour government was that their remit was partly socio-political and partly macro-economic (O'Hara 2009). The social aims were to realise the pent-up expectations of Labour Party supporters and members for remedies to the socio-economic inequalities of capitalism. The economic purposes were to act as engines of investment and industrial reconstruction to remedy the effects of war-time destruction and pre-war depression. Sidney Webb's constitutional subtleties also turned out to have a painful side-effect as far as some interpretations of 'popular administration and control' were concerned.

After 1945 Labour ministers were able to enact what, in retrospect, seemed an inappropriate, one-size-fits-all, model for any industrial sector because of favourable cultural, political and economic circumstances. One factor was the positive impressions on the Left, of the apparent success of the post-1917 Soviet model. From a distance this system appeared to combine elements of worker-management (the original 'soviets' of workers, peasants and soldiers) with centralised state ownership and direction to promote economic growth through coordinated industrial planning. The rival model, of cooperative and mutual forms, seemed to lack this centralised economic potency. Moreover after 1927, a *de facto* electoral merger of the Co-operative Party with the Labour Party in Britain muffled the political case for widespread mutualism as a principle of enterprise organisation, even with the blank canvass of reform provided by Labour's 1945 landslide election victory (Burge 2012).

Moreover, as Berle and Means were arguing in the USA, and Labour minister Anthony Crosland would still insist during the political maelstrom of the 1970s (see below), many believed that share-owned corporations were gradually and accidentally 'socialising' themselves. They had become dependent on the pooled investment funds of diverse owners which now owned most corporate shares. John Maynard Keynes, staunch Liberal and the economist whose theory underlay the post-WWII managed economy, had said as much (Keynes 1926). Yet, despite differences in design, a consensus had built up, across the left and centre of the political spectrum, on the need for an alternative to the apparently failed private enterprise system. Such thinking was only strengthened by the length of the 1930s recession as Britain's political leadership drifted into war with the rising fascist regimes. The attractiveness of collectivist alternatives was only enhanced by centre-right politicians' defence of, and support for an economic system seemingly intimately enmeshed not only with economic failure, poverty and deprivation, but also with resort to a major war. The political and cultural ascendancy of state-collectivist ideas also benefited from the image of centralised control as new, progressive and relatively successful in both the First and Second World Wars. Indeed by 1943, even Winston Churchill, the outstanding statesman and Conservative leader of the war-time coalition, conceded that state-controlled businesses would be needed in the peace-time economy (Schmitoff 1951, p. 557).

For the UK, this emphasis can be traced back to the Labour Party's adoption of the compromise Clause IV on common ownership in its 1918 constitution and its political 'branding' to distinguish the party from Liberal competitors on the right and the emerging Communists on the left. Co-operators, of course, were subsequently disappointed (Robertson 2009); but they had already built up networks of their own autonomous businesses at local and national level. A more intransigent alternative, gaining considerable subsequent importance in the 1970s, was the trade union advocacy of industrial democracy and workers control. As far back as the 1919 Sankey Commission on reform of the coal industry, liberals and socialists had argued the case for worker participation in industrial management (Jackson 2012, pp. 46–8). There had also been a grudging inclusion of worker participation in the running of nationalised industries in seminal Party declarations such as *For Socialism and Peace*. These had proposed that publicly owned industries would be run by bodies on which the workers of those industries would be represented (Labour Party 1934, pp. 22–6).Though subsequently squeezed out of political influence and side-lined within the Labour Party by the 1940s, (Crompton, 2009) trade union and radical political advocacy of workers' control survived to become more vocal and influential later, in the booming labour markets of the1950s and 1960s.

At that later point they combined with a more politically assertive and militant trade unionism, with intra- and extra-Party power bases in the unions, which attacked, from the Left, the weak (by any standards) provisions for worker involvement in the nationalised industries. The workers' role in these was not very different from that in the more progressive private firms. Even in the nationalised coal industry, its vociferous and frequently militant trade unions had to accept a back-seat role in the running of the National Coal Board and restrict themselves mainly to conventional collective bargaining. Throughout the national-isations between 1946 and 1951, the Labour government confined worker participation to the relatively trivial forums of consultative committees in basic industries: coal, long distance communications (the Post Office, the Cable and Wireless company), railways and iron and steel.

3. MODERNISING THE NATIONALISED INDUSTRY MODEL

By the 1960s the contradictory expectations of 'nationalised' industry for both economic efficiency and social justice were fuelling dissatisfaction on both the left and right of the mainstream of the Labour Party. As early as 1951, observers were pointing out the potential conflict between the spheres of ministerial prerogatives and the managerial policy-making (Schmitoff 1951, p. 571).The post-war political consensus limited the Conservative Party's instinctive hostility toward public ownership. Gov-erning from 1951 to 1964, the Tories restricted de-nationalisation to early re-privatisations in the more contentious sectors such as iron and steel and road transport, where a more plausible case for private competitive enterprises could be made. Conservative Harold Macmillan had been a prominent advocate in the 1930s of a 'Third Way' between unregulated capitalism and comprehensive socialism. Under his extended post-war premiership (1956–1963) of the Tory government, the party of 'free enterprise' was prepared to 'live and let live' with the nationalised sectors in a mixed economy. However, under the avowedly technocratic and interventionist Labour governments of Harold Wilson, between 1964 and 1970, the role of state ownership and economic direction was further revised. The Wilson cabinets paid lip service, where necessary, to socialistic pleas for more radical approaches to collective, state, owner-ship. However, their main interest in, and justification for the latter was to boost economic growth and efficiency – widely seen to be flagging after the early post-war period of growth and affluence.

Although steel was again nationalised and some forms of public transport were added to the existing operations in the 'public sector', the 1964–70 Labour governments attempted no other direct assaults on corporate ownership. The main thrusts of economic interventionism were well-trumpeted but ineffective: target setting in a national planning bureaucracy and support for the modernisation and revitalisation of manufacturing industry through the directive and publicist efforts of a

Ministry of Technology. There was also a kind of state-owned merchant bank: the Industrial Reorganisation Corporation, aimed at efficiency-inducing corporate mergers. Labour lost the 1970 election, in part because of the failure of these and other initiatives to expand economic growth. But the incoming, short-lived Conservative government of Edward Heath quickly dropped its pre-election pro-market liberalisation philosophy and also adopted Wilsonesque dirigisme. Commentators and activists on both the Left and Right then began pressing their own widely contrasting recipes for economic recovery. The Right, grouped around nascent neo-liberals such as Keith Joseph and campaigning forums such as the Selsdon Group – named after the venue where Heath's Conservatives had formulated their ephemeral rejection of statist economics – had another answer. This was denationalisation, de-regulation, tax cutting, and a transfer of national spending from the state to the private sector.

Although these campaigns were at first confined to the political fringes, problems with the nationalised industry model persisted. Rising unemployment and political expediency forced both Conservative and Labour governments to nationalise more manufacturing firms in the 1970s. British Aerospace, Rolls Royce, British Leyland and British Shipbuilders were only some of the struggling and failing corporations taken into the state's embrace. Though not all adopted the public corporation model of the earlier phase of nationalisation, by the mid-1970s a fifth of total UK capital investment was in state corporations (O'Hara 2009, p. 508). But crisis thinking was beginning to focus on the first-wave nationalised corporations. Their labour productivity, which was improving through the 1960s, deteriorated in the 1970s. Attempted reforms only heightened confusion over both their accountability, and the criteria of efficiency – competitiveness? or public contributions? – by which they were to be assessed (Floud and McCloskey 1992, pp. 181–2). Wider-ranging critiques, such as those of the subsequent Green movement icon E.F. Schumacher, pointed to the contradictions between political overlords demanding both profitability and their imposition of social objectives on nationalised industries. As a former chief economist for the National Coal Board, Schumacher was well placed to criticise also the over-centralisation of operating decisions by industry chiefs and the absence of significant inputs from what today would be called 'stakeholders' into the industries' policies (Schumacher 1973, pp. 225–6).

But from 1970 Labour Party radicals, smarting from that unexpected electoral defeat, began formulating various alternatives to the Heath government's initial, neo-liberal case for disengagement from state control. Labour resumed office after the 1974 miners' strike had led Heath to call a premature and hasty general election. The Labour leadership's ideas envisaged a more porous public sector that could attract private sector finance and provide a more liberal, competitive and decentralised alternative. As Labour PM, Wilson oversaw the policy translation of such ideas which eventually degenerated into an Industrial Re-Organisation Corporation, whose main focus became to promote ultimately unsuccessful mergers between large private manufacturing firms (O'Hara 2009). The financing of these became tied to the traditional City of London financial institutions. Meanwhile, from elsewhere in the Labour movement, committee reports and annual conference motions in 1971 began referring to the concept of industrial democracy as, at least, an adjunct to orthodox management and union-employer bargaining. Sometime minister and emerging leader of the Labour left, Anthony ('Tony') Wedgwood Benn, even proposed, as early as 1971, annual registrations of private companies that would be conditional upon affirmations of their integrity from workforce representatives (Armstrong et al. 1984, p. 436). The implicit and general sentiment was that social redirection of businesses would need a new element to transcend the unproductive stalemates over pie-sharing with traditional enterprise managements (Hatfield 1978, pp. 54–55).

The post 1960s general climate of agitation for greater participation, and greater accountability of society's power holders included forums such as the influential Institute for Workers' Control. The IWC eulogised both previous episodes of worker control and workplace participation in other countries. Marxist-inspired protagonists celebrated the period of shop-steward control of workplaces on 'Red Clydeside' in Scotland during the First World War. Others made a case for adopting the model of worker self-management in the Yugoslav system of state enterprises (Coates and Topham 1968/1970, pp. 349–436). Less dramatically, the case of the systematic representation of workers on the works councils and supervisory boards of West German companies – as 'codetermination' (*Mitbestimmung*) – suggested a potential link with greater productivity and economic profitability (Batstone and Davies, 1976). By 1968, even leaders of some of the biggest unions were calling for reforms to make managements accountable to a system of workers' councils in the nationalisation of the biggest private firms (Scanlon 1968).

General principles of worker participation had a broad appeal beyond trade unions and the socialist left. They could be interpreted as another 'Third Way' between capitalism and Soviet-style state-ownership of enterprises. The early 1970s also witnessed a spate of worker occupations: 'sit-ins' and 'work-ins' to try to stave off job losses and factory closures (Spencer 1991, pp. 187, 197; Gold 2010). Such episodes were linked to the worsening economic climate of rising inflation and flagging aggregate demand which had given a sharper edge to the militancy and political radicalism of the shop-steward movement. The latter had been growing in scale and influence through the wage militancy of the 1950s and 1960s. In some industries these unofficial networks, some encouraged by the more radical union leaderships, began to out-flank the official trade union structures in countering employers' authority. On one estimate there were more than 250 workplace occupations between 1969 and 1979 (Tuckman 2011).

One influential solution to economic and industrial failings, which also crystallised the ethos of the sit-ins and occupations and the wider popularity of workplace unionism, was the January 1975 plan of the powerful Lucas Aerospace company's Shop Stewards Combine Committee (SSCC). To counter management proposals to close factories and cut jobs, the Lucas stewards came up with their own alternative investment and production plan. With a membership that included qualified designers and engineers, the Committee, which had already defeated Lucas management in one dispute over wages and jobs, was well equipped to frame technical alternatives to the Lucas division's manufacturing specialisation in military aircraft equipment. The SSCC plan proposed a change in the product line to medical and other socially useful technologies including medical diagnostic and treatment equipment and – ahead of its time – a range of alternative energy sources such as solar collecting equipment and wind generators (New Scientist 1975; STEPS, 2014).

This combination of worker activism and 'socially-useful' alternatives to the orthodox products of struggling capitalist firms had an immediate appeal to a broad swathe of the British Left in and beyond the Labour Party. But it was of particular relevance to the faction of opinion which had, by 1974, established an influential position in Labour's policy making machinery. This faction was led, politically, by the former Minister of Technology, Tony Benn – a recent convert to the political role of workplace unionism – and intellectually by a Sussex University lecturer, ex-civil servant and soon to be MP, Stuart Holland. Their aim was to revitalise and control British industry while transcending the limitations of the older nationalised industry model. During Labour's four-year spell in Opposition to the Heath government this informal set within the Labour Party managed to get the following proposals accepted as Party policy.

- New forms of public enterprise involving strategic shareholdings in key firms by a National Enterprise Board;
- Planning agreements between public bodies and private firms covering up to 100 firms;

- Use of a National Enterprise Board to channel investments between strategically crucial firms;
- New nationalisations of sectors such as aircraft manufacture;
- 'Major legislation to extend industrial democracy' (Hatfield 1978, p. 173).

The 1974 General Election was called precipitously by the Heath government to resolve its bitter conflict with striking mineworkers. Labour's pre-election Manifesto commitments did not explicitly connect industrial democracy with the proposals for extended and reformed public ownership. However, this link was clearly envisaged by the ascendant Bennites and Left trade union leaders within the Party. It was not until after the Bennite Left's exclusion from governmental power that these ideas became systematised into their Alternative Economic Strategy (AES). But that programme made explicit the existing, implicit theme of squaring the circle of remote and unfocussed public ownership and the movement for industrial democracy. The British Labour Party's post-WWII formula of nationalised industries organised as public corporations had become widely regarded as unsuitable for the broader renewal of industrial vitality in the 1970s. The proto-AES sought to tackle a problem of Left politics after the upsurge of 1960s radicalism – how to combat economic stagnation – but also sought to meet supporters'/radicals' demands for more democratic accountability (Callaghan 2000).

4. THE CLIMACTERIC OF COLLECTIVE CONTROL POLITICS: INTELLECTUAL CONTEXT

The Bennite recipes for transcending the traditional Labour model for public ownership also broke new ground in the intellectual and academic ideas and debates from which they emerged. Academics in Britain and North America had been analysing and debating the nature of the 'new capitalism' since Berle and Means' seminal 1930s book *The Modern Corporation and Private Property*. This thesis was given added significance by business's role in the uninterrupted post-war economic boom. The crux of this debate was whether the combination of 'enlightened' managerial corporations and progressive, Keynesian, state intervention, had definitively broken with the exploitative and disruptive tendencies of classical capitalism. Had it re-established economic growth on a new institutional basis? For the proponents of this latter view, a key feature was the allegedly transformed nature of the 'modern corporation'.

Taking their cue from Berle and Means, 'managerialists' argued that the loosening of director investor controls over corporate managers had left the top executives with sufficient autonomy to respond to prevailing social norms. If the latter cooperated with their counterparts in the administrative hierarchies of government, it was argued, state organs and corporations could coordinate policies for economic growth to benefit both the expansionary aims of the firms and the social welfare objectives of governments. This argument was buttressed by ancillary theories that the evolving class structure had created commonalities between the roles and interests of the top managers in both the private and public sectors. After some proselytisation of Berle's managerialism by Party insiders (see Brooke 1991), the managerialist perspective's support within the British Labour Party was persuasively advanced by a senior figure and Minister, Anthony Crosland. The intellectual conflict was therefore between Berlian, managerialist corporatism and Euro-socialist industrial democracy. Representing the former, Crosland and his supporters were the main opposition to the democratising counter-philosophy of the Bennites and their intellectual champion Stuart Holland.

Crosland, in his book *The Future of Socialism* (1956) and in other publications, argued that the *de facto* splitting of ownership from control meant that top managers were effectively no more than salaried officials. It was claimed that these were, at least potentially – with the right government prompting – responsive to public interest rather than profit-maximisation aims. Crosland raised the beguiling prospect of a 'share-owning democracy' via the pension, insurance and other savings funds which had become the biggest investors in private corporations. The rhetorical question was: aren't these funds in effect working in the public interest? Crosland's affirmative response was that these investors simply coordinated the savings of millions of ordinary citizens. The funds, it was further argued, were also run by neutral managers rather than self-interested, individual capitalists.

The only remaining conflicts of interest, where governments still needed to intervene to correct economic processes, concerned macro-economic conditions: distortions in the national balance of payments, imbalances in investment between regions, and the deleterious impacts of industry and economic development on local environments. The national balance of payments was a recurrent concern of governments under the Bretton Woods international monetary system: for example, in the UK case, excesses of imports over exports threatened to destabilise financial systems. However in Crosland's view, state economic instruments and policies could smooth out these various frictions; for example through financial incentives to induce firms to invest in regions suffering local decline.

The more radical model of publicly controlled – if not owned – industry came from Labour advisers such as Stuart Holland, an influential member of the Party's key Industrial Policy Group in 1972. This position gave him a stronger platform than advocates of other forms of enhanced state intervention such as the prolific Richard Pryke. In this capacity Holland led the drafting of most of what became the Party's industrial policies for the 1974 General Election, which returned the Party to power. Holland's take on large corporations differed sharply from that of Crosland and the managerialists. In background papers and books, Holland argued that top managers were using their quasi-independence from shareholders to wield the power of their firms' resources in what he called the *meso*-economy: a level of activity cutting through the *macro*-economy, with which conventional policy makers concerned themselves, and the *micro*-economy of families, small firms, individual employees and consumers. Trends to monopoly strengthened top managers' powers: enabling them to 'manage' shareholdings, to keep investors happy and thus secure virtual independence from share capital. Up to this point, Holland's analysis resembles that of the managerialists. However, Holland and other critics drew radically different interpretations about the effects of corporate executives' independence.

Their very size meant, said Holland, that a few giant firms dominate the meso-economy. The top managers of giant firms thus control key economic developments and factors, enabling them to thwart both shareholders and governments, rendering ineffectual conventional economic policies: such as balanced growth and equitable employment, which may clash with corporations' supra-national aims and interests. The Labour Party's aspirations for economic planning to secure socio-economic improvements would only succeed, argued Holland, if these firms and their executives were more publicly accountable through a comprehensive system of planning agreements. These would bind corporations and trade unions together in joint commitments to govern prices, investments and wages (Holland 1972, pp. 7–18, 39–44; Hatfield 1978, pp. 121–7; Callaghan 2000; Thompson 2006, p. 195, n. 15). As a result of their inclusion in the pre-election *Programme* documents of 1973 (Labour Party 1973) and after bitter internal Party debates, public holdings in private corporations, planning agreements and National Enterprise Board, all appeared in Labour's manifesto. Labour's subsequent narrow victory in 1974 could therefore justify claims to have, at least partly, gained electoral support.

Benn, Holland and key Left factions had proposed that the planning agreements, covering 100 major manufacturing firms, other large enterprises and the existing nationalised industry corporations, would be supplemented and sharpened by new forms of public holding in 25 of the most important industrial firms. These strategic holdings were to be funded through a new 'national investment bank' (later re-labelled the National Enterprise Board), controlled and mainly funded by government, and organised as a state holding company. From the vantage point of today's virtual consensus on 'free' markets, these proposals now seem outrageously radical. However, state shareholdings apart, there were definite similarities with the industrial policy framework attempted by Roosevelt's National Recovery programme in 1930s America, as well as the contemporaneous French system of state-directed economic planning. Holland himself drew explicitly from the similar institutions, notably the state investment body the Istituto per la Ricostruzione Industriale, which Italy's post-war governments had adapted from the Fascist era system of industrial organisation (Holland 1972).

The radical political currents of the 1970s contributed one more, distinctive thread to the planning and accountability proposals. Labour's 1972 *Programme* document gave a specific commitment to the introduction of 'industrial democracy', 'especially in the public sector', though without specifying the forms which this should take. The 1974 manifesto limited the application to: 'socialise existing nationalised industries ... to make the management of existing nationalised industries more responsible to the workers in the industry and more responsive to their consumers' needs' (Labour Party 1974, para 4). At the time, industrial democracy was generally regarded as meaning union, or at least worker, representation at senior executive levels of decision-making. Though it had not originally been part of the proposals for corporate planning and supervision, industrial democracy began to be regarded, by its Left and union supporters, as one of the three distinctive pillars of the emerging industrial-economic policy (Wilks 1988, p. 48; Thompson 2006, p. 195). The dominant assumption was that union participation could be achieved by yoking the existing ethos and institutions of company collective bargaining to the proposed planning system. However, there was also an aspiration in some Left and Party circles for industrial democracy and for planning to be linked to parallel proposals for worker-directors.

The powerful TGWU leader Jack Jones had been advocating a process of 'bottom-up' union participation to culminate in worker/union directors for some time (Purdy n.d., p. 10). This view was potentially strengthened by the seal of approval for the latter given by the recommendations of the influential Bullock Committee on Industrial Democracy which reported favourably in 1977. Alas, by that time Holland, leading leftist (ex-) minister Tony Benn and their allies were fighting a rear-guard action on the whole programme for corporate accountability through 'democratic planning'. As early as its return to government in February 1974, the Labour leadership was seeking to reassure the business lobby that it would maintain 'a clear frontier between what is public and what is private industry'(Forester 1979, p. 8). In a heady next few months Benn flew too close to the political sun by leading the 'No' campaign on membership of the European Economic Community. The defeat of that campaign in the national referendum of June 1974 gave Prime Minister Harold Wilson the opportunity to remove Benn from his cabinet post and power base as minister for Trade and Industry (Hatfield 1978, pp. 248–9; Purdy n.d., p. 9).

But the campaign for industrial democracy had a longer half-life. Indeed it developed a separate existence for a few years. Wilson's successor as Labour Prime Minister, James Callaghan, saw industrial democracy as part of a strategy of winning over union power brokers to the stabilisation of economic crisis. So he was minded to support board-level representation of unions, as advocated by influential union leaders (Phillips 2011, p. 17; Morgan, 1997, p. 561). If implemented in either its strong (the 'Majority Report') or weaker form (the 'Minority Report') the Bullock formula could have changed the links between large corporations, other stakeholders and the public policy-making process, through union-backed directors at, or just below, board-level. The business representatives' Minority Report recommended employee representation on 'supervisory' boards – similar to the German two-tier system of control. The union and other members in the majority report wanted unitary boards with equal numbers of worker representatives and executives. Deputy TUC Secretary and Bullock committee member David Lea recalls that without consensus the Labour government's willingness to turn the Report's recommendations into law was undermined. However, Lea acknowledges the several problems that would still have had to be addressed. 'How would they operate in multi-national corporations? Where would other stakeholders (e.g. consumers) fit in? How could they be operated in the public sector?' (*History and Policy* 2010).

Momentum was also lost because the unions disagreed amongst themselves on whether to support or oppose Bullock's main recommendations. Meanwhile organised business waged a concerted and vociferous campaign against it (Useem 1982). Government-union relations were being worsened by the unravelling of the vital Social Contract element of national economic policy. Set up to deflate union-led wage increases in return for price controls, the third round of the Contract ('5% maximum at a time of rising double-digit inflation') was impossible for union leaders and militants to accept. This visible breakdown of union-government collaboration made ambitious industrial democracy proposals seem even less important. Rejection of the Social Contract model also dealt a death blow to hopes of both industrial democracy legislation and 'corporatist' economic planning. Worse, media depictions of unrestrained and militant collective bargaining and strikes in the 1978–79 'Winter of Discontent' discredited Labour's governmental credentials.

Tantalisingly though, Labour had agreed in 1978 to legislate on a version of the Bullock business representatives' Minority Report. Though far from the shared parity of representation proposed by the Majority Report this could still have opened up corporate governance through its specification of sub-board participation for two years, followed by establishment of a 'Rhenish' two-tier board system with one-third of supervisory board seats reserved for employees (UK White Paper 1978). The White Paper particularly singled out nationalised industries as appropriate for these innovations (Davies 1978, p. 268). But then, before legislation could be prepared, Labour lost a confidence vote (by one vote) in the House of Commons after the continuing conflicts over incomes policy were portrayed as public chaos. Labour's subsequent election manifesto promised only to give 'working men and women a voice in the decisions which affect their jobs' (Labour Party 1979, p. 4). Such nuances became irrelevant as media images of union-inspired public chaos helped Thatcher's Conservative Party to an election victory in June 1979. This triumph ushered in wholesale rejection of both democratic and public involvement in corporate accountability for three decades.

5. SUMMARY AND LESSONS

The Conservative neo-liberal victories over Labour, and the wider labour movement from the late 1970s, not only discredited, falsely in some respects, social democratic politics. They also shattered any rehabilitation of the nationalised public corporation model. Henceforth the accountability of all large business undertakings was promoted through market, or crypto-market mechanisms. The post-WWII nationalisation model undoubtedly suffered from political, social and economic flaws. However, despite the concomitant resource and fiscal constraints under which they were run, their contribution to national economic welfare was, on several criteria, not necessarily worse than private firms' performance. Nationalised industries were perennially subjected to government restrictions on their pricing policies and to fluctuating criteria on the returns expected from their state financing. But the 1970s economic crises accentuated these handicaps. The 1970–74 Heath government controlled nationalised corporations' prices but not those of private sector firms

(O'Hara 2009, pp. 518–9). Public spending cuts from 1974 reduced nationalised industry funding by £1bn p.a. (£8.8 billion at 2014 prices). More limited was their internal governance and social responsiveness (Schumacher 1973; Ferner 1988; Heath 2004). The political Left in 1970s Britain interpreted the public corporation's limitations as rendering its original format an unsuitable tool for further, significant reclamation of big business for the public good.

Instead, the political strategies developed by the Labour Left in the 1970s to renew and extend state-controlled common ownership aimed to embody both economic regeneration and greater social accountability. The Left nearly succeeded in reshaping corporations' contributions to economic welfare by both upward and downward accountability. Strategic government shareholdings in key companies through a state-holding company as part of a national planning framework would have involved executives and representatives from a wider range of 200 companies. The planning institutions would have linked to the second strategy of 'downward' social accountability through industrial democracy; as trade union participation in national industrial strategy making; with executive-level roles for worker-union representatives on company boards. These forms of participation were seen as the institutions that would help to both restrain and harness the powers of the 'new class' of corporate managers in the international meso-economy.

This approach and even the more business-favoured form of participation based on contemporary West Germany's *Mitbestimmung* system, failed because of contemporary political dynamics. Yet the next chapter will show that the privatisations which have succeeded the nationalisation model have not been significantly more successful. Indeed there was little evidence at the time of their introduction that they would be more efficient. The major obstacles to democratic planning policies included the organisational complexities and oppositional potential of non-British MNCs such as Ford and IBM. By 1980 an accelerating 10 per cent of UK capital investment belonged to foreign firms, although, unlike today, the FTSE 100 was almost entirely British (Dunning and Archer 1987, p. 22). What intensified the importance of these difficult obstacles was the influence that organised business was able to project into the parliamentary and governmental arenas to undermine the credibility of Bullock's majority report (Useem 1982; Phillips 2011).

However, all of these elements need not necessarily have prevented exploratory or modest attempts at either public stakes with partial planning agreements, or of worker representation in some forms. Indeed, experiments with worker directors proceeded at the nationalised British Steel, British Telecommunications and the Post Office before and after the demise of Bullock. Labour was also inching towards implementation of legislation for dual boards and minority worker representation. What was lacking was broad political and popular support. Though less attractive to the industrial democracy activists, the German system is apparently successful from a business point of view; but even that did not attract decisive support. The Bullock Minority Report had recommended German-style representation on supervisory boards, which is described in chapter 7. But most 1970s 'industrial democrats' rejected this idea as inadequate. Today, it seems substantially superior to any subsequently attempted UK reforms.

This addition of worker representative democracy could have made the public corporation distinctly more socially accountable. The negative power of trade unionism and influential unionists' attachment to a restricted and adversarial role militated against it. Enclosed within an ideology of workerist socialism, their political supporters neglected to consider the Marxist dictum of assessing the 'balance of social forces' in pursuit of their strategy. It was entirely understandable that participation and accountability were defined mainly in relation to the then powerful labour and union interests. But organised labour is only one social interest amongst several. When the political climate turned against union power from 1979 onwards, there were no other sections of society pressing for corporate accountability. One lesson is that movements for corporate reform, as well as decisive government backing, will also need a coalition of social forces, not just one sectional interest.

Over-riding and shaping the political factors was macro-economic crisis. The Labour government veered towards monetarism and fiscal stringency after the IMF crisis of 1976. Ironically, however, implementation of the Bullock recommendations might have persuaded enough unions and their militants to maintain some semblance of an incomes policy under Labour. If this had happened it could have averted the industrial relations crisis of 1978–79, which divided the Labour movement and strengthened support for the Tory opposition (Ackers, 2010). As it was, high inflation and state wage controls deflected even sympathetic unions back to aggressive collective bargaining basics. Reflecting these forces, sharper political divisions emerged within the Labour movement.

Unlike in 1970, the resurgent Tory Party was more successful in agreeing a break with state-interventionist 'corporatism' and all it stood for; winning support instead for 'market forces' forms of accountability. In this vision, nationalised industries were an easy campaign target. In the 1980s, the Conservatives' nascent neo-liberal government and its ideological support were able to dismantle or undermine the political infrastructure of state industrial intervention. It also broke those social forces – the Labour movement organisations – which had generated the collectivist solutions to corporate autonomy and hegemony. By the 1990s, it seemed to many that the failure of this route to social embedding of corporate power had ended democratic forms of account-ability for ever. In reality the broader issue of accountability had only been postponed to the present crisis of economic failure and businesses' social legitimacy.

NOTE

1. As 'nationalisation', the political pedigree of the campaigns for public ownership was associated by Webb's intellectual and marital partner, Beatrice Webb, with the more ideological socialists in the labour movement: '[The Independent Labour Party's] Tom Mann said the progressives on the LCC (Labour Coordinating Committee) were not convinced Socialists ... No one should get the votes of the ILP who did not pledge himself to the "Nationalisation of the Means of Production" ... It was melancholy to see Tom Mann reverting to the sectarian views of the SDF [the former Marxist Social Democratic Federation] ... Keir Hardie [Leader of the ILP], who impressed me very unfavourably, deliberately chooses this policy as the only one which he can boss.'

    However: 'We [the Fabians] should continue our policy of inoculation of giving to each class – to each person – that come under our influence the exact dose of collectivism they were prepared to assimilate' (Beatrice Webb, 23 January 1895, p. 1369).

PART II

Social embedding and disembedding of
business systems

4. The neo-liberalisation of big business: disembedding or re-regulating?

> Regulation ... is not a substitute for competition. It is a means of 'holding the fort' until competition arrives. (Littlechild 1983)

> ... the superstructures, etc. – are never seen to step aside when their work is done or, when the time comes, as his pure phenomena, to scatter before His Majesty the Economy as he strides along the royal road of the Dialectic. (Althusser 1990, p. 113)

INTRODUCTION

Central to the agenda of the UK Conservative governments under Margaret Thatcher was the political destruction of the social democratic business paradigm of publicly owned/controlled industries, centralised trade union bargaining and Keynesian management of the economy. This was a political assassination because, as Vogel comments in the case of the telecommunications industry, 'neither British Telecommunications (BT), nor telecom equipment manufacturers, nor users ever demanded that the government privatise BT or introduce competition in basic telephone services' (Vogel 2005, p. 4). Rather, the new regime replaced social democratic institutions through a gradual but eventually systematic application of neo-liberal policy and ideology. This mission turned the accountability conundrum inside out. No longer would the accountability conduits run from society – albeit via government – into business. Instead the exchange relationships, believed to be at the heart of the business enterprise, would be expanded so that 'market disciplines' would render executives accountable to investors, and contracting businesses accountable to public authorities in terms of price and delivery efficiencies. Other businesses were regarded as accountable to a society conceived as a mosaic of different contractors or 'customers'. Market institutions would be regulated by market institutions. Contemporary corporate power cannot be understood without analysis of this neo-liberal re-engineering of business accountability.

The insurgent neo-liberals characterised nationalised industries as being dogged by 'inefficiency, excessive costs, uneconomic investments, old and outdated products, little innovation, little responsiveness to customer preferences' (Littlechild 2003, p. 4). In hindsight they can also be seen to have lost, or have been deprived of, their sense of social purpose: 'their public mission' (Florio 2004, p. 367). Neo-liberalisers promised to cut the Gordian knot of the manifold financial and efficiency problems attributed to nationalised industry and publicly owned enterprises by 'privatisation': a simple conversion into ST/EM corporations. In this status they would be directly accountable to investors and customers in competitive markets. A key parallel development, assisted by financial authorities and academic economists, was an attempted resolution of the conundrum of shareholder rights *vs* executive independence. It was believed that the simple expedient of treating executive managers as shareholders and remunerating them with shares, would enhance executives' interest in 'shareholder value', making them work more consistently for the mass of investors.

Intellectual justification came from the elaboration of principal-agent theory in which share owners were treated unequivocally as 'owners' (Fama 1980; Fama and Jensen 1983). The sum total of these policy changes – augmented by massive programmes of sales of public property such as council housing and withdrawals of overt subsidies for struggling industrial firms – created a regime committed to market accountability. The initial impacts of this new system soon displayed predictable effects of disembedding from public institutions: excessive executive rewards, destructive mergers and insolvencies, regressive labour relations and exploitative customer services. As a result, existing original and new 'light-touch' regulatory arrangements soon had to adopt, or be adapted to, a strengthened and extended complex of notionally independent, sometimes 'voluntary', regulatory systems and financial rules. Beyond the ex-nationalised firms, analogous problems led to more subtle frameworks of semi-voluntary regulation being introduced for and by other big business enterprises. These will be examined in the next chapter.

The tirades of free market economists on the inefficiencies and costs of regulation (Vogel 1996, pp. 10–11), did not overtly acknowledge it, but the (re)introduction of these complexes of contradictory constraints were tacit acceptances of a brutal fact: that re-empowered corporations did not comply with the text-book ideals of market forces. However, for neo-liberalisers like Stephen Littlechild, cited above, state regulation was only to be a temporary arrangement until full competition emerged to exert market disciplines. Yet regulatory institutions have developed into a twilight world of quasi-, often manipulated, market mechanisms and power-based bargaining strengths. The rest of this chapter describes the stages by which the managed capitalism of social democracy was reconfigured into a triangular stalemate between states and regulators, corporate managements, and a range of financial investment institutions.

Essentially, privatised corporations – and some of their pre-existing private counterparts – were disembedded from their previous social democratic frameworks and enmeshed in new bureaucratised markets, remote from public accountability and civil society, but *not* inside the pure market utopia of economic theology. As the analyses of the privatised utilities will show, whatever the aspirations, superior benefits to consumers have scarcely figured in the regulation of these firms. The present chapter examines the transformation of nationalised industry businesses into oligopolistic corporations and the regulatory problems this conversion has entailed. Together with the concurrent rise of the philosophy and practice of shareholder-value described in more detail in chapter 5, these developments add up to the effective reduction of market accountability to competition for financial advantage. The cases of executive pay and corporate tax avoidance examined in that next chapter illustrate the limitations of the system of voluntary compliance in UK corporate governance codes.

1. ORIGINS AND MOTIVES (1979–83)

As the previous chapter showed, in contrast to the USA, the UK had by the mid-1970s a much broader spectrum of publicly owned enterprises. The inflationary storm of the 1970s recession pushed the social-democratic governments of that period into adding state subsidies, take-overs, or part-nationalisations of other industrial firms, such as the vehicle manufacturer British Leyland, to the roster of nationalised utilities and transport enterprises already taken into state control. The story of the Thatcherite response to this panoply of public obligations (and assets) has been often told, and from several standpoints (*inter alia*: Clarke and Pitelis 1993; Feigenbaum et al. 1998; Jenkins 1995; Martin and Parker 1997; Monbiot 2000; Saunders and Harris 1994). For our purposes, its main features are that the first two Conservative neo-liberal governments faced continuing pressure on public finances while at the same time, for electoral-ideological reasons, aiming to reduce levels of taxation. The revenues from the initial privatisations helped to create the space for tax cuts, as well as stimulating the merchant banking sectors of the financial industry. There was an additional, ideological bonus. Together with the simultaneous sales of public, council-owned, housing to tenants, dependent proletarians could be transformed into property and share-owning bourgeois. All of these policies could be, and were, ideologically gift-wrapped in slogans such as the 'rolling back' of the overbearing state and the 'freeing' of private enterprise. The electorate as a whole was deeply divided by Thatcherite policies and the conflicts they generated. None of her three governments was elected on more than 43 per cent of the votes cast, let alone of eligible voters. However, the apparent enrichment of some sections of the electorate by the privatisations and tax cuts was seen as adding to Thatcherism's electoral popularity (Butler and Kavanagh 1988).

As documented by commentators like Stephen Wilks, the denationalisation and privatisation of state-owned businesses in the UK was later supplemented by wider outsourcing of local and national public housing, social and welfare services (Wilks 2013, p. 121–32). But these later commissioning projects, renewed by the 2010–15 Coalition government, have taken on several of the techniques and organisational processes established by the previous Thatcherite industrial privatisations, such as the railways. These earlier phases dismantled partial or total state ownership of: oil (British Petroleum), aerospace, telecommunications, ports, airports, airlines (British Airways), automobiles (British Leyland), gas, electricity, road freight, railways, buses, water, and mutual savings (Trustee Savings Bank). In all 22 companies were privatised between 1979 and 1987. As the privatisation programme was ramped up during the 1980s it attracted emulators abroad. But the UK's programme, standing at £45 billion, was the biggest in the OECD group of countries; with the exception of Japan's staggered privatisation of Nippon Telegraph & Telephone (NTT) between 1985 and 1996 (Takano 2002).

Given the government's ideological mission for a people's capitalism, there was an understandable increase in individuals' share ownership from 6 per cent to 20 per cent of the general population between 1984 and 1988. However, this expansion was restricted to the higher income groups and was mainly amongst inhabitants of South East England. Share purchases in the privatisations were rightly perceived as windfalls, for the shares sold were generally under-priced relative to their market value, on average by 18.5 per cent (Florio 2004, p. 163). The syndrome was repeated with the 2010 Coalition government's sale of Royal Mail shares in 2013 – at least 40 per cent below their subsequent resale price (NAO 2014). Most individual purchasers of the early privatisation shares resold them to make a quick profit, and an appetite for wider share ownership was minimal. A majority confined themselves to shares in one or two companies. Individual investors' proportion of all stock market shares fell from 28 per cent to 17 per cent between 1989 and 1997 (Parker 2004,

p. 8). More significantly, privatisation augmented the size and thus power of the corporate sector. By 2009, 38 per cent of the *Financial Times* (FT) list of 500 top companies was privatised firms. Excluding US firms, their share capital made up 50 per cent of traded shares (Wilks 2013, p. 126).

Improvements in the privatised firms' economic performance were mostly limited and uneven. Judged on conventional micro-economic criteria, efficiency in terms of labour productivity went up, but that of other factors of production, such as capital equipment, went down. Improved cost efficiencies were largely from exogenous price changes, labour productivity from controversial redundancies, union bashing, or a gradual tightening of external regulation (Florio 2004, p. 342–3; Parker 2004, p. 11). Macro-economic benefits were limited, partly because firms were 'externalising' labour costs onto the workers (by reducing wages), the unemployed and state welfare budgets (Florio 2004, p. 345–6). Consumers of services such as energy and water experienced higher prices. But perhaps the most significant development was the non-development of the Holy Grail of competition. Privatisations were trumpeted as bringing 'healthy' competition to public monopolies to the benefit of consumers. But, by and large, a transfer of ownership by itself achieved little price competition (Florio 2004, p. 348–52).

For policy adviser and uber-regulator Stephen Littlechild, 'Regulation is essentially a means of preventing the worst excesses of monopoly; it is not a substitute for competition. It is a means of "holding the fort" until competition arrives' (Littlechild 1983). Yet the construction of elaborate regulatory systems designed, in part, to achieve market mechanisms has had, at best, only mixed results. Neo-liberal policy-makers recognised the dangers of predatory pricing, particularly by the newly formed mon-opolistic and oligopolistic utility firms. Morana and Sawkins (2002) claim that UK privatisations were premised on the assumption that, especially in sectors like telecommunications, technological progress would stimulate competitive product markets, allowing the eventual relaxation of economic regulation until the competition cavalry arrived. So free market beliefs were modified to create regulatory bodies for each of the corporatised sectors created by privatisation: Ofcom (formerly Oftel) – mainly telecommunications; Ofwat – water; Ofgem, for gas and electricity; and the Office of Rail Regulation (UK Parliament, 2007). As Figure 4.1 shows, the powers of these sector specific bodies to check on operational performance and service standards also overlap with more general regulatory oversight. Regulators' concern with price controls has fluctuated but, by 2006, earlier debates on the intensification of sectoral regulation versus tightening of general competition law petered out. Dedicated regulation rather than competition law predominated (Hancher

2007). The following review of the workings of price regulation in the UK's privatised water and energy sectors indicates the relative strengths and advantages of different regulators, businesses, consumers and investors.

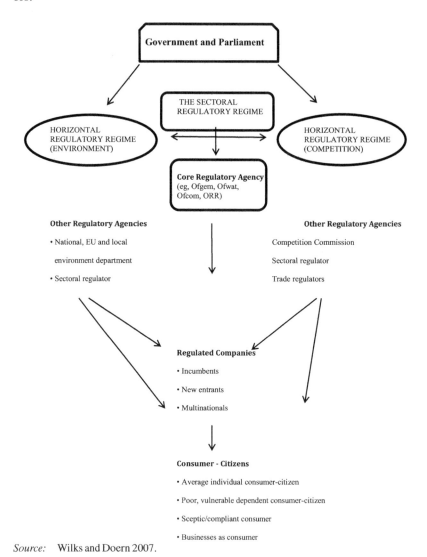

Source: Wilks and Doern 2007.

Figure 4.1   UK sectoral and horizontal regulatory regimes and business and consumer stakeholders

2. INVESTMENT ACCOUNTABILITY VS PUBLIC ACCOUNTABILITY IN PRIVATISED UTILITIES

Probably the starkest case of financial capture in the privatisation and regulation saga is the water industry, as it shows most clearly that the economic regulators' brief was to avoid disrupting the financial security of the industry. According to the 1989 Water Act, the prime duty of OFWAT, the regulator, was not consumer protection but to permit companies a 'reasonable rate of return' on their capital. Regulation had to ensure that it would not jeopardise investors' earnings from loans and share holdings (Morana and Sawkins 2002, p. 185).

Regulators decide price limits for products and services because firms might otherwise use monopoly power in setting customers' prices. But, in doing so, regulators are supposed to take into account what should be regarded as a 'fair' rate of profit. The latter mainly reflects the level of return investors would have received out of profits had they invested in non-regulated firms with comparable levels of risk. So the key factor is not the presence or absence of the prices of alternative products, or the cost components going into the utilities' product. Rather it is the assumption that all utilities have to bid for investment funding from competitive capital markets. 'All that matters is the market cost of capital adjusted for the firm's risk characteristics, irrespective of whether it is a monopoly' (Wright et al. 2003, p. 1). This allowance is known as the rate of return on capital. The accounting formula for these pricing rules is RP–X; where RP is the retail price and X is allowable costs. This equation originated in the protocols drawn up to guide the regulation of BT. Its logic and rationale were drafted in extreme haste, within a week, with one and a half eyes on the political and financial overlords: 'Alan Walters [Margaret Thatcher's Chief Economic Adviser] and BT's merchant bankers considered it better than a profit ceiling, the department's merchant bankers considered it workable, it was politically defensible and indeed attractive, and it carried the day' (Littlechild 2003, p. 35).

Littlechild, who also acted as a regulator for the electricity sector, speaks of investors and others needing to encourage a 'more explicit rate of return approach in the electricity and water sectors' by their 'pressure on regulators to explain their calculations' (Littlechild 2003, p. 47). The limitations of RP–X for stimulating technical investment were eventually recognised; but only to the extent that a 'hybrid model' with both 'price-cap' and a 'rate of return' element was adopted by the water regulator OFWAT (Abou-Seada et al. 2007, p. 10). In that industry, the price cap formula has been explicitly reworked as RPI–X+K, with K being OFWAT's allowance for each company to claim projected financing requirements above inflation for service improvements to customers: again, the cost of capital. What is of greatest significance is that the resulting, projected prices sought/allowed are to pay not only for future operations, but also to cover capital maintenance costs *and* taxation *and* returns on investors' and lenders' capital. Thus shareholders are *ensured* a definite rate of return on their investments.

3.   CREATIVE ACCOUNTING VS CREDIBLE ACCOUNTABILITY

Regulated utilities receive relatively high and guaranteed returns over extended periods. The contributory factors behind this generosity are the accounting conventions employed, inadequate information transparency, and intra-firm accounting practices. Combined with excessive tolerance of debt financing and rivalry between regulators, the net outcome is handsome pay-outs to shareholders and weak public accountability. The opacity of the utilities' financial records handicaps the scope of even the most thorough regulator's scrutiny. The IFS commented in 1997 that there was insufficient transparency in company accounts for regulators to identify equitable price levels and this complaint was still being made in 2013 (Kemp 2013; Utility Week 2013). This lack of transparency is partly the result of the old corporate trick of transfer pricing. Multi-business companies can derive higher allowances from the regulators by manipulating the prices charged by one part of their business to another to inflate their apparent costs (Abou-Seada et al. 2007, p. 18).

After the original privatisations, the energy retailing companies had to buy from a so-called 'Pool' of supplies from energy generating firms. But mergers and take-overs between the supply and retail firms obscured these contracts. Retailers were soon buying their supplies from the generating subsidiaries of their own company. Prices between these could then be set to show increases as necessary and thus justify price hikes to the regulator and for the final consumer (Helm 2013, p. 5). A further factor in the transparency fog is that most private companies do not now use current cost accounting, yet the regulators do. This convention also suits privatised water companies and their merchant bankers because it shows higher repayments due on capital than have actually been paid; thereby releasing funds to pay investor dividends (Cuthbert and Cuthbert 2007). Thus: 'accounting choices have meant that water has been significantly overpriced since privatization and that they make it more profitable for water companies to invest in new infrastructure and/or sweat existing assets, rather than repair or maintain infrastructure' (Abou-Seada et al. 2007, p. 2).

Water companies also benefit from the high capital allowances and artificial investment charges they can deduct from Corporation Tax liabilities. It seems that the sector regulators could reduce the oligopoly of the utilities by referring their behaviour to the Competition Commission. But a vested interest in the status quo has emerged. Jealousy of others encroaching on their authority, and wariness about having their judgments questioned, deter the sector regulators from this option (Helm 2013, p. 10).

Compared to all of the companies in the FTSE All-Share index, there have been few better dividend yields. The generosity of these allowances compared to 'normal' business conditions is illustrated by the fact that the larger merged companies, which took over the original water businesses, generate most of the profits from their UK water operations, rather than from the other trading activities in their ownership (Shaoul 1997, p. 400; Cuthbert 2012, p. 2). A consequence of all of these impasses is lax price-capping allowing disproportionate investor returns. The Institute of Fiscal Studies calculated that between 1991 and 1995, the different types of privatised utilities (including water, energy retailing and transmission) paid out dividends of between 16 per cent and 35 per cent in 'excess' of prevailing market rates (Chennells 1997, p. 14). Utilities' dividend returns have, in general, outperformed the FTSE All Share index. Any claw-back from excessive dividend returns only took place *post facto* after the regulators' fourth or fifth year review, by which time investors could have moved on to new opportunities elsewhere.[1]

4. THE FINANCIAL COSTS OF SHAREHOLDER SUPREMACY

The significance of the corporate diversion of surpluses into shareholders' profits is indicated by the calculations of utility financing expert T. Martin Blaiklock. He estimates that if Thames Water had made no dividend payments over the past 10 years, and had instead used the cash to build up reserves, it could have accumulated £4bn to finance infrastructure works with no extra borrowing, and thus no extra water charges. This arrangement would still have given Thames's investor-owners a two-thirds increase in their shares' value since 2006, instead of the *tenfold* increase they have received (Blaiklock 2013, p. 6).

A related, perverse result of regulators' conventions is the tolerance of excessive debt. They permit high fixed-interest borrowing – which also inflates apparent costs – to make it easier for 'their' firms to raise investment capital. Consequently, the water and other utility companies now rely much more on debt finance. The average level of gearing (debt in relation to assets) in the water industry rose from 41 per cent in 1989–99 to 57 per cent in 2002–03; 85 per cent for water companies such as Anglian and Southern (Abou-Seada et al. 2007). The advantage is that these costs can be offset against special tax allowance for the industry (Chennells 1997, p. 8), further boosting profits for shareholders. One outcome is that Thames, the biggest water utility, is, as one commentary observed: 'crippled with debt, which has jumped from £1.8bn to £8bn over the past decade' under its current owners – private, Luxembourg-based equity funds coordinated by Australian bank Macquarie. 'By maxing out on debt, all the astonishingly high interest payments can be offset against tax, so that in 2012 it paid no tax whatsoever even while paying £279.5m of dividends and minute Luxembourg taxation' (Hutton 2012). The risk is that such over-indebtedness could precipitate a collapse. Paradoxically this puts the companies into a stronger bargaining position with the regulator. Insolvency might require a state-backed bailout, despite the firm having paid little tax to the state that is rescuing it.

So the history and functioning of the regulatory accounting model demonstrates that it biased its methods in favour of shareholders over consumers. Financial analysts' assessments partly confirm the reasons for this confidence. Not only were utilities consistently paying out good dividends, they were able to do so because regulatory rules allowed them to borrow the funds required to pay them (Evans 2013a). Figure 4.2 illustrates the magnitude of this ruse.

Other factors have contributed to regulators' capture by shareholder interests. Throughout the water sector, the regulator calculated that the aggregate costs of capital investment – financing of operations and infrastructure changes, plus returns to lenders and share investors – made up 58.4 per cent of customers' bills for the period 2010–15. Of this amount, return on capital – gross profit – by itself was almost 27 per cent. If regulators want to cut or cap the utilities' charges to consumers they have to accept that the companies will find the necessary savings from one or more of three sources: reductions in capital investment, job cuts, or reductions to shareholders' returns. Yet when regulators have tried to exert restraints it has not been the shareholding constituency that has suffered. Investors have continued to receive relatively high returns, even when investments are no longer a cost to them. Thus in water, for example, companies have increased their interest-bearing debt and not their issued share capital (Ofwat 2011). In other words they seem to have

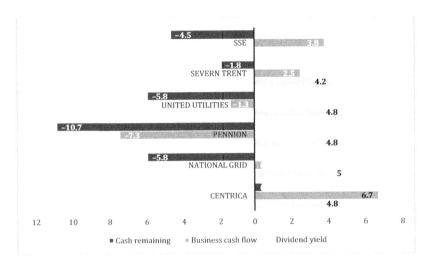

Sources: Compiled from company accounts; Evans 2013; Hargreaves Lansdown dividend overviews available at http://www.hl.co.uk/shares/shares-search-results/

Figure 4.2 Allocation of selected utilities' cash to shareholders

issued virtually no new shares. The logic here is that, *ceteris paribus*, a smaller total of issued share capital benefits existing holders because, when a company creates more shares the price of each share usually declines. In 2010, for example, the electricity transmission utility National Grid saw the price of its shares fall by 7 per cent when it issued two new shares for every five owned (Crooks 2010).

Ofwat drew the following inferences about the consequences if 'their' utilities increased equity (share-capital) financing. A shareholder who does not buy the extra shares created from a rights issue 'concedes ownership rights to shareholders that do.' So these existing shareholders could end up 'seeing their ownership rights eroded if they do not' buy any new shares. Worse, the water regulator, the Water Services Regulation Authority (Ofwat), believed: 'a majority shareholder would lose its majority stake; and that an owner who previously had 100 per cent control of a company would be forced to bring in a minority shareholder, or, in general, that any carefully struck balance of interests among owners is disrupted.'

By avoiding further direct comment, Ofwat seems to suggest that such 'disruption' is to be avoided. That it should not direct the water companies to reduce their risky levels of non-equity borrowing by tapping the stock markets (!) (Ofwat 2011, pp. 27–8).

On this issue, regulatory reluctance is reflecting the attitudes of the utilities' executives. For example, in 2009, United Utilities is reported to have weighed up the merits of a rights issue versus a cut to its dividend. Instead it decided that these would only be pursued: 'if Ofwat's proposals are little changed and it cannot negotiate delays to its capital spending programme with the statutory authorities.' Its counterpart, Thames Water, was reported to be considering an appeal to the Competition Commission and to be 'deeply worried that it will have to cut its dividend' (Dunkley 2009). Following a 'tough' Ofwat decision that year, United Utilities cut its pay-out for 2010–11 by 12.5 per cent and Severn Trent announced a 'one-off' 10 per cent cut to its dividend in 2010–11. But by 2010, despite – or perhaps because – one large investor reportedly claimed Ofwat controls were creating 'inadequate returns for investors', the water utilities were once again pledging returns of between 3 per cent and 4 per cent, *plus* the rate of inflation. There was no further mention of rights issues (*Global Water Intelligence* 2010).

A glimpse into the arm-lock of this shareholder value pre-occupation on privatised utilities, and the consequences of regulator sanctions, is provided by the tensions between the giant transport operator FirstGroup and its shareholders. FirstGroup grew out of the privatisations of regional bus and rail services 'to become one of the world's biggest transport companies with 120,000 employees'. Non-renewal of one of FirstGroup's mainline rail contracts by the Department for Transport in 2012, led to the firm making a rights issue of new shares and cancelling that year's dividend. This decision caused the share price to plummet by 30 per cent, some investors to demand the sale of overseas subsidiaries, and the mooting of executive sackings (*Guardian* 2013; Pratley 2013).

Neo-liberal defenders of the investor-friendly regulatory regime counter-pose evidence such as the higher returns paid out by corporations in unregulated sectors (Littlechild 2003). However, in March 2013, an investors' adviser summed up the enduring dividend potential of investments in utilities, setting out four reasons why they are a 'major contributor to the income in shareholders' pockets' and why their high levels of debt will not jeopardise this status but continue to 'provide them with a high income'. These reasons were: a high level of visibility of revenues from regulation; an inflation-linked asset base; easy and competitive access to debt; and strong cash flows well in excess of profits (Burgess 2013). Burgess points out that utilities gain an 'important inflation-linked advantage when it comes to … dividend policy', because the RPI factor in the regulatory formula is linked to inflation. She adds that regulatory obligations to invest in physical capital such as infrastructure lead to high levels of debt borrowing. On the other hand, the 'visibility of returns make utilities a lower than average credit risk' so that they can secure loans at relatively cheap rates. Regulation also provides actual tax rates that are considerably lower than the reported figures, because of the capital allowances permitted by the tax system.

In 2012, Asia's richest man, Hong Kong billionaire Li Ka-shing, paid £645m to add Wales and West Utilities, the UK gas company, to his portfolio of British utilities, via a consortium led by his flagship firm Cheung Kong Holdings. His reported reasons were that British utilities 'offer stable regulatory environments, common law jurisdictions and predictable returns' (*Financial Times*/Jacob 2012). All but one of the regional electricity companies and six of the ten water/sewage firms have been taken over since privatisation. Yet despite these changes in their ownership, the operating domains of the Big Six energy providers have remained fairly constant. So there is a market for corporate control but otherwise market competition only exists in the form of striving to offer better returns to shareholders. Interestingly, several energy companies eventually became subsidiaries of continental companies – including one still-nationalised French firm: EDF. Ironically the rules of the regulated market, however, constrain them to behave and operate like their ST/EM counterparts in the sector, because the system's logic was designed for an idealised model of the latter.

The independence of the regulators, and their credibility via the RPI-X incentive structure, is supposed to encourage firms to find efficiencies. But it also means that, after the regulator's verdict, firms can maximise profits for periods of up to five years until the next price review: allowing retention or distribution of profits as dividends, bonuses, or reinvestment. Regulators' autonomy and transparency has been complicated by EU market harmonisation and the increased importance of domestic competition authorities. But it is no surprise that firms have learnt to 'love their regulator' and to unite against more direct political intervention, because 'independent regulators were best positioned to guarantee a stable contract price' (Coen 2005, p. 380). Businesses and politicians claim that regulators protect consumer interests by increased competition, assisted by incentive price regulation (Davey 2013; *Telegraph* 2014). This shared, but delusory, faux-competition ethos allows all involved to denounce interventionist policies like windfall taxes as 'in effect back-door re-nationalization' and threats of political intervention as undermining the 'allocative efficiency gains incentivized in the current price-cap model' (Coen 2005, p. 380–1).

Thus the so-called discretionary regime of utility regulation became a system of compensatory trading; transferring incomes to investors and creditors. In this system the regulators conduct *ex-post facto* assessments of what kinds of outcomes a notional market pricing system might produce. They then negotiate adjusted consumer prices with the companies, in relation to what they believe a 'fair' but competitive market for investment funding might require the companies to return to shareowners. Absent from regulators' calculations is the fact that investors can discount risk threats because, ultimately, the utility firms are quasi-monopolistic revenue receivers. In essence, the entire system of privatised utility contracting operates as a form of investor welfare. The ultimate price of privatisation is borne by the consumers of their products and services, who pay guaranteed returns to a class of investor-rentiers (Florio 2004, p. 347–8).

5.   HOW ACCOUNTABLE ARE REGULATORS?

There are major problems with regulators' accountability to the wider society. As Figure 4.1 shows, sector regulators are, in theory, answerable to ministers and, via the Select Committee system, to MPs. But this 'upward accountability' (Scott 2000) is attenuated because regulators' objectives are fluid and weak. To paraphrase Coen and Thatcher (2005): one regulator's aims may conflict with those of another – for example increasing competition yet maintaining social safeguards for consumers. Politically awarded mandates for discretion give flexibility but reduce political oversight and accountability. Yet politicians need to demonstrate some influence over regulators, while also showing an apparent 'hands-off' relationship to maintain regulators' *raison d' être* (Thatcher 2005). On the other hand, if politicians were to fine-tune regulatory goals, the point of delegation to a separate agency would become irrelevant. Yet if governments adopt the hands-off role and use only informal or backdoor political influence, transparency is weakened and upward accountability looks as though it has been reduced. Regulators may also evade close accountability through tacit alliances with regulated businesses (Coen 2005; Mattli and Büthe 2005).

The cultural ascendancy of the ST/EM model as the hallmark of market governance was emphasised from 1997. The New Labour governments began replicating ST/EM structures within the regulatory bodies themselves: replacing the single-person authorities set up by the Conservatives with the same kinds of boards of directors as the corporations which they are supposed to be regulating. Regulatory boards now typically consist of a part-time chairman, chief executive, executive and non-executive directors: a model whose efficacy is dealt with in the next and in the final chapters. This incorporation (sic) extends to the requirement for the regulator boards to conform to the Stock Exchange's Combined Code of Corporate Governance. To adapt the lyrics of the contemporaneous 'Barbie Girl' pop song: they became 'a corporate doll in a corporate world'. However, unlike business corporations, the regulatory bodies' wider potential was used by politicians and civil servants as a cosmetic device for tacking on *ad hoc* responsibilities for security, environmental and sustainability policies. In 2007 Deorn and Wilks reflected that: 'regulators can no longer restrict themselves to the narrower issues of price and quality of service, or limit their major responsibility to consumers in market settings' (Deorn and Wilks 2007). However, in practice, regulators' integration of new duties to promote, for example, 'sustainability' into their primary economic roles have been piecemeal and random (Bartle and Vass 2007).

Thus the bigger problem with the Topsy-like efflorescence of regulation of privatised institutions, and other processes of corporate businesses' regulation described below, is their attenuated and stuttering pretensions to accountability. Officially, utility regulation runs to and from 'an impartial, anonymous civil service' to a single minister, through to a sovereign parliament and finally to the electorate. As in many other instances however, this process has been shown to transmit only the weakest of democratic impulses to the final decision makers. In 2013 a political furore over its ineffectiveness for preventing energy companies' exploitation of customers led to Opposition promises to bypass the whole system to impose lower prices on the firms by legislative fiat. Or, as Deorn and Wilks admitted in 2007, the system has 'effectively broken down'. However, echoing Palast et al. (2003), these commentators also perceived regulatory systems as potential channels for adding 'democratic accountability, trust, transparency and legitimacy.' The last three chapters of this book address the kind of changes needed to achieve such improvements to accountability.

Ministerial declamations, particularly in the case of the energy industries, show vague aspirations to improve the accountability of regulators to topical public concerns. Admittedly, processes and decisions are more open and publicly debated than in the nationalised industry days (Thatcher n.d., p. 16). However, this change may be more of a reflection of the scale of public concern at current conditions. At any rate, there is little evidence of systemic shifts in these institutions' democratic fundamentals. The appointment of regulators, like other major public appointments, remains in the gift of the relevant cabinet minister. Vague moves towards involving Parliamentary Select Committees in the appointment process have not had much impact. In the words of one report on the process: 'most pre-appointment scrutiny serves little purpose except as a "rubber stamp" for the benefit of the executive' (Paun and Atkinson 2011, p. 23).[2]

Other evidence confirms the necessity of closer scrutiny and reform. Here we have focussed on the financial dysfunctionality and biases in the regulatory system. We could also have included in the regulatory deficit, concerns about 'fat cat' pay excesses for corporate directors, poor consumer protection and deficiencies in environmental improvements. A more intrinsic accountability defect is that, unlike their continental European counterparts, UK regulators seem to have close professional ties with business. Between 1990 and 2001, 71 per cent of regulators came from the business sector before their appointments and 93 per cent went into private business on leaving office (Thatcher n.d., p. 5). It is this kind of democratic deficit which has led civil society campaigns and NGOs to press for more direct bilateral engagement with all kinds of corporations. The advent and implications of this 'civil society regu- lation' is analysed in chapters 10 and 11. Here we can simply note that the expansion of these forms of 'soft regulation' is another indicator of the inadequacies of state-organised formal regulation. The central prob- lem with the current situation is the contradiction between, on the one hand, the residues of social democratic and emerging communitarian accountability – CSR and civil society partnerships – and, on the other, neo-liberal accountability by markets. The latter is expressed as financial accountability and responsiveness to investors; but, as the next chapter shows, in its present form it acts as both a contradiction to, and a check on public structures for moderating corporate powers.

6.   UK PRIVATISATION: A MODEL FOR OTHER COUNTRIES?

In chapter 7 we will examine divergences from the ST/EM model in other societal contexts. Could privatisation be a way of exporting the model to these countries? Sympathetic UK observers claim that the Thatcherite privatisations set a trend which the rest of the world followed. Even for the more critical Florio: 'It had a deep impact on policy-making worldwide. Privatization is now an accepted paradigm' (Florio 2004, p. 341). However, in the implementation of privatisation elsewhere the UK model has been of limited relevance. The USA has different regulatory protocols and models, although Arnold and Cheng (2000, p. 124) believe that here too, in sectors such as nuclear power, the setting of utility rates by state commissions means 'distributions of economic wealth depend extensively on state actions and institutions, as well as market forces'. Amongst more recent privatisers elsewhere: in Japan, the Ministry of Finance (MoF) 'considers NTT fully privatized', even though it still controls a third of Nippon Telegraph & Telephone (NTT) holdings company shares (National Property Office 2013, p. 70). In Japan large institutional investors such as trust banks and life insurance companies hold most of the remaining NTT shares (Kushida 2005). Most privatisation executed in the European nations in the 1990s has had the sole aim of assuring financial resources for the state. Privatisations seem to have had limited voter popularity after the first changes (Dan et al., 2012). In general, sales of shareholdings tended to reflect the prevailing investor patterns. In France and Italy big private groups bought the privatised firms without a wider share ownership resulting.

Between 1997 and 2002 the French government sold holdings worth a total of EUR 31 bn (or 2.15 per cent of 2000 GDP) in the (partial) privatisation of France Télécom, Air France, Autoroutes du Sud, Thomson-CSF, EADS and Crédit Lyonnais. More share sales followed between 2004 and 2008 with the disposal of major stakes in energy utilities: GDF and EDF, Paris-Rhin-Rhone and additional share sales in Autoroute du Sud, the airport operator AdP, and France Télécom (Bräuninger, 2013 p. 4). However in most of these French cases the state, as with Japan's NTT, retains a partial shareholding to maintain some critical influence and, perhaps, facilitate future resumptions of majority control. Even in 2011, these partial holdings meant that at the end of 2011 the government owned a majority stake in 1,498 companies employing 784,500 people, including the national mail service (La Poste), railways (SNCF), and Electricité de France (EDF).

Italy privatised in the 1990s and early 2000s, not for ideological reasons, but in order to reduce the size of its sovereign debt (1995: 121 per cent of GDP) and soaring budget deficits (1995: 7.5 per cent of GDP), and fulfil the convergence criteria of the Maastricht Treaty. Breakup of the Istituto per la Ricostruzione Industriale (IRI), a holding company, which owned 1,000 enterprises and employed up to 500,000 in the 1970s – see chapter 3 – was followed by partial privatisations in telecommunications, energy utilities (ENEL), infrastructure (including motorways) and transport. But central government still owns the railway (Ferrovie dell Stato) and the post office (Poste Italiane) and substantial amounts in energy supply and aerospace sector companies. As in France, municipalities own many general services enterprises such as energy supply, water supply and sewage disposal. Post the euro crisis further sales in former IRI firms' shares have taken place; but the approach remains cautious. So that, for example, state-owned historic buildings, castles, palaces or cloisters, are only being leased to the private sector for up to 50 years, rather than being sold off completely (Bräuninger 2013, p. 7).

Moreover, in the energy sector, the more pragmatic French approach has come to haunt the British privatisation purists. Amidst the slew of private UK, German, Spanish and US owners of electricity companies in the UK, France's EDF commands 20 per cent of the British market. Yet EDF is a part-privatised enterprise of which the state sold off only 15 per cent in 2005, following the 22 per cent shareholding of Gaz de France (GDF) sold in July 2005. These part-privatisations were executed to accommodate new EU competition laws. Yet, it is the near monopoly that EDF, for example, possesses in France that facilitates overseas expansions such as its acquisition, and subsequent mergers of SEEBOARD plc, London Electricity plc, SWEB Energy plc and three power generating stations. In 2009, EDF Energy also bought up the nuclear generator, British Energy, from the UK government. (A deal part-financed by selling off some of the electricity distribution business to future Wales and West buyer, Li Ka-shing's Cheung Kong Holdings.)

Following the 2008 financial crisis, the subsequent international recession and the 2011 Euro-currency crisis there has been, what even the pro-privatisation Deutsche Bank, calls 'a clear trend reversal' with 'growing' opposition to privatisations in many countries. Italy dropped transfer of municipal water utilities to the private sector after a referendum in June 2011. The 'counter-movement' involved some governments resuming their holdings in private-sector companies providing 'services of general interest'. In Germany and France some municipalities have re-established a presence in regional and local energy or water utilities, 'often by taking a direct equity stake'. Of France's significant portfolio of real estate and infrastructure facilities, valued at 85 per cent of GDP for 2010, three-quarters, such as hospitals and roads, are owned by municipalities. In France the Hollande presidency has pledged to add selective privatisations to help finance the government's investment programme. However, the 'primary target' is not cash generation *à la* Thatcher, but to meet broader economic policy goals by, *inter alia*, avoiding the sale of strategic holdings while retaining potential influence over companies which it part-owns (Bräuninger 2013, pp. 3–5).

Germany experienced two types of privatisation: the break-up and sale of operations within the former East German state's *treuhand* combines, and the more gradual share sales of parts of West Germany's state-owned businesses. In the west, after the partial sale of Volkswagen, the energy and chemical firm VEBA, and the Deutsche Lufthansa shares in the

1980s. Most German privatisations involved similar part-privatisations including: in the 1990s, Deutsche Telekom, a share offer in Deutsche Post, and the sale of Berliner Wasserbetriebe water company. The federal or regional state governments retained holdings in such firms as well as the commercial bank Bankgesellschaft Berli. A similar pattern is observed amongst the assets owned by municipalities: such as utilities in Bielefeld and Solingen and Dusseldorf. But Germany is also experiencing reverse privatisation movements. A referendum in Hamburg in 2013 voted for repurchase of the energy grid which the city sold off years before and campaigns are under way for Berlin to set up a public enterprise to trade in electricity from green sources. The BBC cites the German association of public utilities as reporting that 'more than 70 new publicly run services have started in the last six years' with more than 200 public projects to supply energy to local people. It is what the association calls a 're-municipalisation' (Evans 2013b).

CONCLUSION

So the UK's 'export' of its neo-liberal privatisation model has been a patchy, partial and temporary affair. Other societies morphed privatisation into more hybrid and nationally specific forms and compromises. What the Thatcherite programme did stimulate, inadvertently and contradictorily, was a proliferating web of more market regulation. Unlike the United States, Europe had few regulatory bodies that were not directly state-run, before the ascendancy of neo-liberal politics. Since the 1980s, such bodies have mushroomed, at least in European countries. Regulating competition, utilities, and financial markets these overlap with supranational, world and EU monitoring organisations (Coen and Thatcher 2005).

Indeed the multiplication of regulatory bodies – sectoral, competition, European and transnational – had by the mid-2000s become so complex that influential voices were calling for three additional bodies to monitor the regulators' success in progressing de-regulation (House of Lords 2007): in effect, a bizarre plea for de-regulatory regulators! In 2008, two decades after the initial privatisations in energy, the regulator was still dreaming of the, as yet, unrealised utopia of a market driven system: 'many consumers are not yet benefiting fully from the competitive market ... the transition to competitive markets needs to be accelerated' (Ofgem 2008, p. 1). A further six years later, this wish showed no signs of being realised but the oligopolist executives and their shareholder doppelgangers continue to secure their bonuses and dividends.

NOTES

1. Severn Trent Water Ltd is owned by Severn Trent plc, an FTSE 100 services company. The group's 15,000 people around the world, including Biffa and Severn Trent Laboratories, generate revenues of £2.015 billion. But the regulated utility, Severn Trent Water, contributes about 47 per cent of turnover and a colossal 77 per cent of profits. Yorkshire Water Services Ltd is part of Kelda Group plc, but Yorkshire Water provides 80 per cent of the group's turnover and 88 per cent of its profits (Abou-Seada et al. 2007, p. 18).
2. For instance, during a hearing with the proposed Chair of Ofcom, jointly conducted by the Department for Business, Innovation and Skills (BIS) and Culture, Media and Sports (CMS) committees, low attendance and early departures led to the CMS committee losing its quorum. As a result the two remaining members had to sit silently for part of the session. One can also find examples of flippant questioning such as an exchange over whether the candidate (again for the Chair of Ofcom) watched the TV show *Strictly Come Dancing*, and which football team she supported (Paun and Atkinson 2011, p. 24).

5. Financialised market accountability and the empowerment of shareholder value

INTRODUCTION

Shareholder interests' near stranglehold over privatised corporations, even as regulatory processes became more complicated, has reflected the broader financialisation of business processes. The legitimacy of these interests was secured in particular by the ascendancy of the philosophy and policies of 'shareholder value' (SV). This discourse overlaps, expresses, yet contradicts more general attempts to govern corporate life through 'soft' or 'self' regulation. It is the broader paradigm within which the privatisation-regulation sphere operates. The financial sector itself – banks, building societies, investment funds, unit trusts, insurance, and so on – was amongst the first to receive this treatment. Banks, stock dealers and financial intermediaries in both the USA and UK were given more freedoms in their spheres of operations and the scale of their lending and borrowing.

The paradigm envisaged that more relaxed, para-statal regulation would be mitigated by state measures which made corporate executives more responsible in terms of adherence to their shareholders' financial priorities. Taken together this liberalising complex made monetary goals, targets and performance measures the guiding principle for most business activity. Financial profits have always been a leitmotiv of capitalist enterprise. However, the function and role of profits varies. Put simply, from often being what they still are in other business systems – that is, a means to other ends: like expansion, innovation, employment, corporate status – financial measures became ends-in-themselves. Financialisation, as 'the increasing role of financial motives, financial markets, financial actors and financial institutions in the operation of the domestic and international economies' (Dore 2008), has become a proxy measure of wider social value for policy makers.

Within this new regime, the principle of SV was aimed at injecting market transactions into the corporation's internal processes. The aim became the achievement of greater distribution to shareholders by reducing managerial control over resource allocation and revenues to control by markets. Lazonick and O'Sullivan's forensic analysis of these developments is of such scope and depth that it warrants extended analysis; even though it applies mainly to the USA. Exhuming the roots of the SV philosophy in 1970s ideas and regulatory changes, Lazonick and O'Sullivan show how these encouraged a new corporate strategy paradigm that they term Downsize and Disinvest (D&D). The assumption was that the primary function of business was to generate financial wealth for redistribution by financial markets: investing in equally, or higher value businesses. In this paradigm, social benefits would accrue from ever higher returns through more physical capital, jobs flowing into the more dynamic and hence more profitable businesses and, where unavoidable, tax revenues for states to purchase public goods and services. Critical examination of this trend, by Lazonick and O'Sullivan and others, in the economic terrain that the UK shares with the USA, shows how it has actually led to the opposite social and economic welfare outcomes to those predicted.

In the UK the last decades of the twentieth century saw the evolution of a system of guided voluntarism in corporate governance. More prevalent than 'hard' state-enforced or directed regulation is 'soft' regulation: businesses voluntarily consent to police themselves and make agreements and compacts with trading bodies, standard setting agencies, para-statal and civil society campaigns. Although not embodied in legal statutes the informal endorsement of the Stock Exchange and related financial authorities made it obligatory for listed ST/EM firms to adopt the preferred model for company board structures, information, shareholder relations and – less forcefully – social and environmental responsibilities. These provisions are supplemented and paralleled by specific legal requirements established through various Acts of Parliament: the Companies Act 1985 covering criminal charges for directors, the Company Directors Disqualification Act 1986, the Insolvency Act 1986, the Companies Act 1989 and the Financial Services Act 1986. (Investor groups, such as the National Association of Pension Funds, have issued their own codes of conduct.)

National hard and soft regulation of corporations is also now enmeshed in various international codes and agreements of varying degrees of obligation and legality. Aspects of these are described in the third section below in relation to corporate irresponsibility in tax liabilities. A more detailed analysis comes in chapters 9 and 10 when we assess the progress of the broader soft regulation of the social responsibility movement. In this chapter we examine the significance of corporate tax avoidance as an illustration of the failure of the neo-liberal package of 'soft' regulation and market forces accountability. Before that, and after considering Lazonick and O'Shaughnessy's US illustrations, there is an analysis of this neo-liberal system of voluntary regulation and market governance of UK executives' pay and rewards. This latter issue is examined because it highlights the flaws in the application of the principle of executives' accountability to shareholders.

1. SHAREHOLDER VALUE I: THE FINANCIALISATION OF MANAGEMENT ROLES

Ideological justification for the SV model came from financial economists' conversion to the creed of 'agency theory', married to the neo-liberal axiom that the market always allocates resources better than organisations. Agency theory, as described above in pages 80–81 designates shareholders as the principals with corporate managers cast as their stewards or agents (Alchian and Demsetz, 1972). This view attributed the stagnating corporate economy of the 1970s to the weakening of market forces. Without market disciplines, it was claimed, managers would not fulfil their role as shareowners' agents. Instead executives were using their control of resources and revenues for 'insider' benefits to reward themselves and subordinates, aggrandise the corporation's social standing and other objectives that diverged from shareholders' interests in improved incomes or stock values. This was a malign recasting of the heroic roles sought for managers by Berle and Means, and Crosland. Using agency theory, financial and business economists in academia and the business world, argued instead for the virtues of active take-over markets to discipline low-performing corporate managers. It was claimed that managers would reward shareholder investors more diligently if they recognised a risk of losing their control to hostile take-overs by other businesses.

According to this story the higher share prices of shareholder-friendly policies would make take-overs of diligent businesses more difficult. Satisfied shareholder principals would then support rather than dump successful controllers, so the costs of buying control would be higher. The rate of return on corporate stock, it was argued, is the best measure of superior performance. It was assumed that this metric also reflected the degree of market accountability. Lazonick and O'Sullivan show how corporations also faced more competition for investment funds as de-regulation opened up alternative destinations for financial investors. In the late 1970s the US Securities and Exchange Commission, and in 1986 its UK counterpart, ended fixed charges on stock exchange deals. Rule changes to the US Employee Retirement Income Security Act in 1979, allowed pension, insurance and related funds to invest in more risky shares and even the highest risk – 'junk bonds'. Then both the US and UK authorities facilitated more competition amongst financial institutions: deregulating the setting of interest rates and charges on loans, permitting junk bond investments and lending to risky new ventures. As investors sought high returns and the stock markets themselves became more volatile/fluid, corporate stocks now had more rivals in attracting investment capital.

Changes in corporate structures and behaviour ensued as investor institutions (mutual and pension funds, insurance companies and their fund managers) encouraged take-up of SV perspectives amongst corporations aimed at increasing shareowners' collective influence over yields and corporate share values. These beliefs began to invert both investment managers' tactics and corporate strategies. Corporations, especially the conglomerates, were thought to comprise too many different lines of business for boards to manage and for external investment specialists to analyse effectively. The underlying values of firms and their profitability potential were deemed to be obscured by the opacity of the accounts in multi-product firms' reports. 'Unbundling' and 're focussing' corporations' diverse activities promised to produce greater clarity and accuracy in the information used to transact companies' shares. These kinds of analytics became popular because they revealed more about corporate internalities and more potential value and cash opportunities for investors in the form of share dividends or sales. The expansion of the M-form of corporate organisation detailed in chapter 2 had already increased organisational segmentation. Now it facilitated downsizing and disinvestment strategies – closures and selling of subsidiaries and divisions consistent with analysts' assessments.

Lazonick and O'Sullivan claim that the rise of D&D displaced corporations' previous emphasis on retain and re-invest (R&R) strategies. These had kept a higher proportion of profits within the firm to invest in innovation, new plant and employee training. Reducing staff numbers via D&D came to be seen as more attractive than upgrading skills and techniques. This shift was further propelled by SV impacts on top executives' status. Previously, top managers were often 'career' employees who had worked their way to the top through the managerial hierarchy. They were acculturated into the business organisation and understood and supported R&R policies. As financialisation took hold, top executives increasingly came from outside the firm and more had financial, rather than production or marketing, backgrounds (Fligstein

1993, pp. 287–94). Focussed on corporate financing, take-over markets and investor relations, executive management became more centralised and remote from the operating divisions. Their understanding of organisational capabilities and types of innovative strategies was reduced. Tax changes aimed at strengthening the identification of executive 'agents' with their shareholding 'principals' favoured reward by stock options rather than salary increments. Together these changes increased differences in average pay ratios between US CEOs and factory workers by nearly 400 per cent from 1965 to 1998 (Lazonick and O'Sullivan 2000, p. 25). The culture of boards became ever more divorced from that of the firm's operational paradigms.

The scale of executive wealth followed D&D strategies as 1980s/1990s share dividends ('pay-outs') rose to distribute more corporate revenues to support share prices. Surplus profits were also used to buy back shares (1996: $177 billion; 1997: $181 billion; 1998: $207bn) to add even more lustre – as well as executive gains – to shareholding's appeal. Indeed there is evidence that some US executives managed the trick of talking the SV talk, without 'walking it'; that is, they emphasised high investor returns whilst primarily enriching themselves (Shin 2012). The wider social impacts belie the promises of increased social welfare from a financialised regime. Enrichment of an executive-investor elite has simultaneously narrowed its composition. By 2001 as the economy neared the 2007 peak, the top 1 per cent of the share investing public owned 33.5 per cent and the next 10 per cent owned almost 43.5 per cent; leaving the remaining 90 per cent owning just 23 per cent. Adding in other financial assets the richest 5 per cent accounted for nearly two-thirds of all (non-residential property) wealth. The bottom half of the population held less than 2 per cent. Ireland estimates that the UK distributions are similar though slightly less concentrated at the very top (Ireland 2011, pp. 61–2, 64–68).[1]

Wider consequences included a marked deterioration in blue- and routine white-collar employment security, falling job tenures and job losses, further worsening the US income distribution. By the 1990s the average American employee's annual working hours exceeded those of the average Japanese worker. From the 1970s and 1980s the attenuated R&R policies in innovative US firms focussed only on 'narrow and concentrated' skill bases of highly educated personnel. Corporations' residual R&D policies favoured higher education training and research and diminished big business interest in upgrading the general quality of US education, which has declined into a highly unequal and internationally inferior mass schooling system. Lazonick suggests that aspects of the D&D strategy, such as excessive returns to shareholders, also apply to the UK (Lazonick 2012). Point-by-point comparisons of Lazonick and O'Sullivan's US diagnosis with the UK are lacking. However, work by the Manchester-based team at CRESC (cf Erturk et al. 2005, 2006; Froud et al. 2006) and others show similar outcomes from the same economic ideology and policies of deregulation and financialisation. As Bowman et al. have put it, the UK government helped sponsor 'a new order private sector built on sheltered services, shareholder value and deregulated credit' (Bowman et al. 2013, p. 171). Even free-market advocates now acknowledge that shareholder value in the UK is 'a snare, or worse' involving 'looting' by executives as they manipulate SV-based remuneration packages to benefit themselves and distort corporate performance (Wolf 2012).

2. SHAREHOLDER VALUE II: GOVERNANCE AND TOP MANAGERS' REMUNERATION IN THE UK

One feature of regulatory liberalisation on which there is ample evidence and concern in the UK, is executive remuneration. The explosion of these incomes relative to those of other occupations has a much broader significance than for corporate governance and finances alone. According to one much-discussed treatise on the growth of inequality and incomes in the English-speaking world, the effect of top managers' pay increases was not confined to the division of spoils within the business world, but became a 'powerful force' for the wider 'divergence of the wealth distribution' in entire societies (Piketty 2014, p. 334). In the present context, 'boardroom pay' highlights the collusive character of voluntary, soft, re-regulation via quasi-business authorities. It also shows the dysfunctionality of the shareholder accountability lauded by neo-liberal theories and policy.

A succession of 'insider' reports by corporate grandees, the Cadbury, Greenbury and Hampel committees, aimed at reducing agency costs and monitoring executive pay and performance These led to the 2000 Combined Code. Promulgated by the various City institutions, this code is only 'overseen' by a government appointed regulator – a company limited by guarantee – and partly funded by government and industry. This is a semi-voluntary model which does not oblige SE listed companies to conform to its model board formula, but requires explanation when they fail to do so: the 'comply or explain' principle. More explicit government support came from the inclusion of these conditions as requirements for SE listing in the Financial Services and Markets Act 2000. The Cadbury Report stipulated a division of the top roles into chief executive and chair and non-executive directors to oversee top executive activity: 'monitors for the monitors'. The Report also set out procedures to ensure that performance-related pay really rewarded performance (Talbot 2012, p. 458).

The combination of privatisation and shareholder value policies, reviewed above, also expanded senior managements' rewards in British businesses (Wilks 2013, pp. 91–3). FTSE100 CEO pay increased from 47 times the pay of the average employee in 1998, to 133 times by 2012 with some firms paying between 300 and 600 times the average UK worker's pay to their CEOs (High Pay Centre 2013, p. 4, 14). Recession and overall company performance seems to make little difference to this trend. As in the USA, the *de facto* bonuses which executives receive are in the form of share allocations, or options. Often defined as 'long-term performance-related pay awards', these awards of shares are the main source of the gross inequalities. Corporations' excuses for these mushrooming increases are, firstly, that it is necessary to pay higher salaries in a competitive international market for managerial talent. Yet the High Pay Centre has shown that overseas recruitment of CEOs from rival firms constituted less than 1 per cent of the appointments by the world's largest 500 companies (High Pay Centre, 2013, p. 13). Secondly, it is claimed that the corporate remuneration committees (RCs), derived from the Cadbury recommendations, ensure competitiveness in awards, and objectivity in their determination because RC members are supposedly impartial and independent of the executives who receive the resultant awards.

Because this membership was to consist 'wholly or mainly of non-executive directors', it was assumed that the independence of the RCs from the executive beneficiaries could be guaranteed, as the 'non-execs' would have little or no vested interest in the remuneration packages recommended (High Pay Centre 2013, p. 6). Other inputs into RC decisions come from Financial Reporting Council guidelines and best practice prescriptions by such groups as the Association of British Insurers (ABI) and National Association of Pension Funds (NAPF). RC recommendations will often also be informed by advice from remuneration consultants and also subject to an advisory vote from the firm's shareholders. The flaws in this system arise from the:

1. typical methodology employed;
2. composition of the committees; and
3. shareholders' role in relation to pay awards.

RC methodology usually involves 'benchmarking' their executives' pay against allegedly comparable groups; but these tend to be ones in the median or upper quartile rates of pay. Hence there is a built-in tendency – explicitly recognised by the authorities – to 'ratchet' pay changes upwards, because each committee in turn looks at the gradually increasing rates awarded by other committees (Financial Reporting Council 2012, p. 22). Ironically, many years previously, neo-liberals pointed to just such an upward-ratcheting effect, to discredit the pay-setting procedures based on the 'going rate' for ordinary workers under the trade-unionised regime (High Pay Centre 2013).

The composition of committees tends to be mainly of current or former CEOs and so these have an indirect interest in approving rises against which their own committees may subsequently be benchmarked. Significantly, where a high proportion of both the main board and the remuneration committee are 'outsiders' – that is, not directly employed executives of the company – then CEO pay corresponds more closely to the firm's results (Conyon and Peck 1998). Successive reforms to UK corporate governance designed to strengthen the pay-performance link through 'professionalising' and making executive pay setting more transparent 'may not have had much of an impact', despite encouraging more termination of contracts for under-performers (Thompson 2005, p. 24). The lack of truly independent voices is indicated by the High Pay Centre's finding that only 10 per cent of the 366 non-executive directors on remuneration committees are not from the same culture of business or financial and accounting institutions (High Pay Centre 2013, p. 10).

So what of the third monitor of executive pay: the shareholders' role? If RCs mainly serve the interests of executives, why do shareholders not react against the awards as the governance codes allow? A comparison of CEOs' pay in the (US) S&P 500 with FTSE 100 corporate categories shows that, despite the incidence of gross inequalities in pay, 'managers of public companies need not create long-term shareholder value'. Yet they are still 'uniquely positioned to enrich themselves, without creating obvious victims, as neither shareholders nor labour directly lose *en masse*'. In other words, considerable, absolute, levies can be extracted by corporate executives partly because these are small relative to profits generated and returns made to shareholders.[2] So executive awards (1) must not jar too starkly with returns to investors; and/or (2) executives must be able to legitimate their rewards by 'playing the numbers game': creating balance sheet figures which indicate progress attributable to their efforts (Erturk et al. 2005). In the latter respect, as Erturk et al. and others have observed, managers and RC sympathisers are helped by the fact that general rises in share prices will lift those of their specific company. While managers will be careful to omit or downplay such secular trends as causes of higher share values, contrarily, they will be likely to blame factors which depress another measure of success – return on capital employed. In this case they tend to cite factors like product market difficulties in the whole of their particular sector, dismissing these as beyond one firm's ability to prevent (Erturk et al. 2005, pp. 62–3).

If all else fails, as we saw above, managers can fall back on devices such as share buy-backs, or even the plant closures and divisional divestitures which will be described in detail for the food industry, in chapter 10 below. There are also possibilities of 'horse-trading' in the more informal information meetings that take place between executives and longer-term, big shareholders. As Pendleton comments, in these interactions 'managers attempt to anticipate what shareholders want because it is in their career and remuneration interests to do so' (Pendleton 2005, p. 117). In other words, adapting corporate strategies to the expectations of such investors may entail the latters' tacit approval of potentially contestable remuneration packages. It is true that shareholder 'revolts' over executive pay levels have become more frequent and public, with embarrassed managements sometimes moderating proposed increases. However, in almost all cases revolts have not yet involved a sufficient majority of shareholder groups to block them. In some headline cases of well-known firms, substantial minorities voted against proposals; but in 2013, across the FTSE 350, 'the vast majority of companies have polled more than 90 per cent investor support on their Directors' Remuneration Report'. Preliminary results for early 2014 also showed large majorities in favour (Towers Watson 2013, 2014a, b).

One reason for investor timidity may be that fund managers themselves benefit from the lack of transparency and accountability in executive compensation schemes. A representative of Worldwide Fidelity Investment was asked if a wider group of shareholders would support this fund's protest against the much-publicised £180 million pay-out to the Chairman and board of Sports Direct in July 2014. His instructive reply was that some investor firms would 'have to address their own Litip (executive reward) schemes before they can address others [in whom they invest]' (Treanor 2014). Similarly, sympathetic 'insider' individuals on the remuneration committees will not be too difficult to persuade that high pay is justified by the performance figures formulated by the firm's executives – not least because they may play the same game with the committees deciding their own remuneration rewards.

Despite the apparently 'disembedded' character of accountability by market forces in the UK's corporate economy there are social-institutional influences which would be anathema to disciples of Adam Smith. Pendleton summarises the partly covert arrangements which have developed to compensate for the kinds of explicitly regulated shareholder-executive relationships found in non-Anglo Saxon business cultures:

> ... tiers of co-ordinated activity, involving active [investor] trade associations and federations, as well as *ad hoc* and informal networks and alliances ... have given rise over the years to a web of rules and conventions that govern corporate actions, and provide mechanisms and opportunities for investor interventions. (Pendleton 2005, p. 120)

This myriad of codes involve trade bodies, such as the Association of British Insurers, and socially connected individual investment institutions. The codes are often informally implemented or adapted 'on particular issues' by the associations, 'groups of investors marshalled by investors, self-selected groups of investors, and individual investment firms'. Pendleton concludes: 'UK corporate governance is characterised by a distinct set of social relationships between key actors in which market transactions may be just one of several instruments' (Pendleton 2005, p. 120). But whether the form of regulation and accountability is explicit and procedural, or *ad hoc* and social, it seems highly unlikely that the arrangements will conflict with the shareholder-value orientation in ST/EM corporations. They seem more likely to strengthen it. Taken together, all of these rigidities and dysfunctions in the official ethos of market accountability indicate that the executives' commitment to broader economic or social criteria, cannot be realised through the institutions and ideologies of market accountability; in this case to shareholder-investors.

One pure form of market accountability over executive performance – central to neo-liberal theories might still seem plausible. This takes the form of the take-over threat in the 'market for corporate control', which, theoretically, deters executives from behaviour that is too self-serving or antithetical to investors' welfare. There is certainly a well-organised set of take-over institutions: rules, codes, investment banks and the like. However, this complex does not seem to exert a great deal of influence over errant managerial behaviour. The prime reason for this weakness is financial cost. Take-overs are expensive and will only be considered when returns can be calculated to offset the extra costs of purchasing shares above market rates and the transaction costs of the purchase (Prowse 1995; Franks and Mayer 1997). Shareholders may see these costs as eating into any future gains promised by the bidding firm and prefer to lobby existing managements to reveal and share with them the lucrative assets detected by the bidder. So it is no surprise to find that the takeover market and hostile take-overs do not predominantly involve badly run or poorly performing companies (Franks and Mayer 1997). In the United Kingdom over 80 per cent of 1991–95 take-overs were 'friendly' (Deakin and Slinger 1997, p. 418), and aimed at securing economies of scale or to expand market share (Froud et al. 2000b) rather than installing superior management disciplines. Thus the in-built tendency for take-overs in the ST/EM system does not function to control either the self-serving dynamic of executive remuneration nor, probably, does it act as a more general form of market accountability over corporate boards of directors.

3. 'GLOBAL' REGULATION AND EVASION

The multi-divisional and international scale of the eventual owners of firms in the privatised sectors was scarcely foreseen in the initial legislation and policy making. But the implications of these enlargements, as with transfer pricing between different corporate divisions, have restricted regulators' powers over the firms' finances and business models. In addition national regulators' roles are, in some respects, confined by the 'new risk regulators' of the international arena: such as the WTO, IMF and even the World Bank. Whatever their economic efficacy, these authorities tend to favour MNC interests, while also further limiting accountability to national public institutions and civil society (King and Narlikar 2003). Other gaps between such inter-governmental regulatory and national powers have been filled by the above-mentioned 'soft regulation' via an array of non-state concords, pacts, and standard agreements; in many cases as 'civil society regulation' with campaigning and other NGOs. These arrangements, some examined in detail in chapters 9 and 10, range from in-house initiatives by individual firms ('self-regulation'), or business associations, to 'multi-stakeholder initiatives' involving multiple actors from NGOs, public agencies and governmental representatives. The Organisation for Economic Cooperation and Development (OECD) identified 246 codes of conduct for standards and 'principles of conduct for business activities in the marketplace' (OECD 2001, p. 3), covering areas such as labour standards, environmental safeguards, consumer protection, and information disclosure. However, until recently, most codes are still issued by companies (48 per cent) and business associations (37 per cent), with only 13 per cent involving 'stakeholder' partnerships with public and civil society bodies (Pattberg 2006).

The chapters below on CSR and social movement challenges, provide detailed assessments of the strengths and weaknesses of these approaches and their potential for providing new forms of social embedding. Here, we need only note that their very existence shows the limited scope and effectivity of neo-liberalism's national regulatory and financialised forms of accountability. But the sheer diversity and 'ad-hocery' of these multiple rules conflicts with publicly and socially accountable standards of corporate, especially international behaviour. Commenting on his investigation of this rule-making by 'public and particularly private elites'– what he calls 'global quasi-constitutionality' (Thompson 2013) – Grahame Thompson writes:

> a major issue of concern is whether quasi-constitutionalization leads to Rule by Laws (RbLs) rather than the Rule of Law (RoL) in the international system? The RoL may be being given away as RbLs replace a comprehensive system of democratically constituted judicial review, which cannot happen in the case of global quasi-constitutionality. (Thompson 2013)

Of course, financially oriented, guided voluntarism does have some influence on the behaviour of those internationalised firms based in the UK. For example Stock Exchange rules require minimal levels of internal governance. Yet corporations' 'globalised' activities provide considerable scope for evading even the most basic responsibilities. A particularly blatant evasion is corporate taxation, identified by CSR gurus, such as Archie Carroll, as one of the basic responsibilities to be fulfilled before corporations can make philanthropic and other social contributions (Visser 2006, p. 37).

An unfolding scandal of multinational businesses has revealed that some of the most advanced corporate participants in CSR and soft regulation organise their accounting and business operations so that minimal, if any, taxes are paid in countries like the UK; from where most of their revenues come (House of Commons 2013, *passim*). Lax tax enforcement and generous rules by UK authorities have encouraged barely legal, but certainly unethical, tax avoidance to dovetail with financial accounting devices. This manipulation has deprived UK authorities of tax revenues so large that, if paid, they could have obviated the need for public spending cuts. Critical tax expert Richard Murphy estimated that £12 billion p.a. of tax revenues were lost from the 700 largest corporations in 2006. In 2012/13 the Coalition government cut public spending, in real terms, by £10.8bn (Murphy n.d.; *Guardian* 2012). Preoccupied with smoothing away national regulatory constraints on global and intra-EU market transactions, the international regulatory authorities and the European Commission have shown only weak interest in regulating transnational tax avoidance. It has been left to the relatively toothless OECD to devise 'advisory' transparency and reporting procedures satisfactory to national governments of the biggest economies and their corporate lobbies (Wilks 2013, p. 155; OECD 2013a). As the multi-national accountancy firm Ernst and Young consoled corporate clients at the time: 'the CAA [the OECD's formula for inter-state information sharing] is only a model and, before coming to an agreement, jurisdictions are able to negotiate amendments to it' (Ernst and Young 2014).

CONCLUSION

In sum, a melange of semi-voluntary and market-friendly policies and politics has followed the demise of the social democratic frameworks of control or accountability of big business. But, like the 'harder' regulatory systems for the privatised utilities, these neo-liberal aspirations have not induced much informal accountability amongst and between market participants. The problem is not one of 'unregulated capitalism'. From the early days of oligopolistic checks through to the complex webs of national regional and international regulation, and the rise of world-level 'soft regulation' of international business, there are multiple, sometimes competing, regulatory institutions. Their common weakness is the scale of the Pandora's Box of corporate powers and social distress released by neo-liberalism which they are meant to check.

The above cases of tax avoidance and executive pay extortion show that, even for core financial integrity, the outcomes of semi-voluntary and market controls do not reverse much of the societal delinquency and dereliction Lazonick and Wilkinson attributed to the SV form of accountability. The problems seem broader than state-devolved and market regulation can handle. Thus the next chapter looks at the social embeddedness of business relations, and chapter 7 focusses on national business systems where closer integration, or embedding, in mainstream society replaces, or supplements, the importance of such regulation. In Germany, for example, executive pay is now subject to agreement by supervisory company boards which include employees, trade union and other 'stakeholder' representatives (cf High Pay Centre 2013). On one estimate the ratio between the CEO's and lowest paid worker's total pay is 12 times in Germany, 22 times in Britain and between 400 and 500 times in the USA (Towers Perrin, cited in Mindful Money 2012).

NOTES

1. Hi-tech giants were prepared to sacrifice capital for innovation in order to enhance stock values. Intel's 1998 spend on stock options to attract/reward top staff involved share re-purchases that were twice its R&D spend. Microsoft's 1999 repurchases of stock neared the value of all its R&D expenditure (Lazonick and O'Sullivan 2000, p. 33).
2. The scale of some executive rewards has, on occasion, threatened to breach even this consideration. In 2013 Barclays Bank plc paid a total staff bonus of £2.38 billion, much of which was received by senior executives. A move which prompted Roger Barker, Director of Corporate Governance at the pro-market Institute of Directors to say: 'It cannot be right in any business for the executive bonus pool to be nearly three times bigger than the total dividend pay out to the company's owners ... The question must be asked – for whom is this institution being run? '(Institute of Directors 2014).

6. Contextualising the neo-liberal model: social embeddedness of economic relations

> The triumph of the shareholder-oriented model of the corporation over its principal competitors is now assured, even if it was problematic as recently as twenty-five years ago. (Hansmann and Kraakman 2001)

INTRODUCTION

As the above quote indicates, the ST/EM corporate form seemed destined to become common around the world. By the mid-1990s neo-liberalism had effectively vanquished Marxist and collectivist ideas in the political arenas. Nevertheless intellectual interest grew in apparently successful business systems which did not conform to the ST/EM type. Explicitly or implicitly, the common attraction of these alternatives was their contrast to that model's dislocation from civil society. Based more on sociology and social anthropology than Marxism, these assessments variously celebrated the virtues of continental Europe's 'Rhenish' model of 'coordinated capitalism' (from countries bordering the river Rhine), the politically and culturally integrated corporate organisations in Japan, as well as the industrial districts of small firms in Italy and elsewhere. More recently the near-collapse of the financial system, in which the corporate system is enmeshed, has even stimulated an interest in the hybrid state-market structures which have continued to power Chinese growth while the West's economies contract (Arrighi 2007, 2009).

Analyses of these various alternative systems are not all based on the concept of social embeddedness. But, as originated by social anthropologist and historian Karl Polanyi, it is a useful tool for comparing the candidate systems and for judging their potential for re-balancing the economy-society relationship. During and after the Second World War, Polanyi synthesised economic anthropology and history into a critique of 'formalistic', neo-classical economics. His ideas have lately enjoyed a substantial revival amongst opponents of neo-liberal economics. Their basic assumption is that the viability of market complexes of economic transactions and business enterprise activities depends upon their nesting, or embedding in more ethical social and cultural institutions.

As explained below, such sentiments are logically opposed to the dominant assumptions of most neo-classical economics and the neo-liberal paradigm which grew out of neo-classicism. In the latter perspective, business prosperity depends upon maximising the distance between, on the one hand social forces and influences, and on the other, corporate autonomy. The embeddedness thesis argues the opposite: that, in order to operate sustainably, economic institutions depend on abolishing rather than extending this separation. The next chapter assesses alternatives to ST/EM capitalism in relation to their social embeddedness. It looks at the ways in which the governance of the German business system and large Japanese corporations avoid the separation of investor and 'stakeholder' interests from executive control. It further examines the integration of small-firm networks and cooperatives in industrial district communities in Italy and Spain. These latter examples offer potential alternatives to the Fordist bureaucratisation of mass production/mass consumption identified as a key feature of the ST/EM firm in chapter 2. Before assessing these cases however, I will outline the broader meanings and significance of social embeddedness as a perspective for analysing and helping to reverse neo-liberal orthodoxy and corporate power.

1. DEPARTING FROM NEO-LIBERAL PARADIGMS

When necessary, neo-classical economics falls back on philosophical axioms about the inevitability of acquisitive, utility maximising behaviour. Thus the behavioural constant in the generic economic institution of the market is claimed to be a universal and perpetual striving for gain (Fukuyama 1995, p. 18). This is said to be an instinct which is accompanied by a faculty and disposition for calculation of the costs and benefits of transactions and, by implication, commodity creation (Hodgson 2012). In this view the propensity to exchange is an inbuilt and universal human disposition. Thus the 'natural' profit-making inclinations can be liberated if the constraining impediments of other human practices and social institutions are excluded. Then individual humans will create, innovate and trade spontaneously to the general advantage of all.

From this a-historical conception it is further deduced that market behaviour, and the wealth-creating activities presumed to follow, can be created or encouraged by excluding inimical social 'constraints'. The usual authority for this line of thought is the work of Adam Smith, the designated John the Baptist of market economics. Most popular is

Smith's much invoked warning in the *Wealth of Nations* that collective associations of business people are, in general, potentially dangerous. For they 'seldom meet together, even for merriment and diversion, but the conversation ends in a conspiracy against the public interest' (Smith 1776, Book I, Chapter 10, para 82). Smith had in mind the collusion that leads to price-fixing through cartel-type associations. However, the presumption that enterprises are better kept apart and encouraged to compete against each other, rather than acting in concert, has become a staple of contemporary economic thought and much policy making. Thus it is believed that economic efficiency is generally better achieved by discouraging businesses from acting collectively in social institutions. Better that they regard competitor businesses as adversaries and act to outperform them.

Smith's broader social philosophy, for example in his *Theory of Moral Sentiments*, had an important place for social ethics. However, the principle most associated with his intellectual legacy is the importance of baser instincts. For Smith, and even writers like de Tocqueville (1946, p. 123) the motive force of market behaviour is self-concern. It would be a travesty for Smith himself to be depicted as believing that this trait could be represented by the vices of avarice or greed, but more recent advocates of free markets have implicitly or explicitly done so. The celebrated equation of the market with individual selfishness comes directly from the *Wealth of Nations*: 'Not from benevolence' says the sage of Kirkcaldy, 'do we expect our bread from the baker' but from self-interest 'as by an invisible hand'. Avaricious or not, such individual acts flow together to promote the general welfare by the force of price competition amongst traders and producers and their search for better goods to increase their sales.

During the 1980s these assumptions became popularised and polemicised. To maximise their political and policy potentials, neo-liberals propagandised and bowdlerised the initial philosophical ideas as: individualistic competition = 'good'; cooperation and collusion = 'bad'. In some quarters they were given a significant boost by an association with other attractive, libertarian perspectives, such as the fundamentalist individualism of the ex-Russian polemicist and putative philosopher Ayn Rand (Rand 1964, 1967). Explicit disciples of a combined Smithian and Randian 'ideology' became economic policy makers; such as long-serving Federal Reserve Bank chairman Alan Greenspan. But, as Greenspan's own rueful self-reflection revealed when the financial crash of 2007–08 exposed the economic limitations of these ideas:

I made a mistake in presuming that the self-interests of organisations, specifically banks and others, were such that they were best capable of protecting their own shareholders and their equity in the firms. (Alan Greenspan to US Congressional Committee, cited in Knowlton and Grynbaum 2008)

But long before this cataclysmic refutation, more socially liberal and sociologically informed scholars and commentators had been proposing alternative theories of the relationship between social institutions and economic, especially market, behaviour. Their opposition to the Smith-derived nostrums of atomised market relationships based on inherent dispositions was simple.

2. WHY/HOW ARE ECONOMIES EMBEDDED? POLANYI'S THESIS

The counter-argument is that anthropological and historical evidence shows that trade and markets have only usually flourished by being embedded in relevant social institutions. The 'substantivist' argument is thus that the dearth of market behaviour in simple and pre-capitalist societies shows that it is *not* a universal or 'natural' human trait. Instead it should be recognised that markets only arise when social and political powers create the social conditions for their success. Figures such as historical anthropologists Polanyi (1944) and Graeber (2011) argue that specific social relationships are needed to ensure that trade and markets work in ways that benefit the societies in which they operate, rather than expanding their powers and functions to exploit and destabilise social institutions.

Thus market practices and participants should be integrated with, or embedded into social institutions rather than, as neo-Smithians argue, separated from them. Polanyi traced the financial crisis, economic slump and national conflicts of the late 1920s and 1930s to the relatively unfettered market freedoms of nineteenth-century laissez-faire capitalism. Thus, he argued, it is downright dangerous to let markets become 'disembedded' from social constraints and conventions and become autonomous and attempt to be self-reproducing institutions. The social constraints on market practices take several forms but they include diverse modes of regulation. Significantly, it was the misguided policy makers of the 1920s – and, we might now say, the 1980s and 1990s – whose 'liberation' of autonomous businesses and traders made markets become destructive. In his 'double-movement' thesis Polanyi described 'market societies ... continually being reshaped by two conflicting movements – the first is the movement for laissez faire-to expand the scope of markets and the second is the movement for social protection to limit the scope of market forces' (Block and Evans 2005, p. 511).

For Polanyians such as Block and Evans the second part of the double movement, the 're-embedding', is realised through state actions. But state action usually depends on prior civil society campaigns and movements (2005, pp. 506, 514). The social reaction sequence on which Polanyi himself focussed was the post-Depression international institutional reconstruction popularly known as international Keynesianism: the IMF, World Bank, GATT (later WTO) troika and 'managed' exchange rates – what Ruggie in 1982 christened 'embedded liberalism' (Ruggie 2003). This was a 'settlement' which assured the economic North the 'trente glorieuse' decades of stable and growing economic affluence. It resolved the crisis of the conflict between international principles based on market liberalism and national policies to protect domestic economies by tying international market processes to the social standards and expectations of national societies (Block 2003, p. 289).

However, this explanation throws up a conceptual and a predictive impasse in the contention of Block and others that market economies can be 'always-embedded' rather than disembedded. It could therefore be proposed that embedding could take, and might have taken, more subtle forms of re-regulation: in the form of corporate 'takeovers' of political systems – or at least key institutions within these (cf Vogel 1996); or even indirect colonisation of civil society in CSR involvement. In other words, corporate market systems might adapt public, civil society and state institutions to deepen market dominance; while at the same time exploiting and disadvantaging other social institutions – workers' and civil rights, welfare systems and so on. If these developments do constitute perverse but durable embedding why and from where should the reforming response in the double movement arise?

Munck (2002, p. 183) acknowledges that Polanyi himself warned of another possibility: that narrow economic nationalism could mean the reform movement taking the form of reactionary and authoritarian politics, as in the European fascist states of the 1930s. However, he also saw the possibilities of smaller regional solutions to the disembeddedness of international market systems. In today's world two distinct, though related forms of social re-embedding are emerging as possibilities. Despite limited progress so far, there is still a case for 'upwards' and outwards re-embedding, via IGOs and international frameworks of governance. Another form would be the kind of multi-lateral stakeholder relationships to be analysed in Part III of this book: downwards and laterally and aimed at some social regulation by civil society bodies. A focus on national aspects and solutions to corporate globalisation might be thought of as unfairly privileging the European or 'northern' societies, where corporate centres are based, above their more exploited counterparts in the global South. However, such a focus could also lay the basis for reforming their wider international operations. The second part of the double movement may therefore have different, though inter-related, national/regional as well as international dimensions.

Probing the Polanyian perspective raises further questions about another universal form of re-embedding of markets and business: like the system the post-World War II Keynesian-social democratic compromise which benefitted the advanced capitalist societies. Polanyian analysts, and others working in the 'varieties of capitalism' school, emphasise the virtuous effects of embedding business and markets in social and political institutions in societies like the German-speaking and Scandinavian countries, and sometime in East Asian states like Korea and Japan, as described below and in chapter 7. But would such forms of upward and lateral embedding of business systems in these societies also work on Anglo Saxon countries' ST/EM corporations? As explained in the next chapter and chapter 11, some may be transferable, some not. But, if the aim should be social accountability to wider ranges of civil society stakeholders, this is not obviously achieved by closer control by state bodies or employee interests as happened with the social democratic model and in Rhenish and East Asian capitalism. Polanyi himself saw the social half of the double movement as: 'essentially, the tendency inherent in an industrial civilization to transcend the self-regulating market by consciously subordinating it to a democratic society' (1944, p. 234). But what constitutes a 'democratic society'?

3. ECONOMICS VS SOCIOLOGY/ANTHROPOLOGY

Polanyi's analysis and diagnosis relate particularly to the national-international levels of economic systems but analogous approaches with similar implications have been developed in relation to both the 'meso-level' of national economies, by the French Aix school, and the micro-level of firms and market transactions by the American sociologist Mark Granovetter (Granovetter 1985). Both these unconnected approaches begin by exposing what they regard as a false dichotomy between actors being depicted as either 'under-socialised' (in economics) or 'over-socialised' (in sociologistic perspectives). Marc Maurice and his colleagues in the Aix group challenge versions of these perspectives that have been applied to industrial and employment change in discrete societies. Recapitulating interpretations of the transition to developed industrialism in different national contexts, they identify the two fallacious explanations as: firstly, that of the convergence school which posits the technological determination of economic roles and institutions and, secondly, the contrasting cultural determinism approach which sees national patterns as directly shaped by the beliefs and norms of the society in question.

For Maurice et al. (1986), both these perspectives are overly simplistic in explaining the commonalities and differences in economic practices and institutions between societies. Instead, the Aix scholars argue, economic institutions such as occupational structures are not autonomous and homogenised outcomes of transnational, technological necessities as the 'convergence' approach claims. But nor are they simply expressions of national culture; as for example, in some depictions of the rising East Asian economies of the 1970s as expressions of 'Confucian' values (Berger 1988; Kahn 1979). The Aix Group argue instead for the operation of 'societal effects'. In this theory economic practices and institutions do vary between societies but variations derive from the development of practices within separate social 'spaces'. The latter are formed and constrained by each society's social institutions.

Thus the range and content of economic functions, for example the scope of particular occupations, varies according to the influence of training and educational systems, regulations and so on. No single societal institution, neither the legal nor political system, or religious and educational cultures, determine differences in economic and business practices between countries. Rather the interactions of these institutions and others, such as industrial relations systems, create the social spaces within which clusters of activities, such as professional roles, are possible in one society, but not in the different spaces allowed by the institutional configurations of other societies.

In similar fashion, Granovetter stood back from the general debate and polemics between neo-classical economics supporters and over-enthusiastic proponents of social determinants. He diagnosed these extreme differences as stemming from what he called the 'under-socialised' versus the 'over-socialised' conceptions of economic behaviour. The 'under-socialised' view, adopted by most economists, sees individuals as opportunists which entails a consequent risk of 'untrustworthy' behaviours unless sufficient individuals either adhere to general moral codes, or are subject to effective institutional controls – such as the legal enforcement of contracts. The shaping of economic behaviour by moral codes is of course problematic for neo-classical economics because of Smith's strictures on the need for individuals' freedom of self-interest. On the other hand, institutional-legal regulation might also be excessively constraining and discouraging of entrepreneurship. Hence the constant problem plaguing public policy makers, and vividly illustrated in Greenspan's preference for under-regulation, is that too much external control can be intrinsically bad for markets but insufficient controls may unleash rampant opportunism and recklessness with a corresponding decline of trust and economic activity. Granovetter's solution to such contradictions is to emphasise that the relevance of moral constraints or impersonal institutional controls depends on the concrete ways that particular market actions relate to social structures; that is – once again – their 'embeddedness'.

In this way he explains that trust is built up through personal relations with specific individuals and not with some 'generalised other'. This formulation is, ironically, not that different to the more general theory of normative action which Adam Smith depicts in his *Theory of Moral Sentiment*. By making trust relations specific to particular social conditions rather than a given trait, the sterile opposition between the under-socialised and over-socialised depiction of economic actors is avoided. Granovetter's formula is well illustrated by his critical analysis of 'institutional economist' Oliver Williamson's influential version of transaction costs theory – known as the 'markets vs hierarchies' distinction. That theory centred on firms' decisions whether to buy a product or service on the external market, or to undertake the provision of these within its own business organisation. Firms will choose one or the other, argued Williamson, depending on the relative costs of the transactions. A branch of this perspective has gone on to become influential in the economic history of large corporations where the growth of large corporations has been attributed to the gains firms made from bringing the acquisition of parts and products in-house, rather than buying these from, usually smaller, supplier firms. (For an account and critique of this explanation see Perrow, 2002, and chapter 1, above.).

But Granovetter's theory is able to show that Williamson overstates the impersonal anonymous character of markets as being a complete contrast to the 'hierarchical controls' within commercial organisations. Granovetter's critique rests on two sociological insights. Firstly, actual markets are quite unlike neo-classical economics' conception of impersonal interactions between autonomous individuals. For markets are actually replete with social connections. They involve, for example, departures from personal utility (or profit) maximising behaviour through reciprocity: the 'give and take' of favours and obligations; as well as the use of personal connections rather than choice amongst market options. Secondly, Granovetter points out that hierarchies, or firms, lack the clear enforcement of decisions assumed by transactions theory. That theory claims that firms perceive and achieve advantage by using the greater authority and economic control over employees to produce a good or service more economically than an independent – and profit-seeking – external contractor would be willing to accept.

Granovetter contends instead that clear, hierarchical controls over the transactions within organisations may not be as easily achievable as Williamson et al. suppose. Instead there may be as much evasion and haggling within and between different levels and social categories within firms as there can be on the external market. The wealth of sociological evidence on the complexities of control and worker-management conflicts built up since the 1970s would support this contention. Though not necessarily universal, disorder *within* firms may be greater than *between* them in markets. Conversely, hierarchical firms which seek to control markets may also encounter social constraints on their aims and strategies. A prime example of this aspect of social embedding is examined in the case of Vietnamese sub-contractors to Western multinationals described in chapter 10.

A corollary of these points is relevant to the socially embedded business systems examined in the next chapter: large corporate firms do not necessarily have cost advantages over smaller firms. The latter can avoid becoming part of big firms' 'hierarchies' if the denser networks of social relations which they inhabit can provide advantages in trust and cooperation. Thus there is, at least in principle, the possibility of a reversal of the Smithian/neo-classical/institutionalist perspective. If markets and economic organisations are 'embedded' in the right social conditions, they may work better than if they are divorced from social ties. A corroboration of this proposition is indicated by assessments of the economic performance of different types of economic regime by Hall and Soskice (2001, Introduction).

These authors observed that since the 1980s national economies have been governed by one of two policy paradigms. They have become either 'liberalised market economies' (LMEs) or 'coordinated market economies' (CMEs). The former, exemplified by countries such as the USA and UK, deregulated many controls over firms and markets and encouraged 'free market' dynamics to foster competition and growth. CMEs such as France, Germany and Scandinavia, by contrast, modified, but did not abandon social institutions regulating business behaviour. In particular they kept some institutional coordination for pay setting, training and redundancy exercises. They did this because they saw competitive advantages from these arrangements, particularly with reference to inflation control, R&D and innovation for example.

CONCLUSION

Although their analyses are too general to pinpoint the exact influence of the forms of social regulation and institutions, Hall and Soskice's identification of the economic outcomes of LMS vs CME frameworks suggest the more pronounced social embedding in the latter case produces economic advantages. CMEs, sometimes termed 'cooperative economies' (Gordon 1996), have performed better than, or as well as, LMEs on key indicators such as levels of unemployment, inflation, and product innovation. Germany was one of the first economies to rise after the 2008 financial crisis and has since outperformed most other European economies, and for employment rates the USA (OECD 2014, p. 6–7). Intriguingly, Hall and Soskice report that even MNCs seem to prefer to retain the advantages of involvement in CME institutions in the operations they have in those countries. These contrasts confirm the existence of different business systems that are at least equally as successful as the neo-liberal ones dominated by ST/EM corporations.

In the next chapter we ask in what specific ways are these societies' economic institutions socially embedded? How much public or social accountability is involved? Are these forms of embedding consistent with the democratic ties which, as chapter 11 explains, were envisaged by Polanyi? When considering the relevance of these forms of embedding to more marketised societies such as the UK, we need to consider the Aix Group's strictures about the societal specificity of the 'social spaces' needed to accommodate embedding institutions. We must also bear in mind whether any of these institutions, or the principles on which they are based, could be introduced into a society in which neo-liberalism has destroyed or disabled the social democratic conditions necessary to embed and sustain them. More specifically, does the UK need some of the 'upward' and lateral ties that have worked in the coordinated economies? Or are downward links to the movements and groups in civil society now more relevant? For example, Fraser (2013) has argued that 21st century re-embedding to promote women's emancipation should now also be an addition to the movement for social re-orientation of disembedded market processes and institutions.

7. Alternative, socially embedded business systems: Germany, East Asia, and industrial districts

If a customer asks you, 'what does your firm make?', tell them Matsushita Electrical makes people. We also make electrical appliances. But first we make people. (Kushimoto 2007, p. 11)

INTRODUCTION

The examples in the previous chapter suggest that more socially embedded business systems may be more successful and durable than others, such as the ST/EM model. For the logic of the latter rests on 'disembedding' in order to endow firms with autonomous freedoms and powers. But at what level should embedding take place and in what social or political institutions? The state-owned, public corporations examined in chapter 3, for example, could be said to have been socially embedded. However, despite achieving indirect social accountability through government oversight and trade union bargaining rights, engagement with the wider spectrum of British civil society's interests and institutions was very limited. Despite early aspirations, neither consumer groups nor unionised workers gained much influence over, or played much of a role in, their direction or operation. In most key respects the nationalised industries were the domain of the political and business elites who sought to influence their key decisions for political or economic gains.

Do the larger-sized firms in the CME-type societies offer greater engagement? How far can such enterprises be said to be socially embedded in this wider sense, rather than merely enmeshed in webs of rules, policed by the state, in the corporatist regimes so criticised by both left and right during the 1970s (Brittan 1975; Dyson 1983; Westergaard 1977)? CME countries have various types of mainstream enterprise which differ from the Anglo-Saxon form. But the two most significant, national contrasts with the LMEs' Anglo-Saxon model for both economic success, as well as for similar but distinctive forms of social embeddedness, are the Japanese *keiretsu* model and the German two-tier company.

Let us consider firstly the similarities of these two societies and then analyse their societal specificities in terms of embeddedness. The quite different forms of dispersed embedding in industrial district communities and in specific mutually-owned cooperatives can then be assessed.

1. GERMAN AND JAPANESE SIMILARITIES

These societies share two stark features which distinguish them from the Anglo-Saxon model. One is the social impact of their defeat in the Second World War and occupation, mainly by the USA. The second is the relationship between firms and finance capital. As a result of the German and Japanese surrender, the Allied powers, and the USA in particular, were concerned that economic reconstruction would not bind the business systems into potentially militaristic state powers, as had occurred prior to the war. The alternative was checks and balances that, *de facto*, linked business closer to the interests and conventions of civil society, rather than an authoritarian state. So initially, before the Cold War changed American sensibilities towards organised labour, management engagement with trade unions was encouraged. In both countries business reconstruction after the Second World War was imbued with some sense of a social mission. The second similarity, setting Germany and Japan apart from Anglo-Saxon practice and institutions, has been the role of financial interests. In the USA and UK corporations float in vast oceans of share trading and investment. By contrast both German and Japanese corporations, in the main, place relatively much less reliance on external financing by independent investors, or on the dedicated funds which manage investors' capital.

1.1 Finance, Investor Relations and Company Governance

In Germany there have been long-term relations between main banks and large corporations. These encourage longer-term provision of 'patient' capital, as well as access to inside information facilitating the reputational monitoring of firms. On some accounts this pivotal role for the banks – reflected in bank directors chairing other companies' boards – has been diluted since the 1990s. But any such relaxation has not led to the levels of stock market influence involved in USA and UK corporations, and stakeholder representation persists (O'Sullivan 2003, p. 25). Overlapping the financial-industrial links is a system of inter-company cooperation involving widespread cross-holdings of shares and also standard setting and technology transfer. Banks and related financial institutions still supply most long-term investment to companies (Vitols 2005, p. 14) and often, in return, have reserved places on 'their' firms' boards of directors.

Financial flows into German business

Globally, cross-border capital flows increased from US$4.9 trillion in 2000 to US$11.7 trillion in 2007. Nearly 60 per cent of this growth was driven by cross-border lending, but most of it was short-term in nature. Since then, cross-border capital flows have fallen precipitously, and they now remain nearly 60 per cent below their pre-crisis peak; approximately half of this drop was driven by a contraction in cross-border bank lending, primarily within Europe (Vitols 2005, p. 13).

Policy concessions to neo-liberal pressures have reduced bank share-holdings and board representation across firms; but these changes have been partly offset by an increased presence of 'patient capital', such as insurance fund investments. Moreover, most bank capital in Germany belongs to public savings and cooperatives, rather than profit-prioritising commercial banks (Vitols 2005, pp. 2–3).

Unlike the UK and USA practice of formal and remote communication of company metrics via reports and analyses to stock market agencies, Germany's system encourages the sharing of information and concern for reputation. Banks are similarly linked, as their supervisory boards contain industrial company representatives, other banks, suppliers, employees, and public agencies. The resulting networks of 'insider' investors allow 'patient' capital for long-term investment without the great need for public financial data or stock market intermediaries which dominate the Anglo-Saxon model. The German system also gives some protection from hostile, external take-overs. While at plant-level, works councils consisting of elected worker representatives and managers are able to negotiate on working conditions and lay-offs.

Executive managers' capacity for unilateral action is limited by the system of corporate governance. Managerial appointments and strategic policies depend upon agreement from supervisory boards, which are composed of employee representatives, major shareholders, senior managers from outside, major suppliers and customer firms. Thus, embedding is enhanced by the role and presence of these stakeholders which limit the firms' managerial isolation from and power over the wider society. Stakeholder ties reinforce external forms of network monitoring and favour consensus decision-making. Rather than formal and remote communication of company metrics via reports and analyses to stock market agencies, this system encourages the sharing of information and concern for reputation. Banks are similarly linked, as their supervisory boards contain industrial company representatives: other banks, suppliers, employees, and public agencies. The resulting networks of 'insider' investors allow 'patient' capital for long-term investment without the great need for public financial data or stock market intermediaries which dominate the Anglo-Saxon model.

Institutions and investment in Japan

Japan's business institutions and inter-relationships arose after the Second World War, partly as attempts to help its economy to catch up – then surpass – Western industries. These institutions also developed in order to overcome intense labour conflicts in the 1940s and early 1950s. For most of the post-war period the Japanese corporation's distinctive organisational forms have been inter-connected federations of firms: *keiretsu*, supplemented by company-specific unions and networks of SME contractors – resembling the industrial districts analysed below in the Italian case. *Keiretsu* are cross-sector federations of firms (for example energy, machines, and consumer goods) with reciprocal holdings of shares amongst the constituent companies.

Keiretsu federations of firms straddle different business sectors, sometimes with a keiretsu main bank at their centre. Large Japanese corporations have some independent, external investors but more significant investment comes from firms within their own group of enterprises, or from the banks associated with these *keiretsu* groups (Boyd 1987, p. 74–6). Again, these provide long-term indirect financing rather than direct share investment. In Japan's high-growth phase during the 1950s and 1960s external bank loans represented as much as 65 per cent to 83 per cent of total capital supply compared to 5.8 per cent in the USA, 4.3 per cent in the UK, 12.4 per cent in Italy and 18.8 per cent in Germany. Share holdings in the Anglo-Saxon societies function partly to facilitate take-overs and mergers. In the *keiretsu*, by contrast, there have historically been widespread reciprocal holdings of shares amongst member firms, both to prevent hostile take-overs in stock markets and to help secure bank finance. For example, this trend accelerated between 1949 and 1960 from a quarter of the top companies owning more than 5 per cent of shares in other companies to 78.4 per cent. A second wave of increased cross-holding followed in the 1960s as part of a strategy to prevent hostile take-overs threatened by a liberalisation of foreign investment (USGAO 1993, Table 4.2, p. 94). However, later calculations on 'stable' cross-shareholdings show a fall from around 18 per cent in 1987 to 10.5 per cent of all outstanding shares in 1999 (*Japan Economic Journal* 2001, cited in Yoshikawa and Gedajlovic 2002, p. 528).

This *keiretsu* system of inter-connected federations of firms persisted for most of the post-war period. Corporate cross-holdings breed norms of group and inter-group growth, solidarity and stability, rather than simply financial profitability (Gedajlovic and Shapiro 2002). Interestingly for British debates about short-term speculative investments, Japanese parlance distinguishes *antei kabunushi* (or *seisaku toshika*) which translates as 'stable shareholders' or 'strategic investors', from *juntoshika* or 'pure investors'. The latter are primarily finance-oriented while the priorities of the former promote investment, growth and market growth. As in the conglomerates so popular in the pre-financialised era in the West, *keiretsu* may be horizontal combinations across sectors, or vertical ones: between large corporations and their sub-contracting suppliers (*kigyo keiretsu*). Or they may have a distribution sector which provides dependable sales outlets and customer information to parent companies.

The protection by stable/strategic share owners has declined in recent years. However, in general, large holdings of stable investors have shielded most large Japanese firms from the take-over threat that their Anglo-Saxon counterparts face, and market shareholders or 'pure investors' still hold less equity than stable investors (Gedajlovic et al. 2004). Where a *keiretsu* group contains its own corporate banks this can be a source of long-term indirect financing. In the hey-day of the *keiretsu* the intra-group financing of six of the biggest manufacturing firms (Mitsui, Mitsubishi, Sumitomo, Fuji, Sanwa Dai-ichi, Kangyo) ranged from 25 per cent to 45 per cent of all borrowed capital (USGAO, Figure 11.2).

Thus in both Japan and Germany, this difference in the role and status of financial investments means that relations between top corporate executives and investor institutions are more personalised, more direct and less 'arm's-length' than those in Anglo-Saxon firms. Various commentators have argued that these more proximate and closer relationships enable corporations to communicate their aims, concerns and underlying prospects more intimately than their Anglo-Saxon counterparts. For the latter interact much more in terms of the short-term parameters of profitability, dividends and share values. It has been claimed that this more financialised relationship both constitutes and encourages corporate autonomy and remoteness from substantive interests in the wider society (cf Charkham, 1990, 1994). As Thelen (n.d., p. 48) points out, the more stable financing of Japanese corporations also makes it easier for them to offer long-term employment in what is often referred to as the *nenko* (seniority pay and career) system.

1.2   Employment and Stakeholder Relations

The reformation of both German and Japanese systems after World War II was partly undertaken to make managements more responsive to labour rights and trade unions – mainly to head off Communist exploitation of potential worker unrest. However, their labour relations and employment systems differ significantly. In the 1950s Japanese large corporations (until recently comprising about 30 per cent of the workforce) adopted the *nenko* system of internal promotion careers (properly called *nenko joretsu*). In this system core workers and managers usually stayed in lifetime employment (*shushin koyo*) with one firm following post-education recruitment. Workers' restriction to one firm entailed internal labour markets for promotions and vacant posts. Labour relations favoured Hirschman's (1970) 'voice' rather than 'exit' as unions are enterprise-based rather than occupational or industry-wide. Some believe the underlying *nenko* system has diminished; but it has been retained in the core firms and its ethos remains strong (Witt 2014, p. 107–8). Particularly resilient is the normative assumption that the corporate structure locks together both managers and workers in a 'Community of Fate'.

Lest we should stumble back into a culturalist assumption here – that these values are expressions of an essential Japanese philosophy – it is worth noting that *nenko* and its norms were essentially a pragmatic compromise adopted as a solution to bitter conflict between corporations and militant unions during the early 1950s (Suzuki 2006, p. 167). But the outcome has been significant. Lifetime employment and its accompanying institutions and values are another factor pressuring managers to prioritise organisational growth and security above profit generation for investors. It should also be noted, however, that outside the *nenko* system are large swathes of secondary workforce, including many women, in less secure and career limiting forms of employment (cf Kumazawa and Matsui, n.d.): an inequality which seems worse in low-paying, sub-contractor firms (Berggren and Nomura 1997, p. 79–90).

Offsetting the poorer status in sub-contracting has been *keiretsu* managers' practice of regular renewal of long-term contracts which enabled relationship-specific skills to develop amongst prime sub-contractors. More commercial forms of contracting were practised with second, third and fourth tier suppliers to keiretsu firms. Sub-contractor businesses were often set up or owned by those with insufficient higher education qualifications to enter the *nenko* sphere. Yet their technical skills and adaptability contributed to the rise in value of Japanese products. The extent of the mutual loyalty between *keiretsu* and sub-contractors has been eroded since

1991 with the decline of the SME sector in manufacturing. This fall was due to: increasing standardisation in vehicle and machinery parts, big firms' anxiety to re-deploy their own under-used workers, and fewer young people wanting to run industrial SMEs; plus overseas competition from cheaper Asian suppliers – for example in China. Exclusion has also been the usual lot of women, who would resign on marriage or childbirth, then support husbands' commitment to *nenko* in the big firms: the 'salaryman' phenomenon.

Germany, since the Second World War, has also often been portrayed as a model of social consensus in economic affairs. But this ethos stems partly from the strength of its industrial relations system which is even more embedded in cooperative institutions. There are strong, centralised and nationally encompassing employers' associations and trade unions, which contrast with Japan's enterprise-specific unions. But German corporate governance also has company-level 'co-determination' (*Mittbestimmung*) with worker or union representation on both the company's upper or 'supervisory' board and the works councils at plant-level. So socially embedded business in Germany, variants of which exist in different forms in other northern European societies, involves both external institutional supports and internal governance arrangements linked to the wider society. Production strategies are reliant on highly skilled workforces with substantial work autonomy, based on the *meister* system which shares technical with managerial authority in the workplace. This system encourages continuous improvements in products and production processes, thereby favouring technical rather than financial competitiveness. Externally, it is buttressed by the dual-system of workplace-college apprenticeships. Firms, employers' associations, regional governments and trade unions help to coordinate the dual system. The much commended *mittelstand* sector of SMEs, rather than corporate firms per se, provides the system's backbone, with local/regional political authorities and financial institutions affiliated to its representative bodies, as well as to the larger firms.

1.3 Neo-liberalisation?

Germany has experienced a variety of international pressures from business schools, intergovernmental organisations and consultancies to 'neo-liberalise' its corporate government to something approaching the Anglo-Saxon model. Pro-market reforms that have taken place in the last 15 years have loosened the insider role of banks but, paradoxically, increased the influence of trade unions (Jackson and Sorge 2012; Wilks 2013, p. 236–8). Under pressures from global competition Japan has seen some convergence towards the neo-liberal model. According to Dore, for two four-year periods – 1986–90 and 2001–05 – though increased value added was similar, wages rose by 19.1 per cent in 1986–91 but fell by 5.8 per cent during 2001–05. The corresponding increases in firms' profits were 28.4 per cent and 90.0 per cent and for dividends 1.6 per cent and 174.8 per cent. In both periods directors' pay increased: 22.2 per cent in 1986–90 and 97.3 per cent in 2001–05.

For Dore these shifts suggest adoption of the western financialisation model by Japanese firms (Dore 2006). However, more general research suggests that the Japanese *keiretsu-nenko* system is making adaptive responses, not a wholesale shift to neo-liberal principles of marketisation, labour flexibility and shareholder value (Berggren and Nomura, 1997; Aoki et al., 2008). Japan's financial system remains bank-led, rather than (stock) market-led. A 2002 law enabling USA-style board structures has led to only 58 out of 4,000 firms adopting such arrangements by 2012; and corporate defences against take-overs remain strong (Witt 2014, p. 104–5).There is more labour mobility between firms and more information disclosure to external investors, but the basic institutions remain intact. These have survived despite the insecurities of a domestic recession, which began well before the global financial crash of 2008. However, Japan – and in different ways Germany – do show the limits to embedding, particularly some destabilising of the rest of the economy and society with growing exclusion of other workers and hence a deepening of inequality (Thelen and Kume 1999, p. 499).

Generally, however, both Japan and Germany have tended to blur their sharp institutional differences with ST/EM firms, rather than experiencing systemic conversion to the neo-liberal model. Institutional persistence therefore seems to derive from the comparative advantages brought by these forms of social embeddedness. In their Anglo-Saxon counterparts, on the other hand, external links are mainly limited to regulatory accountability and financial responsibilities to shareholders. The German and Japanese systems thus continue to differ from the ST/EM model in terms of social embeddedness yet still show comparable or even better economic returns. Their relevance for broadening accountability in the UK's ST/EM business model is explored in more detail in Chapter 10. Yet, in the main the 'community' obligations of the German and Japanese companies are, in reality, restricted to other economic groups: kindred companies and banks plus the material interests of their core employees. To identify business systems which seem to be articulated to a broader range of civil society actors we have to consider the economic networks known as 'industrial districts'.

2. INDUSTRIAL DISTRICTS, CO-OPS AND LOCALISED EMBEDDING

2.1 Initial Paradigm

Accounts of the significance of industrial districts (IDs) and their competitiveness begin with Alfred Marshall's observations on the benefits of entire towns in industrial Britain localising a specific kind of product or trade in networks of small and large firms. He also observed, however, that firms' small size and focus and their specialisation on single production phases were aided by complementary social concentrations of workers with suitable skills and work customs in the same district: the 'mysteries of the trade … are as it were in the air, and children learn many of them unconsciously' (Marshall 1920, p. 271). As Reisman has observed, this insight could be considered as a rudimentary conception of the role of 'social capital' in economic performance (Reisman 2003). The economic difference between small and large firms, argued Marshall, was that the growth and superiority of large operations and firms stemmed particularly from the economies of scale in purchasing and sales; facilitated by high volumes and also by the separation of strategic from operations management and delegation to specialist managers. Or, in his own words 'internal economies' are '… attainable only by the aggregation of a large part of the business of the country into the hands of a comparatively small number of rich and powerful firms, or, as is commonly said, by production on a large scale'. Marshall saw such systems as a contrast between the ID possibility of: 'concentration of large numbers of small businesses of a similar kind in the same locality' versus the 'internal economies of production' achieved by the large operations of a single giant firm (Marshall 1920, IV.X.21).

The role of British industrial districts was bound up with particular stages of technological and international trade development. Yet it is remarkable how much they contributed to that nation's manufacturing in the nineteenth century. Cotton spinning or weaving in Lancashire, pottery and ceramics around Stoke-on-Trent, all manner of metal fastenings, chains, locks in separate areas of the Black Country are but some of the better-known examples. As Marshall intuited, the industrial practices became interwoven into the cultures of the districts, penetrating their life styles, self-images, idioms and humour. In lectures I refer to this as the 'Humpshire' phenomenon. In the English West Midlands the tangle of industrial districts called the Black Country included the lock-making town of Willenhall. This small town was jocularly known locally as

'Humpshire': because of the large numbers of inhabitants with permanently rounded shoulders and hunched backs from crouching over work benches to make locks. Coal mining and shipbuilding areas are not necessarily regarded as IDs, because of their products' limited capacity for differentiation. But these areas, especially the monocultural ones in Wales, Scotland and the North-east of England, have been celebrated in a plethora of studies which also illustrate this intense fusion of community cultures and industrial institutions (Bulmer 1978; Day 2006, pp. 75–89; Dennis et al. 1969; Roberts 1993; Warwick and Littlejohn 1992). Such intensive identification of local workforces and institutions with trades and industrial processes involved reciprocal, though sometimes conflictual relationships between firms and communities. The firms could draw on know-how, trust and pre-disposed local institutions. For their part the communities could expect employment, incomes and collateral, extramural, social activities and causes.

So why did this successful paradigm decline in the UK? Growth in size of firms, the greater mobility of capital and spread of product markets ruptured the socio-economic fabric from the inside. Some districts metamorphosed into large dominant firms – such as Wedgwood in the Potteries and Pilkington Glass in St Helens. These firms internalised many ID operations and businesses but still tended to retain their local embeddedness in order to draw on workers' skills and to exploit local ancillary trade and services. More serious departures from ID embeddedness came with changes in ownership structures, multidivisional organisation and their dis-articulation into potential purchases for other large firms. The commercial success of Fordist manufacturing methods also furthered the demise of ID-embedded businesses. As Marshall himself observed (Marshall 1920, Book IV, Chapter XI), not only did standardised mass-production limit the importance of many types of specialised skills and know-how in the workforce, it could tempt intervention by industrial policy makers (Barber 1967, p. 192). In fact, as chapter 3 showed, merger-induced business concentration became central to UK government policy after the Second World War, as a formula for industrial success.

By then, British governments were encouraging mergers and takeovers, assuming these would create economies of scale in bigger operations that would therefore be more internationally competitive. They promoted the construction of mega-plants in new locations which had little previous experience of such industries. Following the USA's Fordist model, the profusion of small and medium-sized firms that had supplied the West Midlands car assembling giants, such as Austin, were gradually absorbed into, or became dependent on, volume suppliers to the assemblers (Loveridge 1982). New steel works were concentrated in 'deep water' coastal places to facilitate the import of materials and export of products. New motor car factories were set up in high-unemployment areas such as the west of Scotland and Merseyside. Perhaps more significantly, corporate strategists began to prioritise financial and logistic benefits above the socio-cultural inputs as they planned new plants and closed down older ones. Internal cultures of management innovation began to replace the role of external knowledge transfer and acquisition from local know-how. By the 1960s the industrial district complex was seen as an archaic and inefficient model for both industrial and business policy. This view was challenged in the international recession of the 1970s and 1980s.

2.2   The Other 'Italian Miracle'

Although their renaissance has subsequently been documented through-out the industrialised world (Piore and Sabel 1984; Pyke and Sengen-berger 1992), it was in Italy that crucial new roles and dimensions of IDs were first discovered during the recessionary 1970s and 1980s. National economic data suggested new growth, outside of the main industrial regions of north-west Italy, between the Milan-Turin-Genoa industrial triangle and the under-developed regions of Rome and the South. This 'Third Italy' in the Veneto, Tuscany, and Emilia-Romagna possessed few large, Fordist firms but profuse clusters of SMEs focussed on special textiles, fashion garments, metal engineering products and industrial machinery according to the district. At first this vibrant growth was characterised as backward and based on exploitative cost-cutting: either as a result of increased out-sourcing by big firms seeking to avoid militant labour unions; or because of low-waged, perhaps 'black economy' employment of untaxed workers and minors. But gradually another picture emerged. In this perspective higher-skilled, technologi-cally adroit and well-paid workers and artisans had risen above any early dependence on crude exploitation and the sub-contracted scraps from the big firms' tables (for example Bagnasco 1977; Beccatini 1979; Brusco 1982). Many small firms were led or staffed by skilled workers expelled from large firms in redundancies and labour purges of the 1960s and 1970s. Because this pattern involved a capacity to innovate and to design products in-house, independently of big firms' sub-contracted orders, observers such as Brusco and Sabel – on whom the following account is based – labelled this new phenomenon 'flexible specialisation'.

Variations on this new ID model have been identified throughout the Third Italy. But it was the prominent status and distinctive features of the clusters in Emilia Romagna that highlighted the significance of its social dimensions. Like other Third Italy economies, enterprises in the Emilian clusters relied upon 'natural' social institutions: friendship networks and family ties providing labour, supplementary production and 'borrowed' know-how to complete orders and solve problems. But the political culture and organised institutions added an extra edge which confirmed the importance of distinctive social frameworks. Despite their 'petty-bourgeois' status, many of the small firms shared some of the Socialist or Communist political beliefs of the main trade unions and political parties, to which many SME owners had or still belonged. Regional particularism and antipathy to the national political Establishment fostered shared identities and the Socialist-Communist local governments funded industrial infrastructure and technical education. At the core of these cultural-economic complexes in Emilia have been the artisanal firms.

Legally constituted by Fascist-era laws, firms in Italy headed by worker-owners, with less than 15 adult employees, enjoy special taxation and other rights. They tend to belong to regional and national 'artisanal associations', which are usually allied with one of the main, national political parties. The dominant association in Emilia Romagna, the CNA (*Confederazione Nazionale Artigianale*), had close links with the Communist party (the PCI) and espoused ideologies of working class solidarity and social progress that might seem bizarre in small business contexts elsewhere. Though such principles may have been little more than ideological liturgy, they helped to embed underlying values of trust, solidarity and mutual respect which, in turn, underpinned more practical economic functions.

Although Emilia-Romagna represents an extreme case of the political and cultural embedding of small business IDs, its structural features are prevalent in other Italian regions. They may be thought of as a hierarchy: building up from the informal links and supports from business and social friendships, plus family, through representative bodies, such as the artisanal associations, to the local government and education systems – which have a conscious remit of servicing and promoting 'their citizens' businesses (cf Brusco 1982; Jones 1997, p. 217–43). The shared definitions of exchange, reciprocity and trust, emphasised by sociologists such as Granovetter, are social ingredients which perform functions beyond the scope of legal contracts and governance regulations which preoccupy neo-liberal and transaction cost analysts.

Clusters of firms within these IDs therefore deservedly merit the appellation 'a factory without a roof' or, more appropriately for our analysis, an 'enterprise without a constitution'. The commercial evidence for such ID is now almost overwhelming. At the socio-economic core of the model are dense networks of small firms sub-contracting amongst themselves and for larger firms, innovating more nimbly than big firms and using their social and skill capital to switch between different products or from one component to another. Looser versions of this model have since been identified or championed throughout the industrialised societies, by policy makers and business school pundits (cf Porter 1990). However, doubts persist about the longer term viability of the socially embedded IDs as opposed to those expedient clusters of specialists, as in some IT sectors, which cohere because of contingent geographical and economic gains.

To return to our main theme: are socially embedded and non-hierarchical, non-Fordist enterprise structures only feasible because of historical and cultural specificities in cases such as Emilia-Romagna? We can answer this question by looking at the state of the Italian IDs after two decades of globalised corporate competition and at evidence of new but comparable cases in the global economies' new heartlands. Piore and Sabel argued that flexible specialist forms in these IDs and their variants in Germany, Austria, East Asia and even, in niches, in the USA could survive and prosper, provided key conditions prevailed: no 'sell-out' to Fordist firms, avoid trying to become big themselves, and keeping the support of local institutions for example, for training up skills.

Others have been less sanguine. Harrison, and others, predicted that the big firms had begun fighting back, with tighter controls over sub-contractors, adoption of their own in-house flexible systems and 'off-shoring' operations to eastern Europe and East Asia (Martinelli and Schoenberger 1991; Paniccia 2007). However, current evidence indicates evolution and diversification of the Italian IDs, rather than decline and absorption. The Bologna motorbike industry and Forlì furniture industries lost firms responsible for product design and retained only component supply functions. However, contra Harrison and in the main, Emilian local firms have not been taken over by foreign multinationals. Instead local business groups increased their role by small firms establishing subsidiaries and by take-overs within and outside the districts (Rinaldi 2005, p. 249). Paniccia also identifies some reduction in the numbers of firms and employees in the more specialised IDs. Sometimes more concentration is observable as small firms have merged or formed into larger groups. However, Paniccia also claims other manufacturing IDs have become more diversified, along with some 'tertiarisation' as clusters that were previously manufacturers have moved into intermediate and advanced services. Overall, ID firms that practice flexible specialisation are said to be surviving, but some of these have needed to adopt modified and hybrid forms in order to do so. Meanwhile there is clear evidence that IDs have made a significant contribution to China's rise to a major manufacturing power (Christerson 1997; Bellandi and Di Tommaso 2005).

2.3 Cooperative Variants

A similar pattern can be found in a rather different kind of ID: the federation of Basque cooperative enterprises known as Mondragon. This well-known alternative to conventional business models is usually discussed for its democratic ethos and organisation. As a cooperative it is run by, and for, its members, who are the majority of its employees. Through a system of interlocking and federated institutions, policies and decisions are set by representative and elected forums, which also oversee the executive management. This system is, admittedly, a more formalised, and at the same time, a more focussed form of social embedding than the privately owned networks of firms in IDs. Mondragon's formalised organisation differs even from those socially integrated into local political cultures such as the Emilian case. In addition, Mondragon's uni-focal organisation through worker democracy has no necessary allegiance to other social interests. On the other hand, there are grounds for regarding Mondragon as a kind of ethically organised industrial district; or an ID *with* a constitution.

In the same way that political solidarity made the Emilian networks successful, Mondragon began partly as a response to economic adversity and was fuelled by sentiments of cultural distinctiveness. Under the fascist Franco regime, the Basque region, like other parts of the Spanish republic, had cause for feeling victimised. It had supported the Republican cause in the Civil War and was definitely not rewarded for its disloyalty to the Francoist Nationalists in the decades of dictatorship that followed. After the Mondragon cooperative's foundation in 1955 as *Talleres Ulgor*, it served as a significant source of revenue and jobs in its locality. Also, like football clubs in other independence-oriented regions, Mondragon was partly a vehicle for regional patriotism amongst a population with its own language and separatist traditions. Like the engineering firms in Emilian districts such as Bologna, the co-op has drawn on the local technical schools for its skilled labour. The original workshop, making heaters, was inspired by the efforts of communitarian priest Jose Maria Arizmendiarrieta, in the village of Mondragon. In the 1960s spin-off, co-ops in the same valley formed a wider Mondragon federation to share resources, rather than growing into one larger, centralised organisation. In the 1970s this federation expanded, in classic ID fashion, into workshops in the adjacent Orbide, Learko and Goilan areas (Luzarraga 2008).

Spinning off, or seeding partner firms in related products, Mondragon evolved into a commercial complex of over 150 businesses and tens of thousands of employees. Like other IDs, Mondragon draws on local institutions, like technical colleges, for its social resources. But it has also established its own social security and health care benefits, schools and a university. Unlike the Italian IDs, its organised evolution has been continuously based on a cooperative democracy of 'one member (employee), one vote'. It is organised through a system of tiered representation from the workplace to the Governing Council, which appoints and oversees managers,

Mondragon can also claim to have avoided the economic marginalisation that has befallen many worker cooperatives in other industrialised countries. It has not become a single giant organisation mirroring the bureaucracy of corporations. Nor has it been hemmed in and isolated by the growth of Fordist and multinational firms. It has survived and ridden the waves of market globalisation very well in economic terms. In 2014 the federation comprised 289 businesses (100 being co-ops) with approximately 80,000 employees, including overseas branches (65 plants) in Central/South America, China, India and west and central Europe, the USA and Japan (Mondragon n.d.; Luzarraga 2008, p. 390). Mondragon has also largely avoided the dilution of employee ownership or control which has sometimes occurred in otherwise successful co-ops (Hunt 1992; Cornforth 1995). But, like the Italian IDs, it has had to adapt to internationalised competition and to neo-liberal policy making. Spanish authorities forced the effective privatisation of its banking arm. The Fagor division encountered financial difficulties in 2013. But, unlike, say, a Japanese *keiretsu*, Fagor went into liquidation when the rest of the Mondragon federation refused it financial support. Mondragon did, however, fund relocation, retraining or early retirement schemes for 1,200 of Fagor's Spanish cooperative member workers (Higgs 2013).

On the other hand, Mondragon enterprises have shown that they can exploit global markets as adroitly as any MNC. Several divisions have established overseas branches in order to get closer to cheaper supply lines and their customers. There are around 14,000 temporary and conventional employees overseas. These new overseas enterprises are organised as conventional subsidiaries of Mondragon. However, the need to meet international competition means democratic co-ownership has not been extended to the substantial minority of 14,000 non-member workers mainly employed in foreign subsidiaries. The co-op's management claim that this is to accord with local legal conditions and the eventual plan is to convert them into cooperative enterprises like the Spanish and Basque operations. The most striking feature of four of these overseas locations – in China, Czech Republic, Mexico and Poland – is that they replicate several of the features of an industrial district. For example, four different Mondragon co-ops have plants in the same industrial park in Shanghai. These clusters do not all share the same practices and suppliers but they tend to cooperate on wage rates, training, and provision of services such as IT, legal, and marketing (Luzarraga 2008, pp. 383–406). Thus they can be considered as ID transplants organised on similar grounds to domestic ones: an alternative to the overseas branch plants of MNCs.

Outside of the manufacturing sector one final example of localised cooperative initiatives that exemplifies social embedding is the more recent mushrooming of alternative energy co-ops in Denmark's Jutland peninsula. These enterprises are not strictly industrial districts but they do arise from similar conjunctions of local cultures and institutions of legal and informal cooperation. Such businesses exist as complexes which are consciously distinct from large corporate enterprise in their aims and operations. The municipality plays a key role, 'one of the highest in Europe' in a local democratic culture (Santisteban 2006, citing Knudsen, 1993). Like Emilia, this culture emphasises proactive economic involvement. However there are no Danish national or regional associations, like those in Italy, to organise small firms at the local level (Kristensen 1992) and connect local enterprises, politics, and national political administrations and parties. Instead local industrial clusters benefit from professional, craft and educational organisations which provide training and research functions (Santisteban, 2006). Since 1981 some of this culture of local expertise and municipal involvement has helped spawn a wave of locally owned energy cooperatives, most usually generating wind power. These are owned by associations of local residents and municipalities who finance wind farms which sell the energy into local and national grids. There is intense local commitment to local forms of wind power and the exclusion of big energy corporations from the sector. As a result, and unlike, say, the UK, such renewables contribute 28 per cent of Danish electricity generation (Cumbers 2012, p. 195).

CONCLUSIONS

Proponents and champions of the Anglo-Saxon ST/EM corporation frequently argue that it is, or is becoming, a universal model for the economic conditions of neo-liberal globalisation. Yet all of the cases examined here – the stakeholder-oriented corporations in Germany and Japan, the Italian IDs and the Mondragon cooperative are strikingly different. They can also be said to have adapted well to economic change and adversity: much of it unleashed by neo-liberal de-regulation of national and international markets. It is true that each of these models has been modified and has evolved away from some of its founding characteristics. Yet they have also retained their essential difference from the logic of the ST/EM corporation. In different, and certainly uneven, ways they remain embedded in key institutions of their societies. These relationships constitute various degrees of tacit and formal accountability to community mores and solidarity. By contrast, firms within the Anglo-Saxon model move from one crisis of confidence to another within their host societies. So the resilience of alternative, socially embedded systems at least raises severe questions about the necessity of the ST/EM's continuing logic of autonomous and a-social development.

These cases have shown, in particular, that neither the giant organisation for Fordist mass production and mass finance nor the neo-Fordism of corporations' dependent supply chains is universally necessary. They also show the possibility of economic success (for example, through the embedding of big firms in Germany and Japan) that avoids social and economic segregation between executive managements, shareholders and stakeholders. Speculative, short-term investments, which accentuate the lack of accountability and powers of executive management, can also be avoided. Stock market flows play little or no part in most of the above cases. Finally, forms of collective ownership in the form of cooperatives have proven to be still viable; although they have been severely tested by the price competition and financial volatility unleashed by the forces of globalisation.

The very fact that the kind of embeddedness varies from country to country, and even from region to region, shows that the Aix Group's 'social spaces' could reform corporations' roles in the Anglo-Saxon societies. The similar roles played by Mondragon-style co-ops, Italian socio-political institutions and Danish technical and educational bodies demonstrate that the principle of community embeddedness does not depend on peculiar local conditions. Each of these variant models has been subject to the pressures of globalised markets, induced by neo-liberalism and corporate backers. German and Japanese businesses, IDs, and co-ops have all been bombarded by acute price competition from 'offshoring' and the low-wage developing economies. There have also been pressures from international opinion-formers and policy lobbyists for the adoption of Anglo-Saxon forms of governance. International economic authorities and institutions have also succeeded in partial opening up of their economic environments to financial incursions for direct investments, take-overs and speculation in shareholdings. The supportive political cultures of the socially embedded alternatives have been affected; but they have survived, adapted and, in some instances, prospered even more. The continuing global economic crisis and its destructive potential for internationally exposed markets may even, as Polanyi predicted, make further recourse to forms of social embeddedness an economic and political priority. We will return to their specific relevance to the UK in chapter 11, but let us also keep these relative successes in mind in the next chapter, when assessing the movements that have arisen in the core 'Anglo-Saxon' economies to make corporations more responsive to their civil society.

PART III

The pursuit of responsible capitalism:
campaigns and political recipes

8. Communitarian solutions: business as moral integration

> Riches joined with liberality, is Power; because it procureth friends, and servants. (Thomas Hobbes, Leviathan, i. x. 41)

> CSR in the UK is not just a poor substitute for the dismantling of institutionalized social solidarity. Some of the things currently done in the name of CSR – new governance forms of accountability, innovation, partnerships, supply chain employment and environmental standards – did not get done in that other world, the world of the post-war compromise. (Kinderman 2012, p. 51)

INTRODUCTION

When the fraud-stricken Enron, Worldcom and Tyco corporations collapsed in 2002, Lawrence Lindsey, Chief Economic Adviser to President G.W. Bush, had a pat solution. Did this fairly orthodox, 'supply-side', liberal economist call for more competition between financially suspect firms? Did he advocate a break with the cosy relationships between corporations and the handful of giant accountancy firms; or greater scrutiny and oversight by shareholders? Astonishingly, this economist stalwart of market fundamentalism called for sociological change.

> You need a higher ethical standard than the one that existed in the 1990s. You can't have an anything goes mentality and expect to maintain the trust that is necessary to make markets work. It is a more profound sociological change that is being called for than passing some legislation. (Lindsey in Beattie 2002)

Some might allege that Lindsey, having had exposure to Enron's business practices as a member of its advisory board, was drawing on direct experience of his former associates' dubious integrity (Goldfarb 2006). Less charitably, Lindsey's solution could have been because normative change entails less of a loss of corporate autonomy than having tighter financial controls. But Lindsey could also rely on a call for ethical responsibility chiming with swathes of US corporate opinion in what had become an intellectual reflex amongst the American business and policy establishment.

Neo-liberal ideology generally presumes against legal regulation. So, by 2002 its supporters and fellow travellers were increasingly sympathetic to the idea of moral re-integration as a counterweight to the risks of unregulated avarice and fraudulent expediency in business. Deriving most coherently from the communitarian intellectual movement, Lindsey's 'sociological' solution had been gathering credibility for several decades under the banners of 'corporate social responsibility' or 'corporate citizenship' as an alternative to neo-liberal fundamentalism. The 'moralisation' of business and the practice of its close counterpart of corporate social responsibility (CSR) stemmed from parallel concerns to the previous chapter's neo-Polanyian and sociological theories of embeddedness. But, unlike those perspectives, business communitarianism saw change as coming from within business institutions: a 'reaching out', rather than a drawing back in. The relative popularity of communitarian CSR necessitates close investigation of its scope and the substantive differences between the sociological and communitarian discourses. To do this we need to pin down the distinctive logical structure of the latter and the reasons it crystallised into the intellectual basis of corporate social responsibility. Chapter 10 complements this discursive analysis with evidence from detailed empirical cases of the scope and limitations of CSR practices: codes of conduct, stakeholder relations and environmental sustainability.

The present chapter dissects the communitarian ideas which became the tacit doctrine behind the surprising success of the upstart British CSR variant. By comparison, even its more mature US original version has been relatively less prominent. This overview identifies, firstly, communitarianism's political context and popularity. Secondly, it examines its influence on the promulgation of contemporary CSR. Thirdly, it describes how CSR was institutionalised as the UK's neo-liberal formula for social embedding; i.e. by melding communitarian ideas with indigenous practices. The chapter ends by describing the limitations of communitarian-CSR's values-driven attempts at social integration based on notions of treating the company itself as a community.

1. COMMUNITARIAN THEORY AND 'THIRD WAY' POLITICS

Neo-liberalism's apparent political success in liberating and expanding markets in the 1980s and early 1990s could not conceal the policies' palpable failings and negative consequences for social integration. Whatever its provenance, Margaret Thatcher's 'no such thing as society' sentiment seemed to exemplify the indifference of neo-liberalism to, and incomprehension of the consequences of its policies in community disintegration and social distress.

1.1 Amitai's Answer: An Ethical Turn

Amitai Etzioni's 1988 book, *The Moral Dimension*, may not have inspired a major sociological campaign against neo-liberal economics. However, it did articulate communitarian ideas which fuelled Third Way politics for the New Democrats in the USA and New Labour governments in the UK. Their perspectives, in turn, recognised CSR as an alternative to both direct state promotion and governance of social welfare and to the neo-liberal abdication of social problems to market solutions.

Explaining the mixed fortunes of Etzioni's sociological enterprise, Beckert (2008, p. 137) observes that *The Moral Dimension* 'might have been too close' to the normative action paradigm in the ideologically suspect, conservative Parsonian tradition. Beckert (2008) contrasts Etzioni's premises with those of sociologists like Mark Granovetter (1985), whose view of economic embeddedness as social networks we examined in chapter 6. In other words, these latter analysts argue for structural explanations of economic outcomes and avoid action theory's perspective of actors' capacity for normatively based voluntarism. Too normative for sociologists perhaps, but this normative-ethical emphasis in Etzioni's version of embeddedness and – as we shall discuss – its limited concern for structural change, was probably just what made it attractive to Third Way politicians such as the Clinton and Blair administrations.

Etzioni's version of embeddedness – as 'economic ethics' – offers philosophical underpinning for discourse and policies about corporations' normative responsibilities and hence the CSR movement, or movements. The framework of its actions also focusses on business relations with stakeholders (cf Hollstein 2008, p. 147). The significance of the perspective is highlighted by a comparison with the paradigms of market economics. Analysts of the 'performativity' of neo-classical economics (Callon 1998; MacKenzie et al. 2007) maintain that this paradigm functions not just to describe economic activity but to promote 'performativity'; that is, to cajole and persuade actors to adopt the behaviours its theories of rational action prescribe. The aim of this performativity is to ensure that 'subsequent economic processes will indeed conform to the descriptions in economic theory' (Beckert 2008, p. 140). So if economic theory's utility-maximising, interest-calculating behavioural model can become reality, why not an Etzionian normative action paradigm as a justifiable alternative and countervailing force? However, as our subsequent discussion of CSR practices will show, the performative potential of the 'economic man' model is facilitated by the supportive institutional structures of capitalism – trading norms, financial incentives, legal codes and cultures of individualism. Etzioni's other-regarding formula, on the other hand, has few, if any, independent institutional supports in the business sphere.

Logically enough, Etzioni's communitarianism begins with the 1980s preoccupation with relations between individuals and states and markets. In order to escape the oppressive poles of overbearing states on the one hand and atomising markets on the other, he commends a need: 'to attend to our responsibilities to the conditions and elements we all share, to the community ...' Etzioni assuages neo-liberal fears of building on government controls or fear of authorities. Instead, it is the functioning community which supports individuals, 'backing them up against encroachment by the state and sustains morality by drawing on the gentle prodding of kin, friends and neighbours and other community members' (Etzioni 1993, p. 15).

The neo-liberal interpretation of Adam Smith – that market-acquisitiveness is the key latent instinct in human actors – is rhetorically replaced by Etzioni's claim that 'some values command our support because they are "habits of the heart". As such these sentiments can act as rallying points for a more ethical society in which certain actions are viewed as "beyond the pale"'(Etzioni 1993, p. 24). By encouraging such values, Etzioni claims, the socially destructive behaviours fuelled by market individualism can be moderated. As he succinctly and simply puts it: 'The "I/We" balance will be tilted closer to the "we"' (Etzioni 1993, p. 15). Specifically in market contexts, Etzioni appeals to the collective interest of business actors. Reprising the economic necessity of trust in economic transactions, he challenges the viability of market-economics' performativity: 'The more people accept the neo-classical paradigm as a guide for ... behaviour ... (the) more the ability to sustain a market economy is undermined ... [the] more people pursue immediate gain ... [the] higher the transaction costs' (Etzioni 1988, p. 250).

Citing the example of the de-regulated New York taxi system – in which both cab drivers and customers suffered – Etzioni argues that, without 'trust', transaction costs escalate. Free competition without rules, becomes conflict which damages the common good. But 'rules' may be either externally imposed or voluntarily adopted by the transacting parties, depending on (largely unspecified) circumstances:

The communitarian position I have come to share with … colleagues *and public leaders* assumes that there is a tension between the individual (and their rights) and the common good (and hence one's social responsibilities) and that a good society seeks a carefully crafted balance between the two, relying as much as possible on moral suasion and not on power. (Etzioni 2008, p. 170–1) (emphasis added)

1.2   Ethical Business?

This reliance on moral voluntarism is not indicative of naivety on Etzioni's part, as his caustic view of the bias inherent in the neoclassical economists' paradigm shows. That perspective, Etzioni says, cannot explain, for example, their view that judgements which favour anti-poverty policies 'come from some other, unaccounted for world – or are indeed lacking'. Such economists, he says 'favour lower taxes for income from capital [rather] than on income from labour, and favour still higher pay for CEOs!' (Etzioni 2008, p. 171). Similarly he is alert to the implications of corporate hegemony, recognising that big corporations may use economic power more effectively against polities that are smaller than their national government; for example with local governments and in dealings with smaller states (Etzioni 1988, p. 226).

To counter its corrosive force, competition needs to be 'encapsulated' – the Etzionian version of embedding. Otherwise, corporations will use their political power to reduce input costs while keeping up their 'competitive' prices to consumers, as his examples of energy suppliers and tax-break beneficiaries illustrate. However, the solutions are again said to lie in the arena of appeals to ethical values, or 'moral suasion'. More effective norms mean less resort to government sanctions and an alternative to what Etzioni sees as the equally ineffective role of government incentives. The Thatcher and Reagan governments cut government expenditures and thus taxes, but corporate behaviour did not substantially alter. 'Moral suasion', however, could change it. Nor, Etzioni avers, need economic performance suffer. Cooperation, involving more trust relations between firms, is as likely to improve 'competitiveness' as de-regulation is to increase competition.

Yet when Etzioni applies his formula to the nature and reform of corporate amorality, the broad scope of moral suasion becomes modest to the point of triviality. The prognoses include the claim that corporations which embrace a communitarian approach may prosper more if they move (managerial) employees around less between locations. To avoid threats of legislation which could limit plant closures by slowing down transfers, corporations should involve communities to help or find new buyers. They should also respect the autonomy of employees' private lives by not seeking to control non-work related activities and life styles. Instead they should help employees' work-life balance through paid leave for both parents (Etzioni 1993, pp. li, 27).

However, the prospects for creating 'moral managers', in a conventional philosophical sense, are dimmed by contemporaneous analysis and research, which gives two reasons for rejecting any general conversion. Firstly, there is the organisational-authority constraint that: 'morality ... in the corporation ... is what the guy above you wants from you' (Jackall 2010, p. 115). Yet conventional ethical criteria stipulate that giving or following orders to act in an ethical way does not constitute moral action (MacLagan 1998). Secondly, Etzioni's 'habits of the heart' are not in evidence when firms do change their ways in line with wider social norms. For then they are simply conforming to a specific social expectation, not expressing or internalising such beliefs as an authentic ethic (Jones 2007).

On the other hand, *The Moral Dimension* and similar communitarian treatises are not naively trusting in ethics as a panacea. They do address the societal level of normative versus utilitarian conflicts. They do recognise the need for sanctions in extremis. Commenting on Enron-style misbehaviour Etzioni ignored moral suasion, contradicting Lindsey's ethical nostrums, and simply recommended harsher financial penalties (Etzioni 2001). No doubt Etzioni himself would recommend state intervention rather than normative nudging in the case of systematic business abuses. Moreover, almost as an afterthought to his main statements, Etzioni has more recently also argued on a 'moral' basis for stakeholder rights in the governance of corporations, equivalent to those of shareholders (Etzioni 2014). However, as it has come to be translated into CSR, the basic communitarian recipe for corporate reform is no more radical than the examples just cited. Indeed, as we shall, see, CSR as a whole can function to preclude public controls over corporate autonomy.

2. COMMUNITARIANISM AND CSR: EVOLUTION IN BRITAIN AND AMERICA

By the 1980s business responsibility movements had already been established as flourishing, albeit niche, influences on mainstream corporations. In the USA, more proactive and instrumental social involvement, aligned to brand consciousness, was supplementing the traditional philanthropy amongst tycoon capitalists such as Rockefeller, Heinz or Stanford (Heald 1970; Marens 2012). Yet, as Carroll observes, the adjective 'corporate' had yet to be added to social responsibility which was still, in the philanthropic tradition, discursively associated with the actions of individual businessmen (sic) or executives (Carroll 1999, p. 270–1). The implicitly and explicitly anti-corporate movements of the late 1960s and early 1970s prompted more urgency and intellectual focus amongst business leaders. The Committee for Economic Development's quasi-manifesto of 1971 is clearly a reaction to the campaigns of social movements such as environmentalism, described in the next chapter (Carroll 1999, p. 274–5).

In the UK, business initiatives such as those of multinationals like IBM, Shell and BP can be seen as business 'doing its bit' for the economic crisis that engulfed western economies after the oil shocks and recession of the 1970s. By the 1980s these were being supplemented and buttressed by embryonic business-government schemes such as Business in the Community – initially intended to support the new 'local enterprise agencies' (Marinetto 1998, pp. 53–4) – as later Thatcher cabinets attempted to provide a more emphatic government steer to businesses' social contributions (Kinderman 2012). But on the whole these activities lacked a unifying discourse of philosophical and acceptable political concepts. Explicitly, or by indirect osmosis, communitarian ideas began to fill that gap.

Etzioni had the opportunity to seed communitarian ideas into business education during his 1987–89 tenure of the Thomas Henry Carroll Ford Foundation Professorship at the Harvard Business School. But, despite this platform, his full paradigm seems to have had relatively little impact on the general CSR movement in the USA (Arjoon, 2005). Commentators have speculated that this limitation was because 'integration into higher ranking economic or sociological macro theories is generally lacking in these business ethics approaches' which are: 'primarily concentrated on practical questions of everyday business life' (Hollstein 2008, p. 143). It might be more accurate to say that Etzionian 'action-oriented' manifestos made little impact in US business circles because CSR there had been heading in his direction for some years. Many of his ideas were predated in the writings of evangelists such as Keith Davis (1967). Etzioni's business responsibility recipes were probably just retuning existing practice in some quarters of the US business world. The already-converted, therefore, had little need for another evangelist. On the other hand, the broader political philosophy undoubtedly had some influence in the Clinton and early Bush administrations (Milbank 2001); and probably reinforced its support for CSR as a general policy steer. The European receptiveness – which we will examine soon in the British context – therefore need not be mainly attributable to a more catholic philosophical framework for business ethics (Holstein 2008). Blairites in the UK were receptive to communitarianism because it offered the alternative to both collectivist social-democracy and neo-liberalism for which New Labour were groping. As future (New) Labour cabinet minister Chris Smith argued:

> enterprise is not based simply on two pillars but on four: the customers of the company are a third, and the wider surrounding community a fourth. We are seeing the gradual development of a more complex and interdependent relationship between all these parties than was ever dreamed of. (Smith 1996, p. 12)

Communitarianism also provided a Trojan horse into other European states because both it and CSR were relatively new concepts. Thus the New Labour government gave significant policy boosts to the trans-Atlantic import of CSR because it chimed so clearly with their new found enthusiasm for communitarianism (Brejning 2012, p. 34).

Systematic data is not collected on corporate assistance to, and involvement in, traditional public welfare and civil society activities. On the other hand there is circumstantial evidence of a deepening involvement during the 1990s (Vogel 2005, p. 6) as reports in areas such as sustainable development and environmental improvement indicate. Peter Melchett, former Greenpeace UK Executive Director, put it this way: green campaigners began to focus more on business than on politicians because 'there had been a shift in power from politics to business ... asked for by business and given by politicians' (Rowell 2001a). While John Elkington, a campaigner for corporate transparency, claimed that NGOs 'much less worried about accepting the corporate dollar ... will increasingly need to do so to fund the growing scale of their operations' (Elkington 1997, p. 225–6). We probe these relationships in more detail in the next chapter. However, in the early phases of the neo-liberal era, corporate social involvement was more established in the USA than in the UK, if measured in terms of its sophistication and levels of financial and 'in-kind' contributions to the charity and CSO sector. On the other hand, in corporate-public sector relations such as public-private partnerships, the US pattern has been more eclectic and locally variable (Jones 2005).

2.1 Government Interest in CSR: The Public Duties of Private Enterprises

Neo-liberal changes in corporate fiscal liabilities were the main form of overt governmental support for CSR. These helped to 'nudge' corporations' public roles in the USA and, ever conscious of the precocity of their Big Brother across the water, precipitated British governments' shift towards CSR. Corporate tax allowances in return for social contributions had been higher in the United States than the United Kingdom (Jepperson 1991, pp. 149–53). In addition the 1980s had seen general reductions in corporate taxes; by up to one-third in the last decades of the twentieth century. UK governments probably played a more directive role in prompting businesses to imitate the 'social involvement' of their US counterparts (Marinetto 1998, pp. 15–17). Fiscal legislation in 1986 and again in 1991 was explicitly aimed at stimulating 'corporate giving' towards US levels (Brammer and Millington 2003). The tax payments of many corporations were reduced further by special concessions and allowances.

These reductions induced both more scope for business involvement in public programmes and greater political pressure to get involved: through gifts, sponsorship and the more commercial contracts in 'public–private partnerships' (Cannon 1992, p. 43; Hertz 2001, pp. 176–82; Klein 2000, pp. 30–4; Moon, 2002). Neo-liberal policies meant smaller state budgets and reductions in states' capacity for direct intervention in both existing commitments and new problems in the spheres of employment, personal welfare, human rights overseas and the environment (Teeple 2000, pp. 79, 105–17, 144–5; Swank 2002, pp. 219–37). Such constraints arose also because business was paying lower tax revenues (OECD 2002, pp. 94–6; Pearce and Martin, 1996). The US example of General Electric (Greider 1996) illustrates national trends in the increased scope these shifts gave business to make discretionary contributions to such causes.

Consequently, business sponsorship in the United States increased 700 per cent between 1985 and 1999 to $7 billion (Klein 2000, Table 2.2; IEG 1999). Specifically, CSR-related, 'cause related marketing' contributions rose by almost a thousand-fold to hit $1.08 billion by 2005 (Epstein, 2005). In the United Kingdom, allowing for appropriate lags, it rose continuously after corporate tax levels fell from 52 per cent in 1980 to 34 per cent in 1991 (Commission of the European Communities, 1992, p. 173). From an estimated £4 million in 1970, sponsorship – which includes much corporate 'giving' – came to be 'worth at least 100 times that' (Cooper 2003). General charitable contributions in the United Kingdom rose steadily for 20 years. Then they quadrupled from 1985 to 1999 with the biggest 100 firms increasing donations by 26 per cent to £630 million between 2002 and 2003 (Brammer and Pavelin 2005, p. 24; Campbell et al., 2002). A more chequered US growth recovered to an estimated $13.77 billion by 2005 (Conference Board 2007, cited in 2007). After recovery from the 2007–08 financial crash, cash and in-kind contributions were estimated to have reached a total of $20 billion from just 240 companies (CECP 2013).

2.2 Trends in Corporate Giving

From the 1980s, United States federal budget cuts for welfare services were premised explicitly on compensatory charitable, corporate and third-sector initiatives (Reich 1998; Responsive Philanthropy 1996). These shifts had both instrumental and cultural causes. In both countries increased social involvement was probably prompted by corporate fears that public concerns and controversies over business privilege might mean media and public backlashes, or hostile electoral opinion. The perceived risks were that such reactions might pressure politicians to regulate or otherwise control 'irresponsible' businesses (Wilks, 1997; Sparkes 2003). The fear was that deregulatory trends in such sectors as financial services, telecommunications, transport, and energy utilities might then be threatened.

However, by adopting and publicising social responsibilities, corporations and neo-liberal politicians could counter such threats. Labor Secretary Bob Reich was blunt about the role President Clinton's administration expected of business: for the US federal government CSR was the quid pro quo for lower taxes and less government welfare (Reich 1998). It was also surely not coincidental that some of the biggest and earliest adopters of CSR activity in the UK were the newly privatised, and status-insecure utility companies (Kinderman 2012, p. 43). Indeed corporate responsibility practitioners now recommend CSR as a key management tool in the planning of privatisations (David Halley, UK Business in the Community 2008, cited in Kinderman 2010).

3. CSR: CULTURAL SHIFT OR GOVERNMENT POLICY?

CSR in the United States had a well-established practical basis in its propitious fiscal regimes. However, despite the tradition of business charitable foundations and socio-cultural roots in local business associations (Galaskiewicz 1991), a philanthropic faith rather than a coherent, new, national and ideological focus was sufficient for these institutions. When 'CSR' began to be coined in US business schools in the 1970s and 1980s, it was just one more of several labels and ideas interwoven into the longer traditions of more conventional philanthropy and paradigms of ethical business that stretched back into the nineteenth century. Britain, on the other hand, developed top-down, discursively coherent CSR movements in a much more singular and organised fashion. Its official endorsement by UK governments was part of the break with the post-World War II consensus which had placed the welfare state at least on a par with the status of the market sphere. At the time of its establishment, in 1983, the status of Business in the Community (BITC), as a national CSR association, was internationally unprecedented. BITC described 'the promotion of corporate social responsibility' as a main objective as early as 1984 (BITC, 1984: 2, cited in Kinderman 2012, p. 34).The subsequent UK evolution of CSR has been so successful that some observers have ranked it above the US, or as the leading regime internationally (Vogel 2005, p. 7; Kinderman 2012, p. 32).

In Britain, as long as Thatcherite politicians held sway, the ideological scope for CSR was still uncertain; still limited by the primacy of economic freedoms for business (MacLeod 2007, p. 233). However Tory administrations did seed support for the dissemination of CSR-compatible practice. The Ministry of the Environment convened the Sunningdale Park conference in April 1980 for 17 British government and business representatives, plus 10 officials from the US. One Sunningdale participant saw this as part of 'a growing interest [in corporate responsibility] ... a response to the new Government's intention to reduce the State's activities in society' (Department of the Environment 1980, p. 16, cited in Kinderman 2012). Contemporary sources suggest that a major test-bed for British CSR was the local employment initiatives by which downsizing British firms sought to limit worker opposition to closures and restore their public image (Kinderman 2012, p. 33; Mason 1987; Richardson 1983). Sunningdale was particularly concerned with shifting the limited UK interest in business responsibility closer to what was perceived as superior US status (Kinderman 2012, p. 38). Associations such as BITC were soon giving organised form to such aspirations. Indeed, despite its uncertain relationship to neo-liberalism, BITC experienced its biggest growth, to almost 500 member-companies, between 1986 and 1992 in the heyday of Thatcherism.

3.1 Ideological Elevation

The British Thatcherite governments and the Reagan administrations in the USA gave some encouragement to what was emerging as CSR. However, discursively speaking, support was sotto voce. Corporate responsibility ideas were already facing up to contradictions and objections from the US and UK neo-liberal fundamentalists (cf Friedman 1970; Brittan et al., cited in Mullerat 2010, p. 444). But by the mid-1990s these critics were swimming against the ideological tide. Against the Friedmanite defence of the inviolability of corporate/shareholder interest – which should not be reduced by corporate giving – academics had begun arguing the juridical case for CSR. Corporations can take moral positions and be moral actors precisely because corporations are legal subjects, Goodpaster and Matthews (1982) had claimed some years before. Employment could and should be non-discriminatory, family friendly and based on equal opportunity. Companies can prioritise investment that is not environmentally damaging, does not support political repression, militarism, or hyper-exploitative investment locations. Production should avoid/limit polluting or health threatening products and processes (Waddock et al. 2002, p. 134).

Because the Clinton and Blair governments broadly continued the neo-liberal economic policies of their conservative predecessors, they needed more social responsibility from business to distinguish themselves from those political adversaries. Communitarian advocates such as Etzioni were therefore officially welcomed into Whitehall and the White House as communitarian ideas appeared in CSR discourse. Consider the similarities between Etzioni's celebration of individual citizenship cited above and the following justification for corporations acting as citizens, which:

> ... involves a mutually reinforcing relationship between individuals and communities: individuals fulfil the responsibilities of citizenship, because some of their personal needs can only be met through communal action ... Corporate citizenship likewise suggests a two-way relationship between society and corporations: some of a corporation's needs will ultimately only be met by taking actions ... oriented towards meeting communal needs. (McIntosh et al. 1998, p. xxi)

New Labour's house philosopher, the sociologist Anthony Giddens, wove Etzioni's ideas into the Third Way perspectives he contributed to Blair's governmental project (Marinetto 2003; Calder 2004). Significantly, BITC's second biggest membership rise coincided with the communitarian phase of New Labour between the mid-1990s and 2002 (Kinderman 2012, p. 34).

New Labour rhetoric originally brought corporate responsibility into its communitarian ideology through the ambiguous concept of stakeholders. However, this was later displaced by the less threatening emphasis on individual and community responsibilities (Driver and Martell 1997). New Labour did promote CSR up the governmental ladder. It established, for a while, a junior minister with explicit CSR duties. Under Labour

BITC was directly supported with government funds which it had not received from the previous Conservative governments.

BOX 8.1   BUSINESS IN THE COMMUNITY LTD

- By 2007 BITC could claim a membership of 750 firms, links with 70 of the FTSE 100 companies, plus 2,000 via international networks.
- Another 1600 firms participating in BITC activities, covering 20%+ private sector employees (BITC 2007).
- The total number of companies, many large, stock exchange corporations, exceeded 800 by 2010; 'more than any other business-led CSR coalition in the OECD' (Kinderman 2012, pp. 41, 34).
- However, its 2013 Annual Report suggests that most of BITC's financial donors are public and voluntary sector organisations, not companies (BITC 2014, pp. 40–41)!

---

4.   COMPANIES AS PARTNERS AND COMMUNITIES

Chapter 10 will look at detailed case studies of the actual practices of CSR-focussed businesses on the communities in which they locate. The rest of this chapter examines the policy and discursive underpinnings of this critical community dimension of CSR. As far back as the Sunningdale period British CSR was becoming more distinctive than its US counterpart in linking up with public and civil society organisations for specific projects. British government regulations have helped push these different partners together. Across a range of urban regeneration and community development programmes, government rules required local community initiatives to have business 'partners' before they can qualify for central government funding: for a review and case study evidence see Clement (2010).

'Regeneration partnerships', which operate under these constraints, are also significant because they represent new forms of welfare intervention beyond the operation of traditional state departments such as social security, health and housing. While ostensibly concerned with environmental and economic improvements their objectives also include improvements to the social fabric and health standards of communities. The corporate involvement in such programmes may not be as visible as quantitative and financial data on national, public welfare categories. However it may have extremely influential effects at the local level, not least in propagation of commercialising urban projects (cf Jones and Bull 2006). Within the wider range of public-private partnerships for urban regeneration in the US there are also some 'social partnerships' similar to the more recent, British, local regeneration partnerships. These US arrangements are also usually focussed on neighbourhood revitalisation; but there, private foundations – which are often funded by firms – are more likely to be involved (Reuschke 2004).

The significance of corporate partnerships with non-business organisations is part of the more complex and critical issue of 'stakeholder relationships' analysed in chapters 10 and 11. What we need to note here is that, although the jargon of stakeholder partnerships is liberally bandied around, these actually fall into three distinct categories:

1. bilateral agreements between single corporations and single NGOs or public bodies aimed at singular social or environmental problems;
2. multilateral arrangements, of several firms in the same or related business sectors and several NGOs/public bodies to regulate a problem caused by, or related to, those businesses' activities;
3. multilateral projects – 'partnerships' – between businesses and civil society/public bodies to promote socio-environmental improvement across a range of issues: as with the urban regeneration partnerships just mentioned.

Hence 'partnerships' may sometimes be a form of 'soft' or voluntary co-regulation of negative business activities – something distinctive to contemporary CSR. Sometimes they involve the harnessing of business expertise and resources to tackle public problems for which the businesses have no direct legal or ethical responsibility. In the latter case the business engagement may be a 'social contribution' closer to old-style philanthropy or, in some circumstances, entail direct commercial pay-offs: as in construction firms' involvement in urban regeneration. Thus the extent to which CSR ideologies, such as communitarianism, play a role, varies from one type of partnership arrangement to another.

4.1   The Company as its Own Community?

So 'community involvement', especially in the more traditional forms of corporate engagement practised in the US, can sometimes be used as almost another label for CSR. As such it fits easily into the communitarian discursive mould. However there is another business use of the community concept, highlighted by Etzioni, which has even more contentious ramifications. This is the idea, made especially fashionable in the 1980s and 1990s, that the corporation can be made more internally responsible by realising its potential as a kind of community in its own right. This thesis followed on from the discovery – or rediscovery – of corporate cultures by organisational analysts. It led to quixotic aspirations, in business schools and corporations themselves, for moral reintegration of the fissiparous divisions of interest and identity between managements and employee groups. The rise and decline of this idea is worth examining for the light it may shed on the scope and contradictions of broader CSR trends.

Etzioni's take on corporate responsibility focussed on maintaining and deepening community ties. Mention was made above of his advice for firms to help communities to find new buyers in the face of plant closures. Help in stabilising employees' work-life balance, minimising transfers of managers around the firm, and respect for employees' autonomy in their private lives and life styles were also cited. Such recommendations are hardly revolutionary. They are consistent with a history in paternalistic firms, especially in the USA, of corporate welfare for employees (Jones 2007). The recessionary crises of the 1980s did limit the scope of corporate welfare coverage. With the rise of secondary and peripheral forms of employment entitlements began to narrow to 'core' employees such as managerial staff. But as late as 1990 Charles Perrow was drawing attention to the wider problems with such corporate paternalism (Perrow 1991). By the 1970s, he claimed, some corporations had established such a mind-boggling array of schemes and services for their (core) employees that the obligatory 'fringe benefits' amounted to as much as 45 per cent of labour costs. Perrow's (1991, p. 754) sample list of these covered the following:

- counselling, sex therapy, medical care, funeral services;
- educational opportunities, formal training, tax investment advice;
- retirement planning & counselling, relocation services;
- religious facilities;
- paternal/maternal leave, child care;
- sports facilities, vacation planning, travel services.

Perrow's concern was that such benevolence internalised services and benefits that might earlier or otherwise have come from the family or local community. As a consequence, he claimed, the large corporate-organisation, or its satellites, has 'absorbed society'. Or, to put it another way, the corporation as community is actually undermining the external community.

Other criticisms can be added. What about the increase in inequality between the patronised core employees and the excluded non-core employees? What about those employees whose firms are unable or unwilling to provide such levels of welfare? What are the consequences for the external (real) communities of the loss of participants in social activities? Perrow's observations are of more than just historical significance. The contemporary fragility of such arrangements in a financialised business system is demonstrated in chapter 10. The rise in rewards for senior managers and professionals and related forms of corporate exclusivity can have damaging effects on wider social and political solidarity (Lewchuck and Wells 2008; Rowlingson 2011; Paskov and Dewilde 2012).

There is also a fundamental incoherence in the theories used to apply communitarian principles, either explicitly or implicitly, to integrate corporate employees into the firm-as-community. Peter Dahler-Larsen has subjected the fashion for extending organisational cultures into projects for creating corporate micro-societies to a devastating critique. Dahler-Larsen interrogates the Durkheimian sociology used to posit the firm as a community or mini-society. He points out that the expected moral re-integration – encouraging shared values and motivating employees to work for the common good of the company – is unlikely to occur because employees will still defer to the morals of the wider society. Are corporate values compatible with the wider values? Or, because the former are usually devised tendentiously and independently of society, are they likely to conflict with societal values? Dahler-Larsen also asks, in passing, whether employees may merely 'act out' compliance with corporate values, rather than experience them as 'habits of the heart'. More fundamentally he shows that, according to Durkheim, society is held together by 'sacred', sometimes religious values. Businesses, on the other hand, have to prioritise 'utilitarian' norms: interest, calculation and contract. In the Durkheimian paradigm traditional society tends to regard these as the opposing 'profane' values. Thus a re-creation of moral solidarity, by treating the firm and its employees as a community, is difficult to justify on the same sociological grounds as those which are the implicit basis for the communitarian project.

CONCLUSION

Communitarian ideas, combined with stakeholder policies to be described in chapter 10, were institutionalising CSR by the end of the last century. The extensive success of this adoption has led some relatively dispassionate observers to describe it as the achievement of social embedding within a neo-liberal economic order (Utting 2005, p. 381). Others, such as political analyst Colin Crouch, have speculated that CSR could form the basis for a social re-embedded corporate order to succeed the neo-liberal one (Crouch 2008, p. 485–6). The more significant empirical problems affecting these possibilities will be examined later. This chapter has identified key discursive weaknesses and contradictions in the social theories which have driven this movement. Certainly the somewhat bland welcome that CSR received in some academic and policy circles in its early days has been hosed down with numerous analytical critiques by academic commentators and third sector representatives (Bakan 2004; Banerjee 2007; Jones 2007; Pendleton 2004; Vogel 2005). These have particularly emphasised: the impracticalities of ethical ventures by businesses, the implausibility of a business as a normative community, and the shallow and unbalanced powers in corporate-stakeholder partnerships and 'communities'.

However the true Achilles heel underlying all of these problems is one which straddles both the discursive and practical dimensions of CSR. This weakness was actually and perceptively identified at the outset of the CSR upsurge in the UK. Harvey, Smith and Wilkinson studied a paternalistic, but socially proactive, pet foods company in 1984. They identified the potential, tensions and contradictions in the emerging paradigm. But then they concluded that the older ideology of social democracy – the welfare state plus limited, but strategic, public ownership – created considerable autonomy for business. When necessary it allowed business to cast the state as 'scapegoat' for social problems, because the public sector had all-encompassing social responsibilities. However, these authors concluded that, if a communitarian-esque mission, of what is now known as CSR, replaces social democracy then business's sheltered position will be exposed. Or, as Harvey et al. put it:

> ... if the current re-advocacy of private solutions is more than rhetorical, then the implicit contradictions ... will be highlighted. Without a coherent supporting philosophy, and with little practical guidance or experience, managers would need to become involved in new socially valuable activities. Their personal and political moralities would be tested, the ideological target of state involvement would recede and their tacit commitment to social democracy would be tried. In effect another form of managerial revolution would have to take place. (Harvey et al. 1984, p. 149)

Communitarianism and its CSR cognates provided such a 'philosophy' which, despite its logical and empirical flaws, has provided an ideology to try to soften the cold market forces logic of neo-liberalism. Its other main weakness, explored in the next chapter, is that it promises but does not provide the need for some sort of social accountability. Chapter 10 examines what this managerial revolution has subsequently meant for some of the foremost corporate practitioners and the critical issues CSR is supposed to tackle. Before moving on to those issues we need to chart the separate role of the most significant civil society movements in shaping other key aspects of this emerging form of social responsiveness into CSR practice.

9. Environmentalism and social movement influences on corporate responsibility

> Capitalism does not need a fundamental reform that many CSR advocates wish for ... Better that CSR be undertaken as a cosmetic exercise than as serious surgery to fix what doesn't need fixing. (Crook cited in the *Economist* 2005, Special Report, p. 4)

INTRODUCTION

Of the several social movements bursting from the 1960s cultural revolution, environmentalist/'green' campaigning has probably affected the 'advanced' societies more than any other; except perhaps for gender equality campaigns. 'Environmentalism' and its offshoots have changed corporate agendas in two ways. Firstly, by directly influencing how investments, operations, products and public relations are managed. Secondly, by setting templates for how corporations relate to civil society bodies. This chapter deals mainly with the second of those impacts, which has shaped practical concepts of 'responsibility' and 'accountability'. As the previous chapter showed, a considerable body of opinion believes that these new arrangements constitute a plausible way in which corporations might be surrendering power and autonomy for a social re-integration of business.

Many MNCs, mostly 'Anglo-Saxon' ones, now report on socio-environmental issues and consult with NGOs and campaigns in ways which began as responses to the environmental movement emerging in the late 1960s and early 1970s. The extent and utility of this corporate responsiveness is debatable. But it has certainly formed some useful instituions for corporate responsibility policy makers. On issues such as pollution and community dereliction, businesses early on showed interest in cooperating with environmental campaigners and organisations (Marinetto 1998, pp. 80–85). One survey, by Britain's Business in the Community (BITC) organisation, found that by 1991, 75 per cent of firms rated environmental issues as topics of 'active concern' (Gillies

1992). A compatible framework for corporate responses to an increasingly contentious environmental agenda also came from communitarianism's advocacy of voluntary, non-state forms of ethical activity; and related practices like 'engagement' with civil society groups. Concepts of accountability were vague. However, the canvas offered by communitarianism and its CSR companion, was sufficiently broad to allow corporations themselves to define 'the environment' in terms consistent with their more commercial concerns.

To assess the broader implications of these trends for corporate autonomy and accountability we need to trace the history of environmental campaigning against delinquent business practices. This history explains the nature of corporate responses to both this challenge and to broader civil society movements. Other types of campaigns have also blended with, or been added to green concerns; so that their focus has often widened to include social as well as natural sustainability in global contexts. The story begins with the transition of North American environmental campaigning from a supplicant relationship to corporate paternalism to one of militant opposition; softened partially by pragmatic deal-making, as big business sought new ways of accommodating the green threat. The narrative takes in British developments but increasing concern over systemic global environmental problems means that the account has to include the international level to take account of the parallel expansion of multi-national enterprise and international green campaigns. Growth in the number and scope of transnational corporations has been mirrored by an expansion of NGOs and NGO networks concerned with international, 'global' issues.

Environmental and economic development issues for the poorer countries of the global 'South' began to merge in these networks' campaigns against TNCs, and the discourse of 'sustainable development' encompassed: 'issues such as child labour, sweatshops, fair trade, the rights of indigenous peoples, toxic chemicals, oil pollution, tropical deforestation, and other forms of environmental degradation' (Utting 2005, p. 376). A complex series of developments ensued which can be summarised as follows. There has been a gradual and piecemeal pattern of concessions by corporations to the specifics of environmental concerns, coupled with adroit manoeuvres to outflank the more substantive threat to overall business sovereignty. The question is whether campaigns of environmental and related movements have opened up corporations sufficiently for them to be regarded as genuinely accountable to sections of civil society. The interpretation offered here is that the broader environmental/sustainability movement has drawn corporations into what the latter regard as 'manageable' accommodations with the movement. Nevertheless, rising expectations and commitments have also created a momentum towards restricted but critical forms of enhanced accountability. Polanyi's 'double movement' has drawn business autonomy slightly back towards civil society without dislodging corporations' overall isolation from society.

1. DEFINING ROLES

Wildlife and waterways, for example, are not beings capable of contesting businesses' definition of the remedies to their condition. Their notional introjection into corporate affairs was made possible by the dissemination of the stakeholder paradigm by business school academics from the 1980s. Conveniently, corporations could thenceforth interpret representatives of green issues as another 'stakeholder': as proxies for nature. In this guise they were deemed suitable for 'stakeholder management' (Freeman 1984/2010, p. 56). Freeman and Reed's seminal (1983) statement made clear that the enormous 'turbulence' of the 1960s and 1970s in US society could be prevented from damaging corporate autonomy *if* adversaries were redefined as stakeholders and relations with them were *managed* so as to stifle demands for more 'democratic' involvement.

Until the 1960s, nature's self-appointed human representatives were unlikely to dispute seriously a modest role as clients of corporate charity. By the 1950s US corporations and trade bodies were helping finance research into industrial pollution (Conley 2006, p. 23). Then, from the 1970s onwards, business's relationship to environmental causes became more fraught and controversial. Changing social conceptions of ecological problems identified business as a primary cause. At least some of the civil society organisations (CSOs) promoting solutions became more critical and adversarial towards corporations.

The subsequent saga ebbs and flows around different and reciprocating strategies of 'green' campaign groups and corporations' environmental and CSR policies. On the corporate side the key stages and influences have been changes of strategy from denial and piecemeal amelioration to proactive engagement. On the side of the environmental movement, there has been a gradual switch from broad campaigning through national governments, to focussed pressure and projects with particular firms, industry groupings and multilateral international bodies. Groups' and organisations' orientations towards environmental action in general, and business's responsibility in particular, are shaped by their ideological and discursive assumptions. The rise of the 'sustainability' paradigm has been particularly influential in this respect. These forces, with some differences between North American and European societies, have pinned businesses down to some significant commitments. On the other hand, corporations have tried to exploit the CSR paradigm's concentration on voluntary, informal and 'soft' regulation by incorporating green campaigns as 'stakeholders' into those activities.

Campaigning bodies' and movements' pressure for corporate environmental accountability has developed on two fronts. One has moved towards more focussed campaigning on corporate responsibilities for specific, but systemic environmental problems, such as climate-changing carbon emissions. The other, linked to the discourse of 'sustainability', has merged campaigning topics with those of other social movements mentioned above. These trends have also often been elided into the campaigns and rhetoric of anti- or alter-globalisation. But essentially they have formed an institutional structure, a 'movement of movements' which has increasingly centred on both corporate responsibility, as conventionally seen, and a more radical quest for corporate accountability (Utting 2005, p. 383). Amongst activists, corporate responses to these currents have brought into sharper focus critical features of corporate transparency, accountability and governance.

2. COMPOSITION AND SCOPE OF THE ENVIRONMENTAL (SUSTAINABILITY) MOVEMENT

Since its expansion onto public agendas in the 1970s the environmental movement has developed into different, sometimes overlapping, sub-movements, each with a different perspective or paradigm. Clapp and Duvergne's heuristic classification divides these into the following categories:

1. Market liberalism;
2. Institutionalism;
3. Bioenvironmentalism; and a
4. 'Social green' perspective.

These categories are ideal types; so they only approximate to the stances of specific environmental movement organisations (EMOs). These may fluctuate between one or the other perspective in specific cases and times.

However, they do help us to clarify different green movement orientations towards corporations.

Adherents to the *market liberalism* perspective, for example, assume that economic growth and high per capita incomes are essential to both human welfare and the maintenance of sustainable development. Consequently, from this perspective, business's growth-maximising role is unobjectionable. As providers of economic prosperity, corporations appear as potential contributors to environmental solutions. '*Institutionalists*' partially share these assumptions. They focus on inadequate coordination of the dominant political and economic institutions at international and global levels – international economic bodies, MNCs, and so on. Thus they do not recognise any inherent incompatibilities between these institutions' ethos and purpose and their goals of environmental improvement.

By contrast the other two perspectives, *bioenvironmentalism* and '*social green*' perspectives, trace depleting natural resources, waste and pollution to systemic flaws in capitalism's dominant trade, growth and demographics and institutions. These two latter paradigms differ mainly in the extent of their respective emphasis on the 'social' dimension. For bioenvironmental campaigners humans are, *per se,* progenitors of ecological devastation, while social greens emphasise the role of inequalities in the ecology of the economic system. As these inequalities penalise the poorest populations, especially in the global South, the latter are regarded as similar victims of the system. Thus for social greens, environmental sustainability goes hand-in-hand with greater social justice and sustainability. Both perspectives, however, regard corporations as inherent causes of problems and in need, at the very least, of strong controls and major reforms to their operations (cf Clapp and Dauvergne 2005, pp. 14–15). Different environmental movement organisations (EMOs) have adopted or moved between Clapp and Dauvergne's four paradigms and their corresponding attitudes to corporate powers. This evolution has followed on from bigger shifts in the scale and nature of environmental issues and concerns.

Especially in the US, but in some respects in Europe, in the last 40 years an increasingly radical environmentalism has arisen. This newer wave has rivalled but also influenced the activities and objectives associated with conventional conservation EMOs, such as the Sierra Club in the US, or the UK's Campaign to Protect Rural England, and National Trust. In the 1980s the UK government tried to coordinate corporate sponsoring of national and local 'conservation' groups (Forrester 1990). But EMOs such as Greenpeace and Friends of the Earth had been increasingly successful in promoting greater radicalism and their activities increasingly developed international dimensions. From the 1980s onwards, campaigners adopted various adversarial stances against corporations. Yet these were tempered by a complementary, pragmatic willingness for selective cooperation with business on specific issues. Such collaboration provoked the rise of alternative, and even more militant and aggressively anti-corporate groups, such as the Earth Liberation Front and Earth First! These newer activists adopted more intransigent acts of direct action protest (Doherty 1999).

All of this was a step change from the middle decades of the twentieth century when the main business focus of EMOs was largely confined to challenging and seeking rectification of specific environmental abuses by industrial corporations. Polluting discharges into waterways and the atmosphere were early targets, as were the waste-making consequences of industrial and consumer packaging, especially in the USA. However, this narrow focus took a decisive shift with the seismic publicity generated by the first 'Earth Day' in 1970. Earth Day events included the picketing of corporate head offices in New York, and a mock funeral service for the internal combustion engine in Minneapolis, with slogans such as 'Stop Pollution', 'Stop Ecocide', and 'GM [General Motors] Takes Your Breath Away' (Conley 2006, p. 64).

The new dimension to this environmental movement was its extrapolation from the broader 1960s protest campaigns against the politico-economic order. In their student and anti-war manifestations these had already included attacks on chemical corporations as producers of the toxic 'Agent Orange' defoliant used by US forces in the Vietnam War. Responding to the protests about domestic issues, and mainly to more traditional environmental campaigning, the Nixon Administration set up the Environmental Protection Agency at the end of 1970. The EPA's remit was concerned with the conservation of nature parks and the like. It also began coordinating implementation and enforcement of the stream of piecemeal pollution legislation piling up from the 1950s onwards. These measures were principally the 1955 Air Pollution Control Act, Clean Air Act (1963), Motor Vehicle Air Pollution Control Act (1965); with more air pollution legislation in 1966, 1967, 1970, 1977; and water quality acts in 1965, 1966 and 1970. Following this legislative flurry there was a relative lull as industrial corporations sought to stave off further, costly, controls and laws.

3. CHANGING CORPORATE STRATEGIES

Their resistance took two, linked forms which have been business's default approach to green challenges ever since. The first tactic is lobbying to discourage further controls and legislation. The second consists of concerted public relations campaigns to split the opposition by convincing 'moderate' environmental groups and the wider public that corporations are taking initiatives themselves to curb and improve their industries' environmental problems (Cave and Rowell 2014, pp. 146–152). Conley's account, which could as well be applied to the UK, summarises the corporate response in the chemical, energy, and manufacturing sectors to the 'mounting public alarm' and the 'overall decline in public trust and confidence in corporations and their leaders'. This response, he argues, combined: 'maximum feasible opposition to new environmental laws with public-relations and lobbying postures stressing *voluntary* industry initiatives as the most effective means' to deal with pollution (Conley 2006, p. 61). Corporations and industry associations promoted voluntary programs to create an impression of their role as partners in a national 'environmental clean up' (Conley 2006, p. 61–2). While one PR consultant, Clifford B. Reeves, opined in 1970 that: 'the "environment" could thus become a consensus issue, with industry viewed not as a villain but as a partner in the popular drive for environmental protection' (Reeves 1970, cited in Conley 2006, p. 70).

A particularly significant strategy for future developments was launched in 1970. This glass recycling movement was an early case of business's turn to a communitarian, stakeholding stance, being adapted to the environmental cause. The packaging industry and its commercial clients were trying to respond to criticisms of the amounts of litter and solid waste they generated. However, industry was keen to avoid reverting to an earlier system in which consumers paid a refundable deposit on glass containers to incentivise their return to designated depots. Instead the Glass Container Manufacturers Institute (GCMI), assisted by Carl Byoir and Associates, a major public relations firm, stimulated community recycling schemes as an alternative and as a counter-weight to the PR damage coming from 'amateur ecologists and environmentalists' as well as 'the industry's perennial critics' (Byoir et al. 1970, cited in Conley 2006, p. 93).

Here was a scheme that deliberately created the impression of a grass roots movement, in partnership with industry, even though corporations themselves were behind the initiative and the funding. This *faux* citizen campaigning, later known as 'astroturfing' (Cave and Rowell 2014, pp. 123–30) has become popular with UK lobbyists. But it also fore-shadowed the more plausible partnership model which increasingly attracted social movement organisations (SMOs) with a market-liberal, or institutionalist perspective. A more focussed partnership from those points of view was that agreed between the fast-food chain McDonalds and the Environmental Defence Fund in 1990 (McIntosh et al. 1998, p. 221). But this takes us ahead of the evolution of environmental movement organisation (EMO) challenges to, and relations with corporations. Though execrated by some EMOs, as face-saving 'greenwashing' for corporate reputations, these 'partnerships' became popular with many others: an involvement that was attributed to a more general shift in the triangular relationship between states, business and civil society movements which neo-liberalism redefined from the 1980s onwards.

These shifts arose from a simultaneous lowering and raising amongst EMOs' strategic targets which corresponded to the rise of both neo-liberal state policies and a globalised economy. Partly reflecting increasing frustration over thwarted campaigns for better state regulation, and partly reflecting a perceived shift in power from the state to MNCs, environmental campaigners began to target the latter more than the former. The stance was justified by sometime Greenpeace UK chief executive Peter Melchett, on the grounds that: 'there had been a shift in power from politics to business... asked for by business and given by politicians' (Rowell 2001a, 2001b). Other EMOs also believed direct dialogue with firms could be a more effective route to environmental amelioration, because corporate concern for their public image made them more trustworthy than governments (Van der Schot and Van de Veen 1997 cited in Glasberg and Groenenberg 2000, p. 1). Amongst more radical EMOs, however, larger MNCs were becoming more punitive targets.

This targeting culminated in the successful 1995 campaign led by Greenpeace UK against Shell's planned demolition of an oil rig, the Brent Spar, into the North Sea. This episode cost Shell many millions of dollars in reputational damage, extra disposal costs and lost revenues from a boycott of its petrol stations. It also began a shift from a corporate policy of Decide Announce Defend (major developments) to a consultative process of Dialogue Decide Deliver (Watkins and Passow 2002). This phase also involved a shift of focus from EMO campaigns for individual 'pipeline' solutions against 'pollution', towards critiques of systemic abuse of natural resources. In the USA, the more market-liberal and institutionalist EDF and NWF pushed for the EPA to regulate against dioxins and related compounds. Greenpeace, on the other hand, started a much wider campaign, extending the targets as far as the many organo-chlorines emitted by the pulp and paper industry. Since 1985 the group had worked on pulp and paper pollution in Europe (Conley 2006, p. 234).

From the late 1980s, and especially after the Brent Spar fiasco, large UK-based corporations, like the oil majors, began to develop their public environmental profiles and new cooperation with green groups, some-times with government encouragement and promotion (Marinetto 1998, pp. 83–6; Forrester 1990, p. 22). Even the more radical Greenpeace and Friends of the Earth began tempering their bioenvironmental 'direct action' tactics with 'solutions campaigning' designed to promote better environmental practice by institutions such as corporations (Rootes 2003, p. 22). The twentieth-century peak of environmental protest and partici-pation in the 1990s focussed particular attention on the automobile, oil and roads complex. High profile campaigns were carried out against the construction of new roads, the dismantling of the Brent Spar oil rig, and Shell's involvement in the degradation of the Ogboni people's environ-ment in Nigeria (a social green campaign). Indeed, corporate business was ineluctably implicated in four of the five most prevalent topics of the late 1980s and early '90s: transport, animal welfare, pollution and energy (Rootes 2003, p. 26, 29).

4. GLOBALISATION, SUSTAINABILITY AND THE LIMITS OF CORPORATE COOPERATION

This rise in the campaign horizon stemmed from and interacted with the emergence of a transnational arena of issues and protests. This arena was publicly opened up by the UN Bruntland Commission's broadening of perspectives on resource use and misuse through the thesis of 'sustain-able development'. Awareness was also increasing about the scale of the global warming threat and its sources in the global system of production and consumption run by MNCs. Social green ideas for sustainable development as a remedy were partly driven by indigenous initiatives, such as India's Chipko movement, starting in the global South in the 1970s. These campaigns fostered later recognition of the interdependence of environmental and economic deprivation processes (Clapp and Dauvergne 2005, pp. 57–8). The burgeoning international arena also brought activists and SMOs from the environmental movement together with counterparts in the development and global justice campaign spheres to events such as the United Nations Conference on Environment and Development in Rio de Janeiro in 1992, and the more tumultuous Seattle ministerial conference of the World Trade Organization in 1999. The rise of the 'social green' perspective contributed a sharpening of the distinctions between Clapp and Dauvergne's four environmental paradigms. Yet some EMOs continued to complement protest campaigning against corporations with more pragmatic engagements with businesses on specific projects, Greenpeace's involvement with energy companies to develop wind power in the UK being one example (Doherty 1999, p. 137).

Other environmentalist groupings pursued this trend within a more market-liberal stance. Beginning in the 1980s in the USA, ten mainstream EMOs committed to advocacy of only moderate regulation to allow more economic growth that could finance environmental amelioration. Favouring a twin-track approach, the group argued for radical publicity, combined with conciliatory practices towards economic power-holders (Devall 1988). As Arts (2002, p. 33) observes, the Brundtland Commission's 1987 report *Our Common Future*, UNCED's A*genda 21* and other UN-related initiatives boosted incipient partnership trends through their promotion of the ethos of 'sustainability' in the late 1980s. This discourse:

> made the (partial) integration of opposite views on ecological and economic issues possible: on the one hand the view of economists, industrialists and governments (who interpret the ecological issues only in terms of economics) and on the other hand the view of environmentalists and ecological scientists (who tend to interpret economic issues only in terms of ecology). (Arts 2002, p. 34)

It allowed what Arts calls 'remarkable "discourse coalitions" such as those between NGOs and business in green alliances in which both sides retain fundamentally different core values and world-views' (Arts 2002, p. 35).

These and more sustained corporate-EMO engagements did not eclipse continuing campaigns by biodiversity and social green activists against corporate dominance and businesses' perceived attempts to hegemonise the environmental arenas. Indeed, recognition of MNCs' role in setting agendas, at events such as the 1992 Rio conference, spread amongst the more militant SMOs from this point. Such awareness encouraged the more radical focus, not just on corporate environmental irresponsibility, but upon MNCs' general influence and unaccountability. These latter concerns found their way into the outcomes of the 2002 World Summit on Sustainable Development. The aims of the resulting Plan of Action included an aspiration to:

Actively promote *corporate responsibility and accountability*, based on the Rio principles, including through the full development and effective implementation of intergovernmental agreements and measures, international initiatives and *public-private partnerships* and appropriate national regulations, and support continuous improvement in corporate practices in all countries. (United Nations 2002, p. 38, para V. 49) (emphasis added)

This statement reflects a refinement of earlier twin-track strategies by EMOs to work with MNCs on specific solutions while attempting to make some inroads into their autonomy and hegemony. Of particular significance for the broader pattern of responsibility and accountability, within this 'soft regulation' CSR framework, have been 'multi-stakeholder initiatives'. These bring together NGOs, MNCs and, where appropriate, government and trade bodies, to set voluntary standards and enforcement mechanisms for key firms within an industry. Initiatives like the Marine Stewardship Council and Forest Stewardship Council claim successes in their domains by limiting some of the depletion of sea life and forestry resources respectively. However, others perceive such partnerships as achieving only a minor element of fuller corporate responsibility and accountability. As I have pointed out elsewhere, such 'partnerships' may actually be more like patron-client relationships, with EMOs and SMOs as the clients. They also seem inherently prone to conflict and breakdown over their fundamental assumptions (Arts 2002; Jones 2007).

As Arts has recounted, such alliances begin with a 'dialogue oriented', *ad hoc* and open character where there is mutual respect and cooperation. While the later project phases involve formalisation with companies viewing NGOs as 'business partners'. Shared norms then come under strain; as with the Solaris project teaming Greenpeace with the companies Ecofys, Stork and Rabobank (Glasbergen and Groenenberg 2001). When the involvement of other business partners in the solar campaign was mooted, Greenpeace withdrew. Arts's interpretation is instructive.

For this NGO, it was just a matter of routinely reacting to changing circumstances and new insights concerning a project. After all, Greenpeace is quite used to having *ad hoc* and temporary coalitions from which one can easily withdraw. The companies, on the other hand, considered this act as a breach of contract by an unreliable partner. (Arts 2002, p. 33)

5.   EXTRACTING TRUTH FROM POWER: TRANSPARENCY AND THE TRIPLE BOTTOM LINE

Such limitations with partnerships and alliance forms of engagement enhance the appeal of broader counter-corporate demands for accountability. EMOs have thus found common cause with development, human rights and global justice campaigns (Utting 2005, pp. 376, 383). In the UK this trend took on a more overtly political turn with the formation of CORE, the Corporate Responsibility Coalition. CORE comprises over 130 civil society member groups, combining environment, development and human rights groups with 'ethical businesses, women's groups, religious groups, unions, academics'. Environmental NGOs are prominently represented. Its steering group comprises Friends of the Earth and the British section of the World Wildlife Fund, alongside development NGOs TraidCraft, War on Want and Action Aid, as well as Amnesty International UK. CORE's campaigning aim is: 'to reduce business-related human rights and environmental abuses by ensuring companies can be held to account for their impacts both at home and abroad, and to guarantee access to justice for people adversely affected by corporate activity (CORE 2014).

CORE's was one of the most prominent voices in the debates surrounding the last reform of corporate governance in the shape of the Labour Government's Companies Act, 2006. The final provisions of that bill, also discussed in chapters 10 and 11, fell far short of CORE's proposals, even though those efforts were restricted mainly to more transparent corporate reporting. However, the campaign has helped to bring corporate (ir)responsibility and governance to the forefront of debates within the sustainability movement. It also confirms the synthesis of some of the values and aims associated with radical environmentalism and social greens with the concerns of other social movement campaigns. We return to these radical-structural campaigns against corporate autonomy in the final chapters, but more pragmatic forms of pressure, working with the grain of business practice, have also contributed new arenas of contestation of corporate autonomy.

The most obvious of these is the struggle over corporate information disclosure and transparency which has substantially changed the scope of conventional corporate reporting. Until the innovative call for social and environmental statements within companies' annual reports, the latter had consisted mainly of reams of arcane financial data concocted by corporate accountants and probed by investors' agents and advisers. From the work of business outliers like Elkington, came the acceptance of the case for complementary social and environmental reports within the annual report. Corporate concessions in the increasing business accommodation with EMOs included significant opening up of corporate environment reporting, with the extractive industries making early responses in this direction (Doyle and McEachern 2001, p. 137). Greater public awareness arose from environmental disasters in industries such as oil and chemicals, highlighted by the breakup of the *Exxon Valdez* oil tanker and the explosion of Union Carbide's Bhopal plant in the 1980s. Such publicity pressurised multinationals in these and related industries, such as consumer and forestry products, to disclose information on environmental problems and safeguards in their annual reports (Patten 1992).

Gradually, environmental debates evolved a new discourse around corporate disclosure and procedures (see, for example, Smith 1993). Whole industry initiatives and even broader frameworks were also stimulated by episodes like Brent Spar and the *Exxon Valdez* case; and the critical ammunition which EMOs derived from them. Oil and other industrial sectors were targeted by the Valdez Principles code. These Principles were developed by a US coalition of reformist EMOs, such as the Sierra Club and the National Wildlife Federation, together with environmentally concerned investors (the Social Investment Forum), as the Coalition for Environmentally Responsible Economies (CERES). The latter's Principle 8 in particular, required firms to agree to '... disclose to our employees and to the public incidents relating to our operations that cause environmental harm or pose health or safety hazards ... [and] ... disclose potential environmental, health or safety hazards posed by our operations.'

These provisions are reinforced by Principle 10, requiring commitment to assessment and annual audits, consisting of a:

> public ... annual self-evaluation of our progress in implementing these Principles and in complying with all applicable laws and regulations throughout our world-wide operations ... [and to] work toward the timely creation of independent environmental audit procedures which we will complete annually and make available to the public. (CERES 1991, article 24)

The Principles represented a significant sectoral cross-over, being partly modelled on the anti-apartheid Sullivan Principles campaign. They also included organisational prescriptions, such as a board-level executive role, dedicated to environmental issues. But it was their reporting and disclosure provisions which constituted the environmental movement's particular influence on contemporary, corporate accountability trends. The Valdez – later, CERES – principles provided a springboard for even higher international disclosure criteria. The most popular of these frameworks, the Global Reporting Initiative, provides international standards to which corporate subscribers are expected to report. Through adaptations, such as Sustainability's Triple Bottom Line concept (Elkington 1997), disclosure and reporting principles were widened to include such topics as labour and community responsibilities.

In the USA, in the same year, the California Corporate Accountability Project advocated measures for public institutions, like the California state government, to address corporate malpractices (Leighton et al. 2002). Later, a coalition of US groups, including the trade-union federation the AFL-CIO, worked with Amnesty International USA, Earth Rights International, Global Exchange, Oxfam America, and the Sierra Club on a Community Right to Know project, which led to the International Right to Know campaign (IRTK). The campaign urged the US government to require US-based companies, and those traded on US stock exchanges (including foreign subsidiaries and major contractors), to disclose information on the environmental impacts, labour standards and human rights practices of their overseas operations (IRTK 2003).

In the UK, Gray et al. (1995) found that: 'the volume of disclosure by those companies which disclosed also showed a steady rise from a few lines in 1980 to around three-quarters of a page in the early 1990s.' These authors add that the 'most striking rise is obviously environmental disclosure which has grown inexorably from the late 1980s.' In their sample 'community and environmental reporting rose from approximately 10 per cent to 32 per cent of total disclosure'. Reflecting the rise of new social movement organisations and the decline of 'old' social movements, 'the value added statement and trade union disclosure – quietly fade away' (Gray et al. 1995, p. 63). Consistent with the earlier, US phase of corporate responsiveness, these authors observe that:

> environmental disclosures were being used by companies as an attempt to negotiate the concept of 'environment', and to determine the companies' relationships with society in general and the environmental pressure groups in particular. This is consistent with an organization seeking strategically to manage a new and emerging issue with its stakeholders while attempting to assess the extent of the power of those stakeholders. (Gray et al. 1995, p. 66)

Just as Freeman and Reed advocated in 1983, this strategy aims to preserve corporate autonomy and repel democratisation. However, the disclosure and transparency movement has taken on a life and logic of its own, which corporations are, in some respects, now fighting to contain within their preferred limits. By the beginning of the twenty-first century, reporting bodies and academic analysts were pushing the boundaries of corporate transparency further than corporations had probably envisaged when they first released socio-environmental data. Criticisms and awkward questions were being posed about the extent to which indicators were related to actual actions. Campaigners were also highlighting corporate failures to involve potentially critical stakeholder groups in the compilation of reports (Adams 2004).

CONCLUSION

Standing back and viewing the environmental and related movements in the bigger picture of corporate-society relations shows that EMOs and other NGOs had initially focussed on clear-cut, 'non-political' issues. These were, firstly, localised ones such as factory pollution or overseas outrages, such as contamination or famine. But, as their membership expanded – seven major US environmental groups grew from 5.3 million to 9.5 million between 1980 and 1990 – perspectives expanded to international and global concerns like atmospheric ozone depletion. Veteran sustainability activist and analyst Jem Bendell describes this trend as 'a movement of people and resources in the West', mobilising for confrontations and other activism directly against corporations for 'what I believed would have a major effect on the rest of the world' (Bendell 2004, p. 13).

Using the newly-emergent internet, campaigners adopted what Bendell calls 'forcing change' tactics: targeting TNCs' and MNCs' increasingly valuable, but increasingly vulnerable, reputations (Clifton and Maughan 1999). Corporate responses varied both individually and over time. Denial, PR rebuttal and 'greenwashing' initiatives were all tried. But the relationship intensified to a more critical level with those responses which involved various degrees of 'partnership'. During the 1990s, 'civil groups began advising companies on best practices, and endorsing or promoting such practice. Codes of conduct and certification schemes, often as part of multi-stakeholder initiatives, grew significantly' (Bendell 2004, p. 14).

For their own, mixed motives, corporations, their advisers and the growing ranks of the CSR industry, added momentum to this trend. All of this activity helped to justify and institutionalise such projects as being consistent with the burgeoning commercial logic of businesses' social contributions. Not all environmental and sustainability campaigners shared this collaborative mind-set. Indeed, some, such as Greenpeace, switched between collaborative and confrontational modes according to the issue and changing circumstances. By 2002 CSOs and NGOs began to be divided into two groups. One was seen as working for the more practical but less critical advance of 'corporate responsibility'. On the other side were campaigners, frustrated at the continuance of corporations' obduracy, who were pressing for 'corporate accountability': to go beyond the power asymmetries in the 'partnership relations of CSR' (Hamann and Acutt 2003) and beyond the limitations of international 'codes of conduct' (Richter 2001, p. 210). Evidence of the flawed character of partnerships and codes of conduct, together with the detailed implications of the responsibility-accountability distinction are elaborated in chapter 10. That analysis starts from the point of view of many campaigners, that voluntaristic CSR has largely failed to satisfy the expectations it raised and that: 'Accountability requires going beyond voluntary approaches and establishing mechanisms which provide adequate legal and financial incentives for compliance. It must also *empower stakeholders to challenge corporations*' (emphasis added) (Friends of the Earth International 2002).

10. Corporate voluntarism: responsibility or accountability?

> No matter how responsible managers strive to be, they remain in the fundamental sense irresponsible oligarchs in the context of the modern corporate system.
>
> (Kaysen 1957, p. 316)

INTRODUCTION

From an optimists' point of view CSR has stimulated important ethical and social reconnections with social causes and problems. Notable social links include: the 'mainstreaming' of ethical trading (such as Fairtrade) into multinationals' sourcing practices, the adoption of environmental sustainability as a business strategy, as well as MNC participation in forums ('multi-stakeholder initiatives') for so-called civil society regulation. These include the Ethical Trading Initiative, Forest Stewardship Council and the Marine Stewardship Council, and, more broadly, ethical business strategies, corporate codes of conduct (CoC) and the proliferation of 'stakeholder engagement': 'partnerships' with charities, NGOs and community organisations, plus corporations' enhancement of social/environmental reporting. All of these could be cited as evidence of greater concern, transparency and openness by big business. Is this, in business-speak, a 'win-win' situation for social interests and corporations? Or does their very popularity with business indicate little real change and the need to aim for obligatory responsiveness rather than voluntaristic adoption of 'responsibilities'? More critical perspectives point out the limited effect corporate responsibility approaches have had in reducing the autonomous powers and general social insularity of corporations. The extent to which stakeholder engagement and CSR is increasing social re-integration can be gauged from Bendell's distinction between responsibility and accountability (Bendell 2004, p. 18). As chapter 2 and various authors have shown (Jones 2007; Monbiot 2014a, 2014b; Pingeot 2014, pp. 21 et seq.), far from re-integrating firms into society, corporate involvement in social issues can become another form of corporate over-reach, extending business norms and power into the political and civil society domains.

Accordingly, this chapter assesses the various forms of responsibility and accountability in relation to two axes: (1) those which pull the firm's activities and resources towards undiluted financial priorities and shareholder value interests, and (2) the major forms of CSR – stakeholder partnerships, civil society regulation, corporate codes of conduct and so on – which promise to commit the firm to social interests and standards. In this analysis 'responsibility' and 'accountability' are not regarded as polar opposites. Instead they are treated as a hierarchy, or continuum of social integration which ascends from individual corporate initiatives through bilateral and multilateral partnerships to corporations having to account for their (in)actions to external civil society groups and interests. So we will examine the depth and scope of CSR commitments in relation to this continuum by looking at evidence, mainly from detailed and critical case studies, of key dimensions of such 'soft' or voluntary regulation:

- ethical investing;
- information transparency;
- ethical certification and corporate codes of conduct; plus
- community contributions and environmental integrity.

This analysis begins by clarifying conceptual definitions of responsibility and accountability to judge the effectiveness of CSR and civil society engagement at the responsibility end of the continuum. This engagement tends to consist of 'particularistic' reforms within the conventional institutions of company law, shareholder rights and market disciplines. After identifying the capacity and limitations of corporate accountability within this largely unchanged institutional framework we can move on to look into changes involving more structural relationships, such as civil society partnerships. More radical reforms and transformations of corporate autonomy and authority need to be considered if institutional limitations show that these voluntary and 'soft' forms of regulation and accountability are ineffective or unrealisable. As chapter 11 will show, more fundamental changes must begin with re-structuring of ownership relations and internal reforms for more democratic corporate governance.

1.   ANALYTICAL DISTINCTIONS

Debates and recipes for 'socialising' business activity tend to speak indiscriminately about 'responsibility' and 'accountability', as if these principles were largely equivalent (Bendell 2004, p. 17). It is true that 'accepting responsibility' might lead (some) corporations to try to account for their activities to the affected sections of society. A conscientious management might, for example, establish forums to provide opportunities for 'stakeholder' groups – employees, suppliers or local residents – to respond to corporate plans. Here management are 'giving an account' of their actions. However, as Bendell explains, such elements of accountability are a long way from converting the corporate role to one of generalised accountability. Corporations are perfectly capable of ceding minor or subsidiary dollops of apparent accountability while remaining overwhelmingly unaccountable in most of their activities.

For many critics of corporate power it is equally clear that merely 'giving an account' (answerability) is insufficient to ensure the same levels of behavioural change. If there is a need for 'enforceability' of agreements, standards or cooperation then corporations and their managements will have to be subjected to some degree and form of direct or indirect control. Put crudely: enforceability will mean some redistribution of power, while answerability only betokens involvement and, perhaps, influence. Such influence may be important. In particular cases the information provided by giving an account can lead on to more effective pressure for behavioural change. However, as the study of corporate social and environmental reporting shows, giving an account can act as a smokescreen to stall and conceal rather than an incentive to actual correction (Doane 2005; Adams 2004). The emphasis on voluntarism, discretion and selectivity in business approaches to CSR shows that this paradigm's references to 'accountability' assume, at best, answerability, rather than enforceability. With these parameters in mind, consider Bendell's identification of four broad perspectives amongst campaigners against corporate power. It is seen as either: *opportunity,* or *obstacle,* or *obstruction* or *obscenity.*

Opportunity approaches see the power and resources of corporations as resources which can be harnessed to promote social and environmental reform and improvement. Obstacle interpretations see corporate power as a problem only in specific cases where it is used in ways that hinder particular social or environmental objectives. Strategies bound up with these two perspectives seek to counterbalance the constraints of corporate power by tactics aimed at *resisting, restraining,* or *redressing* those powers. By contrast, *obstruction* or *obscenity* perspective strategies aim at the nature of the corporation itself, including its form and function, with tactics to reduce, redefine, or even remove its powers. For 'obstructionists', corporate power is a systemic problem. Particular corporate abuses and outrages are seen as consequences of the stock-market driven logic of capital accumulation, which pressures business to externalise costs on to others. This logic is said to shape business discourse so that it always precludes genuine social and environmental commitments. Finally, the view of corporate power as a moral obscenity claims it is antithetical to 'human self-determination, freedom and democracy'. These various perspectives need not be empirically and organisationally distinct. The same actors may apply more than one approach or view, at different times and in different contexts. As the later cases in this chapter show, it is even possible for an opportunity stance to be used as a means to advance removal of some systemic obstacles. These distinctions derive from an earlier typology by Broad and Cavanagh (1999) summarised in Figure 10.1.

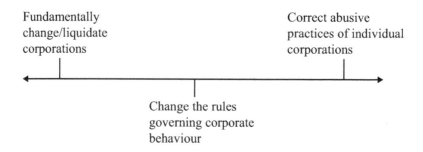

Source: Adapted from Broad and Cavanagh 1999.

Figure 10.1   The spectrum of accountability

Broad and Cavanagh diagnose corporate change recipes as clustering at one of three points on a continuum of aims. Firstly there is a cluster of reforming activity, equivalent to Bendell's obstacle and opportunity perspectives. Campaigners in this category seek only to change individual corporations' specific practices through dialogue or protest to establish voluntary arrangements (Broad and Cavanagh 1999, pp. 5–14). Here change and amelioration or re-alignment of corporations' power assumes no significant systemic changes to their form and function. To simplify the discussion we can label such activities as 'particularistic' approaches. Secondly, around the middle of Broad and Cavanagh's spectrum, are campaigns aimed at the rules that govern corporate behaviour: at either the national or global level. These could include a United Nations code on transnational corporations covering behaviour such as protection for workers and communities; or a world-wide anti-trust authority to break up 'dangerous concentrations of global corporate power'; or international agreements to curb such corporate abuses as bribery of government officials. This cluster may also: 'tend to accept the premise that the market, left to its own, will create certain social and environmental problems that require government intervention' (Broad and Cavanagh 1999, p. 152). So the curbing of global corporations' excesses requires intergovernmental controls. Also in this group are NGO efforts for enforceable codes of conduct on specific businesses, which are examined in some detail in section 3 below.

Thirdly, the far pole consists of approaches seeking fundamentally to change or abolish corporations' present status. The campaigning website Corporate Watch argues that the behavioural change needed: 'is not something any corporation, as currently structured, could handle. It is not within its worldview. Society must create new structures to replace corporations' (Corporate Watch, n.d.). One such is the US re-chartering campaign which seeks a return to democratic control over corporations (cf Korten 1995; Democratic Underground 2009), so that ST/EM firms would be licenced via revocable corporate charters. Renewal of charters by public authorities or by democratic votes, would require proof of acceptable corporate behaviour. Each of these three approaches needs to be considered in relation to its form and degree of social embeddedness as analysed in preceding chapters. This chapter examines the scope of the first two approaches, before setting the stage for an examination of the third, radical approach in the final chapter.

2. PARTICULARISTIC CHANGE WITHIN THE PREVAILING CORPORATE REGIME

Governance theory and legal principles traditionally assume that corporate executives' primary responsibility is to the firm's main investors. Sir Ronald Hampel, chair of the 1998 committee reviewing standards of business corporate governance was clear that his Committee 'stuck to the fundamental principle that corporate prosperity comes before accountability' (*Observer* 1997, in Doig and Wilson 1998). The first potential flaw in particularistic strategies for changing corporate behaviour is this shareholder primacy obligation. Advocated in classic form by Milton Friedman decades ago, its challenge to intra-system reform is that the expenditure on activities which subtract from the profit-maximisation expected by shareholders is both morally and constitutionally wrong.

Actual practice does not support this allegedly primal objection but it does reveal a restriction in the scope of responsibility policies. Since the

19th century the UK courts have allowed expenditure on philanthropic causes, provided – and for CSR this is the critical point – they are 'congruent with commercial interests' (Marinetto 1998, p. 40). Shareholders have not, in general, complained about diversions of resources to CSR from profit-maximisation or share dividends because CSR discourse and rhetoric has come to emphasise consistency with commercial success. Appropriate and well-publicised CSR can increase consumers' and employees' identification with corporate brands. Ergo, CSR contributes to financial returns and shareholder interests. A second reason for investor compliance is that it is difficult in practice for investors dissatisfied with executives' policies to influence or oppose management decisions. Shareholders' disparate perspectives, fragmented holdings and the costs of making interventions make collective action difficult. In addition, protests may also generate bad publicity and thus damage share values.

The last UK Companies Act of 2006 also modified the shareholder primacy principle in that directors of Stock Exchange listed UK firms must also consider their firm's impacts on social and environmental matters (section 172). They also now have to report openly on social and environmental risks and opportunities to their shareholders; as well as on employee matters and risks down supply chains (UK Government n.d., section 417). Further implications of these changes are examined below in section 3. In addition, shareholders have, at least in theory, privileges in respect of information, consultation and general policy making – through board elections, financial reporting and general meetings. Despite the limitation on shareholders' direct influence over company managements, their influence is still greater than that of campaigners for particularistic reforms of corporate activity. They can, in principle, vote for, or against moves to make 'their' business more responsible; even, *in extremis*, removing directors not pursuing such policies. Shareholders also have considerable indirect influence: the risk of a critical mass of investors 'voting with their feet' by selling shares is a perpetual, if largely containable threat to managerial supremacy. The Conclusion to this book examines the significance, limitations and ramifications of campaigners buying shares to acquire some of these privileges using the, admittedly skeletal, system of 'shareholder democracy' to promote corporate responsibility 'from below'.

2.1 Corporate Accountability via Ethical and Activist Investors

In recent years, in the wake of the 2008 financial crash, there has been a general upsurge in what has become known as shareholder and investor 'activism' (Davies and Wilkinson 2014). Part of this unrest has been a reaction against wider abuses of executive power. There has also been an 'ethical' movement involving: (1) proactive decisions to invest only in ethically sound stocks by (2) 'screening' out ones with ethically dubious activities, or (3) taking holdings in companies and then, as shareholders, seeking to get reforms of their unethical practices (MacKenzie 1997). Interventions include lobbying executives or taking active rather than passive stances on policies decided at corporations' general meetings. Ethical stocks and screening seem to have had limited penetration of total global capital investment (Haigh and Hazelton 2004). This means that the second and third steps are more likely to be effective in producing concrete changes to corporate governance. Yet their extension to selections of the UK FTSE top hundred companies appears particularly ineffective. Because, as Collison et al ask:

> will it, in effect, act not merely as a legitimation device, but also contribute to a process of corporate capture ... devaluing the whole concept of socially responsible investing ... we incline to [this] pessimistic view of the potential for the FTSE4Good initiative to effect real change in corporate behaviour – notwithstanding the bona fides of those who are closely involved in the initiative. (Collison et al. 2009, p. 54)

Until recently, at least in the Anglo-Saxon sphere, it was a recognised – if sometimes lamented – fact that shareholders took a largely passive role in the decisions mooted by the boards of corporations and enacted at GMs. Relatively few shareholders would vote, let alone attend the corporation's AGM, unless the issue was controversial or, usually the same thing, involved a merger, or major financial restructuring of the company's shares or resources. In the main they approved board recommendations, or abstained. For shareholders to propose their own policies or motions to company meetings was almost unknown. On the other hand, ethical investors and civil society activists can assume that they can use the same rights or privileges *vis- à-vis* company boards which, theoretically, are enjoyed by conventional financial investors. But recent evidence suggests that, under the present governance system, executives' practices are likely to frustrate all types of shareholders. An investigation by pressure group Tomorrow's Company found that:

> ... companies often 'spin' messages to shareholders and rather than have genuine dialogue they would practice divide and rule tactics – 'you are the only investor to say this'... firms warn... that criticism or negative votes could lead to less future access to the company or damage the share price and therefore shareholders' primary duty ... investors encounter 'resistance' from

some chairmen, CEOs or boards' to greater engagement. [Thus] … share-holder investors' engagement has become limited and ritualistic … representa-tives [have] insufficient status; 'a box-ticking approach to compliance' is adopted and investors restrict their concerns to a few 'specific problems' such as executive remuneration rather than broader aspects of corporate policy and strategy. (Tomorrow's Company 2010b)

NGOs and other stakeholder groups have figured in this recent increase in shareholder activism: buying shares so as to gain a voice in order to pressure corporations to improve their social or environmental perform-ance (CORE 2007). Despite increases in the last few years, the use of CSR-related shareholder resolutions is less frequent in the UK than in the USA (Manifest 2010). How successful have such resolutions been in affecting corporate stances on social and environmental policies and practices? Do they represent a viable means for stakeholders to promote their interests within the present ST/EM regime? Will Whitefield's data from a corporate governance and proxy voting agency shows:

- how many resolutions there have been in the UK;
- who proposed them;
- which topics they addressed;
- which companies were targeted; and
- what levels of support they received.

Whitefield complemented this quantitative data with semi-structured interviews with NGO and stakeholder group representatives who pro-posed CSR-related resolutions. He also quizzed representatives from socially responsible investment (SRI) funds and other investment industry bodies. The research found that CSR-related shareholder resolutions in the UK remain relatively rare, with only 14 in the 13 years to 2008. This low incidence may derive from the level of support they receive. Even including abstentions, the average support is only just above 20 per cent of voting shareholders. However, this is more than double the 10 per cent considered to be enough to influence corporate decision-making. More-over, the very rarity of alternative, shareholder-derived proposals tends to make both managers and investor groups keen to play down any accompanying controversy. This 2009 investigation predated the more recent apparent upsurge in shareholder activism. However, while the level of activity may have risen, the research revealed structural reasons why its scope or impact on boards is probably no greater since then.

The low incidence of 'alternative' motions from ethical investors, NGOs and stakeholder groups, together with the limited levels of support received, indicate systemic legislative and cultural barriers to these parties. These barriers involve procedural obstacles of materiality, time and money, which all derive from aspects of company law. Although NGOs are learning from each other and they are partly negotiating these particular barriers, one trade union representative commented that financing and organising a shareholder resolution was: 'more labour intensive than other tactics that trade unions would normally take' (Whitefield 2009, p. 49). From Whitefield's research the following additional key findings emerge.

Some NGOs consider that barriers are deliberately set up to restrict greater shareholder activism and preserve the status quo, but the barriers may also be more rooted in cultural differences. More general investigations into investor-executive roles in corporate governance have reported that key investors enjoy a wide range of informal opportunities to derive information from executives (Hall and O'Malley 2009; Pendleton 2005). As one SRI interviewee said to Whitefield, formal objections via resolutions are 'just not what "chaps" in the City do; if a chap has a problem with another chap he would talk about it over lunch probably, rather than go through these formal channels' (Whitefield 2009, p. 52).

The deeply rooted financial culture of the City of London means that UK investors prefer to resolve any issues they have with executives through such quiet dialogue (Lewis and Mackenzie 2000; Sparkes and Cowton 2004; Sullivan and Mackenzie, 2006). Stakeholder groups recognised that such sentiments indicated the greatest obstacle to be the firmly entrenched mind-set of the 'City culture'. Because this prevailed amongst all investment institutions – ethical and conventional – it constituted an inbuilt inertia against transparency and accountability.

Similarly Whitefield found that SRI funds and institutional investors interviewed claimed the UK corporate governance system displaces the need for shareholder resolutions because of investors' high levels of informal access to company boards; access which facilitates discussion of contentious issues. But, despite some companies' claims that they treat all shareholders equally (Forum for the Future/PIRC, 2002), it is unlikely that NGO activists or small shareholders representing stakeholder interests would be afforded the same opportunities. There is presently lack of common ground because of a clash between the values of stakeholders and the shareholder-value paradigm. Corporations and investor institutions tend to view NGOs as having a radical ideology, pursuing single-issue interests through whatever means necessary. Such an image undermines their legitimacy in the eyes of company management and the investment community. These commonalities also have important practical correlates.

The key determinant of the amount of support a motion will get, and therefore its impact on the company management, is whether and how campaigning stakeholders and investors interact. Because they are often the biggest investors in publicly listed companies, financial institutions have the greatest potential influence on the outcomes of resolutions at AGMs. So, for an NGO-stakeholder group's shareholder resolution successfully to affect corporate policy making, the group must first convince the institutional investors 'who can exercise power, and mobilise a credible threat within the current system' (McLaren 2004, p. 195). Social or ethical activist shareholder resolutions did have some positive outcomes. These included greater access to company management, increased awareness and education of institutional investors on social and environmental issues, and higher exposure of issues to the general public through the resulting media interest.

Both McLaren's and Whitefield's researches confirm that SRI funds are more stakeholder-orientated than others and this has a considerable impact on the overall effectiveness of campaigners' resolutions. Yet NGOs tended to regard even self-professed SRI bodies as generally predisposed to favour financial returns over social and environmental improvements because of these bodies' legally defined fiduciary duties. These obligations make it difficult for them to act on anything other than financial grounds (Frankental 2006). SRI funds' willingness to push for systematic CSR policies is restrained by the chances that doing so might affect the share price. SRI funds do not want to 'rock the boat' and so jeopardise their primary brief of maximising shareholder return. Moreover, in line with the findings of Haigh and Hazleton (2004) and Hildyard and Mansley (2001), Whitefield's data also shows that SRI funds are often compromised by their commercial connection to mainstream investment companies

2.2 Voluntary and Consensual Regulation: General Codes of Conduct

Chapter 4 outlined the mass of national, European and international codes to which many MNCs now subscribe. In the UK, Stock Exchange rules make adoption of a general code of conduct effectively mandatory for listed companies. Thus any company wishing to list on the London Stock Exchange must either comply with the Combined Code (the Code on Corporate Governance and Code of Best Practice) or provide justifications for non-compliance. These codes are concerned with internal governance and relationships with investors; although they touch on ethical, transparency and general social responsibility issues. The Combined Code has been described as 'an internal, punitive, mandatory code with overall low significance, the text of which is typically not found on corporate web sites' (Bondy et al. 2004). Its crucial feature, however, is that firms themselves can work out the composition of the code provisions which they intend to apply. Individual codes must only cover points set out in the LSE Combined Code. Compared to Canada and Germany, for example, the UK has the highest number of codes which emphasise corporate governance issues. Significantly, the key audience for these codes (in particular for the Combined Code compliance statements) are shareholders and analysts. Apart from Combined Code references, Bondy et al. found there was near parity between emphases on wider stakeholder communities as code targets for CSR engagement and those targeting internal stakeholders to guide and control managerial behaviour (Bondy et al. 2004, p. 301).

Thus the proliferation of UK codes of conduct indicates not 'robustness', nor enthusiasm for regulation, but eclecticism in their character and purpose. Moreover, they seem mainly intended to police more effectively firms' conventional obligations and criteria of accountability to investors, rather than extend accountability to interests in the wider society. Codes also seem to be used to control company's internal risks, rather than guide business-society interfaces (Doig and Wilson 1998; Bondy et al. 2004, pp. 298–9, 461, 464).

> They may be used primarily for self-regulation ... to regulate the behaviour of their employees or suppliers ... as a type of quasi-legal document ... they may have less to do with governance of CSR issues and more with regulating the behaviour of groups influential to the corporation. In other words, codes of conduct ... desire to control the actions of groups within and outside the corporation for risk management purposes and not an attempt to become more environmentally, economically and socially responsible. (Bondy et al. 2004, p. 467)

Of course corporations also adopt codes that are drawn up by international organisations, their trade bodies, or even individual, or groups of NGOs/civil society bodies – the so-called 'Multi-Stakeholder Initiatives' (van Tulder and Kolk 2001, p. 152). In 2000 there were an estimated 246 codes covering environmental stewardship, labour standards, science and technology, competition, information disclosure, taxation, bribery and corruption, and consumer protection (OECD 2001). In keeping with the marriage of neo-liberalism and social responsibility paradigms, self-defined corporate codes and those emanating from NGO initiatives, have increased since 1990. Yet those from international organisations, such as the UN, have declined. Businesses have some leeway about how they implement external codes and some may even draw up codes which appear more stringent than those of outside bodies. Irrespective of their source, codes tend to share some of the same problems which are well illustrated by developments and the following cases from the clothing and food sectors.

3. SELF-REGULATION AND CO-REGULATION: CODES OF CONDUCT FOR SUPPLY CHAIN STANDARDS

The preceding overview suggests that the connections between voluntary or mandatory codes of conduct (CoC) and CSR practices are patchy. However, there is a wide range of codes adopted by corporations to cover their social impacts across different countries and types of operation. This volume indicates that they are significant for accountability debates. One potentially illuminating aspect for assessing CoC as mechanisms for accountability and responsibility is the rectification of abuse and exploitation of workers in MNCs' supplier firms in developing societies: so-called supply chain ethics. These scandals have been highlighted in various industries, but attention has focussed particularly upon high-profile, 'brand' corporations selling consumer goods such as footwear and clothing in the global 'North'. Codes of conduct aim to improve the material welfare of workers in the factories supplying brands and other Western corporations. They purport to curb or remove arbitrary and coercive exercises of managerial power and authority in sub-contracting workplaces, and to secure workers' human rights such as freedom of association and maternity rights. Accountability as 'answerability' is limited in these cases. MNCs still use unjustified excuses of commercial confidentiality for not disclosing either audit reports or suppliers' facilities abroad (Sethi 2003, p. 217–39). Although the scope and quality of the reports are variable, most major brands and retailers in the apparel industries now publish accounts of progress in improving employment standards through their CoC. These kinds of code are significant for three reasons.

Firstly, they push at the outer limits of the reforms that can be introduced within the current and conventional parameters of the ST/EM model. They may entail some limitation of obligations to investors to maximise profits. For example, by reducing the extreme 'commoditisation' of labour amongst their suppliers they may raise their own cost levels. However, standards set out in CoC are hardly revolutionary. The minimal employment rights entitlements with which this type of CoC are concerned are often specified in the national laws of the countries where plants are located; but are absent or weakly enforced in actual workplaces. So CoC can be viewed as simply providing an additional method for remedying deficiencies that are compatible with the 'normal' employment of labour. Moreover, CoC can be formulated internally, tailored to the corporations' specific purposes and interests: entailing some 'answerability' but certainly no external enforcement.

Secondly however, the element of answerability is important if codes are designed in conjunction with external standards, authorities or in multi-stakeholder agreements. In the latter the adopted code – or some key aspects of it – is the joint creation of an initiative composed of external bodies: industry associations, NGOs or public authorities. Examples include the Ethical Trade Initiative (ETI) initiated by the British government in 1998, the Fair Labor Association (FLA) by the Clinton administration in 1996, the Worker Rights Consortium (WRC) by US student activists in 1999, and the (1997) multi-stakeholder organisation Social Accountability International (SAI). These initiatives, together with the Clean Clothes Campaign (CCC), begun in the Netherlands in the early 1990s and later extended to retailers and unions in other European countries, are all joint pacts to which individual corporations surrender a limited amount of organisational sovereignty (Vogel 2005, pp. 80–87). From 2003 a group of MNCs which included Nike, Adidas, Levi Strauss and Liz Claiborne published a common monitoring report for the Fair Labour Association (FLA). Nike, in 2005, published its factories' identities to permit public monitoring. It has also facilitated local and international NGOs to conduct their own audits in its factories (Vogel 2005, p. 84). This initiative may help to encourage imitation by other MNCs. In such instances MNCs are being subjected to systems of rules which may not depart from the essentials of the ST/EM model but nevertheless entail a reversal of its previous evolution. In other words these changes appear to be at the mid-point – the rule-setting category – on Broad and Cavanagh's spectrum of accountability shifts. In the framework of the present analysis: they seem to create some scope for social re-embedding.

The third and more negative reason for critical consideration of these CoC is that they show the limits of individual corporations' powers and their constraint by economic imperatives. Supply chain regulation attempts to change the conditions of workers not directly employed by the MNC itself. Yet both defendants and critics of the operation of CoC assume that corporations' manifold powers are capable of achieving improvements. Unsuccessful implementation of CoC is attributed to insufficient will, effort or organisational competence on the part of corporate managements. In other words, a version of the principal-agent relationship is assumed. These CoC therefore also constitute another test case for this concept. Three aspects of CoC operation have been identified as particularly important:

- their true salience for the global North corporations which adopt them;
- methods of implementing them, through practices like workplace monitoring;
- their effectiveness in improving sweatshop employees' work lives (Jenkins 2001; Pearson and Seyfang 2001; Sethi 1999).

The accountability dimension of such CoC concerns their adequacy in meeting the protests of civil society organisations – usually from the global North – and their conformity with the needs of the exploited workforces in the South.

The predominant evaluation of CoC effectiveness and salience in the above respects is largely negative. CoC are criticised as designed primarily to improve the reputations and brand images of corporations with concerned consumers or sceptical media and NGOs. Some corporations do demonstrate genuine commitment. However, implementation has been shown to be uneven and often ineffective (Raworth and Coryndon 2004; War on Want 2008). The operational effectiveness of CoC implementation has been criticised for allegedly patchy, inaccurate auditing of the supplier firms' practices; and doubts that they have enfranchised workers' rights sufficiently to reverse the prevailing injustices and exploitation (Hale and Wills 2007). However, fresh evidence from research on garment factories in Vietnam by Dong Hoang, raises a more fundamental question about a crucial assumption in the promotion and adoption of CoC as a means of securing corporate responsiveness to social concerns and 'stakeholders'. That question is whether both CoC supporters and some critics over-estimate the powers of MNC hierarchies over the firms and workplaces in their supply chains (cf Arnold and Bowie 2003).

An over-simplification of corporate power and control may exist: one that is erroneously pre-supposed by the principal-agent conception which implicitly underlies many, especially prescriptive, accounts of corporate responsibility and CoC. In the globalised industrial structures comprising sectors such as clothing and footwear, there are disjunctions between the managerial-bureaucratic systems directing CoC and the varying socio-political and cultural contexts within which the sweatshop supplier enterprises are located. Hoang's case studies in Vietnam show that weak compliance with codes arises from the economic position of firms in the 'second-tier' of MNCs' suppliers. The following account is drawn from the summary of Dong's research in Hoang and Jones (2012).

Evidence from the Vietnamese firms shows that it is the shifting interactions between distinct, semi-autonomous categories of socio-economic actors, particularly workforces, which shape the manifest failures, or limited successes, of CoC. In this context, the roles of auditors, factory managers, unions, state bureaucracies, and the workers themselves, involve competition, conflict and collusion on the different objectives of CoC regulation and their operation. Consistent with Murray (2004) this wider, multilateral context suggests that CoC are merely one, albeit potentially influential, variable. Corporations are powerful – but they are not all-powerful. In other words, the corporations may be disembedded, but their attempts to interact with local firms and other social actors do involve complicating social relationships. This situation reprises the Granovetter criticisms of Williamson's model of business transactions described in chapter 6.

Contemporary supply chains are structured more like networks in which corporate buyers source products from many suppliers, rather than simple hierarchies of demand. Suppliers may provide similar products to multiple buyers. This complexity is captured in Rowley's judgement that the position of an organisation in a supply chain network is 'an important determinant of its behaviour as one organisation is a centre point of its own stakeholders but also a stakeholder of other organisations' (Rowley 1997, p. 892). Moreover, in the 'ethical dimension' of the supply net-works, a wide range of international organisations including NGOs, campaign groups, multi-stakeholder initiatives, inter-governmental organ-isations and other multinational firms have been influencing MNCs' adoption and implementation of international labour standards in global supply chains. Campaign groups such as Labour Behind the Label, Clean Clothes Campaign, War on Want, Fair Wear and others have organised numerous anti-sweatshops campaigns. International NGOs like Oxfam, Christian Aid and Verite are involved in research, campaigning, consult-ing, and provision of training for workers. Verite also participates in auditing factories' social performance and some NGOs even intervene in day-to-day, factory management. MNCs' own agents may go into sup-pliers' organisations to 'teach' managers how to communicate effectively with workers; lecturing them on managing culture differences on factory floors (Hartman and Wokutch 2003). But when child labour was found in a factory in Vietnam, consultations with international NGOs and other stakeholders were sought to remedy the problem rather than negotiations with corporate buyers (Hartman et al. 2003).

In addition to this regulatory fragmentation MNCs are also, in some ways, dependent on intermediary firms which commission the actual production firms and on other agencies for the crucial and much-criticised monitoring of CoC implementation in workplaces. MNCs may not know any details of the enterprises which actually make or prepare the products. As they rarely send their own personnel to report on code compliance in the factories there is scope for the local, professional auditors to bend rules and criteria or to under-report abuses. Be too stringent and production may be transferred to other firms, regions or even countries and the auditors lose income. Even if auditors are scrupulous, Dong discovered considerable collusion between factory managers and workers themselves. Because the priorities of the latter are high wages and continuous employment they do not always need to be pressured by managers to deny the incidence of abuses. Better to put up with high overtime and abusive managers than to risk orders, wages and jobs being lost. As even official trade unions may be legitimately controlled by factory management, it is misleading to assume an implicit, principal-agent model of all-powerful, omniscient MNCs, either exploiting or protecting passive workers. CoC will not achieve accountability and social re-embedding if they assume principal-agent relations and other social over-simplifications.

3.1   Corporate Accountability through CoC: Limitations from Economic Constraints

Particularistic and rule-changing routes to corporate responsibility within the ST/EM model are also hampered and contradicted by a set of economic and financial constraints to the workings of CoC in clothing supply chains. The system of globalised production, consumption and distribution entails dedication to hyper-marketised processes in consumer sales and corporate finance. As a result corporations themselves exhibit cognitive dissonance in relations with their suppliers. Aspirations to improve CoC standards coexist with preoccupations to maximise returns to shareholders and to pursue flexibility in commissioning and controlling supplies. In the apparel industry, responding to consumer markets and financial priorities often means deciding on issues such as confirmation of orders, changes in quantity, specifications and delivery times as late as possible; which puts additional pressure on producers (Insight Investment 2004).

Such decisions are, in turn, driven by the structure of consumer markets in the global North, as they have evolved into product proliferation. Five styles of US running shoe in the 1970s grew to about 300 styles in the 1990s. Decreasing product life cycles are now measured in months rather than years, with fashions for some brands lasting mere weeks (Tokatli 2008). Economical high street prices are still expected as are 'faster fulfilment, better quality, and better-performing products for the same price they paid a year ago' (Chopra and Meindl 2007, p. 63). These combined forces require MNCs to seek ever cheaper prices and faster supply times from the contractors and sub-contractors whom they simultaneously require to enhance employees' economic and social standards. Unless MNCs are keen, or constrained by external influences to change their economic practices their CSR contribution to problems such as labour exploitation will be weak.

If the CoC are not being successfully implemented it is not only because of insufficient will, effort or organisational competence by corporate managements. CoC are systems of rules which don't depart from the essentials of the ST/EM model. They are at the mid-point – the rule-setting category – on Broad and Cavanagh's spectrum of accountability shifts. They may limit investors' obligations to maximise profits: in the case examined here they reduced the extreme 'commoditisation' of labour and achieved minor social re-embedding. They push at the outer limits of the reforms within the current and conventional parameters of the ST/EM model and the answerability form of corporate reform. However, mass consumer, short-cycle product business models limit supply chain CoC. Similarly, the failings of model CSR firms in the food manufacturing industry show how over-riding financial priorities of shareholder-value strategies limit and contradict even well-organised CSR programmes.

3.2. Conflicts with Shareholder Value in Food Manufacturing

Although CSR's 'soft regulation may be compatible with neo-liberalism's principle of accountability through market competition, the two systems conflict when pushed towards their limits. As chapter 5 explained, the financialised version of neo-liberalism has led to an internationalised regime characterised by the following features:

- corporations' 'owners' property rights transcend all other forms of social accountability (Dore 2008);
- analysts, institutional investors, and financial executives redefined

corporate efficiency in a preference for 'focussed' rather than diversified firms;
- analysts became less likely to commend conglomerates' diffuse ranges as these were harder to assess; so diversified conglomerates changed into streamlined, 'focussed' firms to improve stock market valuation;
- investors increasingly wanted analysts to predict profits/losses and firms' ability to achieve these;
- as 'money managers' institutional investors reward short-term, relative performance;
- such investors' growing presence in MNC ownership pressured managements to raise returns on capital.

The food and drink sector exemplifies these trends. Case studies of MNCs in this industry (Jones and Nisbet 2011) illustrate clearly the 'disembedding' impacts of financialisation and the limitations which this imposes on voluntary regulation of the CSR kind. Firms like Unilever, Nestlé and Diageo, in the food and drink sector – 'a minefield of cultural and economic sensitivities' (IBLF 2002) – have also invested heavily in CSR commitments.

Because of shareholder value (SV), food MNCs have increasingly been seeking higher financial returns via branding, product innovation and global scale economies; with international growth by acquisitions funded by financial markets. Globalisation and financialisation 'are closely intertwined in corporate strategies' (Froud et al., 2000a; Lazonick and O'Sullivan 2000; Williams 2000). The driving force of SV commitments is clearly shown in extracts from corporations' annual reports and communications for investors. In 2005 Goldman Sachs advised investors: 'take a cautious view of the packaged food industry … uninspiring growth outlook as a key reason for wariness … companies with focussed portfolios perform best' (ConfectioneryNews. com, cited in Jones and Nisbet 2011). Food firms' particular strategies for higher financial returns emphasised: branding, product innovation and globally organised economies of scale in production. Restructuring established large macro-regional factories specialised by product lines serving entire regions: to gain scale economies and productivity increases. International growth was also sought through acquisitions financed by borrowing on the financial markets. So globalisation and financialisation became 'closely intertwined in corporate strategies' (Froud et al. 2000a; Lazonick and O'Sullivan 2000; Palpacuer and Tozanli 2008; Williams 2000). The following statements reported in the

Jones and Nisbet study from the biggest food firms' annual reports illustrated their financial priorities:

- 'a clear sense of urgency. Every day, we focus on what we can … to get growing & deliver superior shareholder value' (Kraft 2007);
- 'Our governing objective … to deliver superior shareholder returns' (Cadbury 2008, Annual Report);
- Cadbury's 2004 Programme: worldwide: shut 33 factories; 6,000 job losses;
- Cadbury's 2007 Programme: worldwide: shut 11 factories; 7,800 job cuts.

A bemused BBC business editor, Robert Peston, commented that 'the company [Cadbury] is doing to itself what a private equity owner would do' (Peston 2007). The Jones and Nisbet research identified several firms executing such socially disembedding rationalisations. But the Cadbury saga is worth examining in some detail because it so clearly reveals the tensions and contradictions between CSR commitments and SV priorities.

One of Cadbury's main production sites was at Keynsham near Bristol, in the west of England. Chocolate products had been made nearby for 200 years, originally as a family firm. The Keynsham site, 'Somerdale', was purpose-built in the 1930s. In October 2007 Cadbury announced that the plant would close in December 2010, with part of its production transferred to another, existing UK plant and part to a new operation in Poland. Most of the site would be sold off for housing and 'light industry' units. In negotiations with unions HR managers offered employees: relocation to other UK sweets factories; redundancy/retirement (40 per cent workforce over 50); and job counselling and retraining (at a nearby college on mostly government-funded courses).

But concern and opposition to these plans was not restricted to employees. The local community began a campaign, which went to the UK Parliament, against the closure because of its predicted impacts on local social capital; that is, more social disembedding. They included:

- potential loss of many sports facilities and down-sizing of a social club;
- end of close ties and support with the local school;
- an end to schemes to re-engage homeless people with work;
- closure of a staff volunteering system helping bodies such as the National Trust.

These assets had been built up over decades through the firm's original CSR schemes for community involvement: 'working with communities'. Local community figures lobbied the firm, the local council and MPs. Representatives put formal questions to Cadbury's AGM.

In the middle of this turmoil Unite, the main trade union, developed a subtle partnership proposal which drew on current CSR ideas and models. Unite offered a 'Partnership' with Cadbury in which the union would endorse Cadbury products to its 2.1 million members; with links to a wider 'community' of 6.1 million people. This deal would be conditional on management backing a 'new Somerdale' plant. The latter would be competitive because it would reduce present labour costs by 50 per cent through voluntary redundancies and incorporated a 'third party' packing area to reduce site costs. Unite pointed out that negotiations had already generated an additional 12.4 per cent production for no more pay, which reduced the rival financial advantages of lower Polish labour costs. In this plan some land could still be sold but a new, more focussed plant with more intensive shift pattern than Poland would significantly reduce capital costs.

By the standard of most UK industrial relations, this was an imaginative and forensic business model. But even more significant for the CSR paradigms was its ecological aspects. The alternative plan proposed bringing back an outsourced organic chocolate line to the UK at Keynsham, thus reducing transport costs and associated emissions; as well as attracting more ethical consumers by marketing the relocated product as a local creation. More substantial were the contrasts drawn between the proposed innovation and the company's 'offshoring' plan. It was argued that Cadbury's green credentials would be enhanced by the lower carbon footprint of the union's 'new Somerdale'. Its heating and cooling requirements would be lower than those needed for the hot summers and colder winters of Poland. More precisely it would avoid the extra carbon emissions inevitably incurred by having to truck the product 2,000 km back to the UK – which would still be its main market. Unite estimated the Polish move would entail an extra 3,421,875 litres of fuel each year at an extra cost of £2.5mn p.a. It would entail a ten-fold (2,847,000 kg) increase of the 'greenhouse gas' CO_2 each year. These impacts were hardly consistent with Cadbury's 'Purple Goes Green' initiative, which promised:

> an *absolute* [emphasis added] commitment to action on climate change ... to shrink our global environmental footprint and set new targets building on the commitments made in our 2006 CSR report (when we committed to develop

a reliance on renewable energy [and] reduce carbon based fuels. (*Talking Retail* 2008)

A day-long meeting between HR and manufacturing managers with local and national union officers combed through the counter-plan. Management then subjected it to detailed financial analysis. Twenty-four hours later, all the proposals were rejected as incompatible with financial criteria and targets.

In 2011 before the closure could be implemented, Kraft swallowed up Cadbury in a controversial take-over. The UK firm's allegedly 'short-termist' shareholders accepted the American predator's attractive offer, which financed the take-over with extra debt of $9.5 billion of bonds bought by global banks: Deutsche Bank, HSBC, RBS, and BNP Paribus. The new owners, predictably, continued the closure and offshoring plans (Slideshare n.d.). The relocation seemed to contradict commitments made by Kraft in 2007 to 'improve our defined Environmental Performance Indicators (DNV-GL, 2007). Moral: the ecological commitments and partnership discourse of CSR is ultimately incompatible with corporations' current financialisation paradigm. There may be companies which manage to combine a measure of community or ecological responsibility with a financialised business strategy. However, the Cadbury case and others identified in such SV prioritised industries, shows that CSR commitments will be dropped when they conflict – as they frequently do – with financial priorities.

4. RULE CHANGING REFORMS AT INTERNATIONAL LEVEL

Another symptom of corporations' inability to maintain CSR policies comes from reports that some corporate leaders have been questioning whether public sector actors need to retrieve some of the increasingly open-ended commitments being asked of CSR firms (Ruggie 2003). CSR limitations have, inevitably, raised prospects of tighter external rules to guide responsible practices – implying reductions in corporate autonomy. Such proposals have been particularly directed at international levels where MNCs have enjoyed more freedoms than within the scope of national jurisdictions.

Civil society organisations have attempted to reform selective aspects of MNCs' behaviour, without challenging corporations' status as sovereign bodies, by proposing externally governed rules. As chapter 9 showed, by the early 2000s, campaigning and charity organisations, long-standing, anti-corporate specialist groups, the alter-globalisation movement and human rights advocates were all targeting international companies (Bendell 2004, p 30). These contributed to efforts such as the UN's Political Declaration of the World Summit on Sustainable Development. This document's 'implementation plan' promised to:

> actively promote corporate responsibility *and* accountability, based on the Rio Principles, including the *full development and effective implementation of inter-governmental agreements and measures*, international initiative and public-private partnerships, and appropriate *national regulations*, and support continuous improvement in corporate practices in all countries. [emphasis added] (WSSD 2002, Paragraph 45)

By implication this, amended, statement – influenced by the Friends of the Earth International position described in the next paragraph – suggests that 'the international community is no longer satisfied with the voluntary approach to corporate accountability' (Justin Alexander of Schroeder's bank, cited in Bendell 2004, p. 19).

The Declaration's announcement at the summit was hedged around with qualifications and dissent (Khor n.d.). International government organisations largely failed to match such calls with concrete measures. Worse, no international process was established to follow through these commitments to strengthening CSR (Calder and Culverwell 2005, p. 86). Consequently, efforts to check global irresponsibilities, including the implementation of the WSSD project, have often switched to national channels, as 'governments are the only actors with jurisdiction over the private sector' and they can 'support the development of effective public governance of the private sector in developed and developing countries' (Calder and Culverwell 2005). These Chatham House recommendations propose progressing the accountability of corporations to sustainable development by 'promoting access to information/transparency, e.g. through appropriate legislation' (Calder and Culverwell 2005, p. 40).

Accordingly, the UK Corporate Responsibility Coalition (CORE) urged UK statutes for compulsory corporate social and environmental reporting, or improved rules regarding broader and more robust financial auditing and reporting. The North American-based International Right to Know campaign, called for national government laws to extend the jurisdiction of national courts to companies' foreign activities and to link foreign legal aid to their extra-territorial performance. A similar sub-ordination of corporations and their officers to international jurisdiction has also been proposed to get national governments to extend the International Criminal Court to cover 'their' corporations. At a higher level, Friends of the Earth International's Framework Convention on

Corporate Accountability and Liability covered some of all these types of regulatory innovation (FoEI 2002); which have been echoed by other bodies (Calder and Culverwell 2005, p. 68). However, international organisations have done no more to tighten or advance such rules that could constrain the abusive roles of MNCs.

CONCLUSION

Corporate autonomy may be more likely to be dented and accountability improved by focussing first on the national level; but accountability as voluntary 'responsibility' is unlikely to advance these aims. In terms of Broad and Cavanagh's continuum, correction of individual firms' abuses has, at best, produced mixed results. In the second zone of rule changes, attempts to reform corporate behaviour have varied between, on the one hand, the soft-regulation of CoC plus multi-stakeholder 'engagement' and, on the other hand, ultimately ineffectual campaigns for international regulation. Ethical investment principles wilt in the face of profitability considerations and executives' stonewalling. Codes of conduct vary in their scope, and lack durability and stakeholder accountability. Pressures from price competition in product markets, or financial market constraints to maximise short-term shareholder value, subvert well-meaning commitments to regulate sweat shops, maintain community welfare or improve ecological performance.

These structural failings point towards Broad and Cavanagh's third focus, of liquidation or re-structuring of the ST/EM model, as the remaining option. But transformations of corporate status would face major corporate opposition and business pressure against government proposals. So, smaller, strategic steps may be necessary. Reforms of the corporate governance could eventually change firms' operational and international policies by opening up decision making. Paradoxically, the slump following the international crash of 2008 may have prepared the ground for such action in national arenas. This possibility occurs because the financially induced economic crisis and the subsequent recession and austerity mind-set have only worsened social conditions in societies across the globe (Ortiz and Cummins 2013).

As a result, and unlike the anti/alter-globalisation movements which targeted international governing bodies, the recent crisis has seen national governments in MNCs' host countries, come under more direct pressure from popular domestic campaigns. Austerity regimes have re-focussed popular protest back to the national level, with protests from movements such as UK Uncut, Occupy!, the Mediterranean Indignados and their successors (Jones and O'Donnell 2014). So it may be that a broadening of corporations' local accountability is a necessary first move by making their executives more amenable to conformity to national rules, which could then be extended to their international activities. Corporate governance is still mainly defined and regulated at national levels. So campaigners may need to follow-up and intensify the UK CORE initiative and refocus their efforts there. Such specific reforms aimed at inducing status changes in corporate, or at least executive, autonomy are examined in the following, final chapters.

11. Embedded accountability: alternative possibilities and political perspectives

> The [corporation] executives ... argue ... that, if it were their own money ... they would not fire lifelong employees a week before retirement, or dump carcinogenic waste next to schools. Yet they are morally bound to ignore such considerations, because they are mere employees whose only responsibility is to provide the maximum return on investment for the company's stockholders. (The stockholders, of course, are not given any say). (Graeber 2011, p. 400)

INTRODUCTION

The previous chapter tried to disentangle ideas of responsibility from accountability and to assess the extent to which different modes of regulation achieve corporate accountability to key sectors of society. This chapter will relate those issues to the alternative types of business system analysed in chapter 7, which are more embedded in their societies. The aim is to pin down whether there are forms of corporate structure and ethos which could inform reforms compatible with the existing institutional UK context. Complementarity seems preferable to extolling a paradigm system that satisfies all of the social, economic and political criteria that rigorous intellectual analysis and political values demand. The following assessment of what reforms are needed has only two guiding principles: (1) to restore a genuine form of social embeddedness to the ST/EM corporation; (2) to create an embeddedness facilitating democratic accountability to civil society, rather than to a remote state – as occurred with nationalisation – or an isolated sectional interest, – as in 1970s 'industrial democracy' or shareholder value (SV).

This chapter begins with a brief re-assessment of the Polanyian theory of social embeddedness and the relevance of the embedded business systems described in chapter 7 as alternatives to the dominance of ST/EM firms in the UK. It goes on to review the claims and problems in the three intellectual perspectives – neo-liberalism, communitarianism/ CSR, and radicalism – which shape and constrain the discourses of corporate reform. Then we analyse the relationship between these perspectives and the policy prescriptions of the UK's mainstream politics. Do the recipes of the political parties offer potential bridgeheads towards meaningful accountability? Or do they remain constrained by the axioms of neo-liberalism and its social responsibility counterpart on voluntary regulation which were described in the previous chapter?

1. WHAT KIND OF EMBEDDEDNESS?

Recall the analysis in chapter 6 which related greater social accountability of big business to models of social embedding derived from Polanyi's insights. In his 'double-movement' thesis the second shift consists of: 'the movement for social protection to limit the scope of market forces' (Block and Evans 2005, p. 511). Chapter 6 also noted the contention of Block and others that market economies can be 'always-embedded' rather than being necessarily disembedded. That idea suggests that CSR's colonisation of civil society could be a form of 're-embedding'. If true, that development would undermine the utility of Polanyian prescriptions because it would maintain corporate market systems which exploit and disadvantage other social institutions – workers' and civil rights, welfare systems and so on. Some contemporary analyses suggest that this CSR dominion could be the likeliest regime to succeed full-blown neo-liberalism (Crouch 2008); but CSR is continuously evolving, as the limitations of its more modest practices are revealed. Are there other developments that would be closer to the spirit of the re-embedding aspect of Polanyi's double movement? As noted in the previous chapter, re-embedding via international NGOs and international frameworks of governance has made very modest progress. Aside from these efforts, a promising starting point is the multi-lateral stakeholder relationships, linked as they are to civil society movements.

Another route could be embedding through social and political institutions like those of the German-speaking and Scandinavian countries. The principles, if not the actual practices, behind embedding in East Asian states such as South Korea and Japan have attractions, as described below and in chapter 7. The following analysis will suggest that some aspects of these societies may be transferable; but often they depend on historical conditions and Aix-type 'social spaces' which are absent in the UK. In addition, the closer control exercised by state bodies or employee interests in 'Rhenish' and East Asian capitalism, may have been permanently discredited by the neo-liberal assassination of social democracy in the UK. Moreover, these forms of embedding are also not obviously

compatible with the devolved movements for corporate social accountability being advanced by civil society movements. To meet this objection, there needs to be an updating of Polanyi's definition of the social
half of the double movement as: 'consciously subordinating [the market]
to a democratic society' (1944, p. 234). A 'democratic society' may now
mean something different from and more than the social democracy
about which Polanyi wrote.

The current crisis involves near abandonment of social democracy as
business and its leaders now evade, colonise and subvert the public
realms of 'democratic' states. Polanyi himself identified the motors of
change specifically with certain types of political party. Yet he also
acknowledged that changes are: 'capable of representation by almost any
type of territorial or functional association such as churches, townships,
fraternal lodges, clubs, trade unions' (Polanyi 1944, p. 154). So might it
be easier and less contentious to build on these developments rather than
prescribe elaborate intergovernmental frameworks or societal restructuring of business institutions? The civil society route to corporate accountability centres on corporate regulation and governance. But before
making a detailed examination of these possibilities we need to consider
whether aspects of the socially embedded systems discussed in chapter 7
could be translated into a corporate homeland such as the UK. So let us
look, in this order, at: East Asian business systems, industrial districts and
their cooperative counterparts, and then the 'Rhenish', co-determined
enterprise most strongly identified with Germany.

2.   LESSONS FROM EMBEDDED BUSINESS SYSTEMS

Media commentary sometimes lauds the industrial success of the company structures of East Asian countries such as Taiwan, South Korea and,
more recently the People's Republic of China. Business systems in these
societies can be said to be socially embedded through strong ties with
state institutions, and often with other business stakeholders. But there is
almost as much variety between these countries' systems as there is
amongst European societies. So no general principles can be drawn from
them. In addition their advantages consist mainly in the capacity to
organise and generate initial industrial growth in the manufacturing
sector. It is not clear how far such advantages and growth patterns would
be applicable to mature, post-industrial societies such as the UK. For
here a major priority is to remedy the predatory relationship between the
corporate sector and a vigorous civil society. It would anyway require a
major shift in the mix of fiscal capacities, political forces and political

culture, to resurrect the kind of state-centric capability which preceded the rise of neo-liberalism and the dismantling of social democratic state institutions. However, one factor in the rise of Chinese industry which is worth noting is the role of local, community-embedded 'industrial districts', similar to those still persisting in parts of Europe (Christerson 1997; Wei et al. 2007). The potential relevance of this, originally European phenomenon, is examined in more detail below.

2.1   Japan – Normative Embedding and Cross Company Stakeholding

Japan's business institutions and relationships have had only limited appeal for would-be reformers of the British and ST/EM systems (Wilks 2013, p. 250). The Japanese system of *keiretsu* groups containing their own corporate banks as a source of long-term indirect financing would be anathema to both autonomy-loving company executives and to the investment strategies of the banks in the UK. However, corporate cross-holdings breed group norms which promote growth and stability rather than simply financial profitability (Gedajlovic and Shapiro 2002). More significantly the Japanese distinction of 'stable shareholders' (*antei kabunushi*) or 'strategic investors' (*seisaku toshika*) from finance-oriented 'pure investors' (*juntoshika*) resonates with recent British concerns about long-term and speculative shareholders. The protection of stable/strategic share owners has declined in recent years but, in general, large holdings of stable investors have shielded most large Japanese firms from the take-over threat that their Anglo-Saxon counterparts face. Moreover, market shareholders or 'pure investors' still hold less equity than stable investors (Gedajlovic et al. 2004). As the discussion of British political perspectives will show, below, a similar distinction is being recognised in the UK.

A more general form of Japanese social embeddedness is the idea of the company as a 'Community of Fate'. This principle persists despite some decline, at the core of the *nenko* employment system and stable sub-contracting to semi-permanent SMEs. This is a factor far removed from the financialised logic of the ST/EM corporation. Lifetime employment diverts a managerial priority for maximising profits for shareholders/investors, to one of collective survival/welfare of all *nenko* employees within the extended *keiretsu* firm. Pressures from global competition have pushed Japanese firms closer to the neo-liberal model in terms of corporate income differentials, returns to shareholders and employment (in)security (see chapter 7). But, in general, the *keiretsu-nenko* system seems to be making adaptive responses, not a wholesale shift to neo-liberal principles of marketisation, labour flexibility and shareholder value (Berggren and Nomura 1997; Aoki et al. 2008). Despite more labour mobility between firms and more information disclosure to external investors, the basic institutions still stand as potential exemplars; despite the insecurities of a domestic recession which began before the global financial crash of 2008. This survival suggests that Japanese-style embedding can co-exist with some neo-liberal conditions.

Japan's main lesson for systems like the UK, consists of different norms of corporate governance to western corporations: investments and profits are not ends in themselves – as with the financialised 'shareholder value' paradigm – but are often means to collective and common goals. Labour market processes could hardly be more different from the UK context. But could the UK system take on the institutional supports of this ethos? For core workers in the large businesses (30 per cent of the workforce), 'lifetime employment' in one firm after post-education recruitment with institutionalised internal labour mobility involves a tacit exchange for strong commitment by employees. This commitment is the quid pro quo for firms' long-term sunk costs in training, because employers know skilled workers are unlikely to be 'poached'. This corporate responsibility contrasts with the UK's worship of flexible and individualistic labour markets. These latter are, ironically, closer to Japan's less secure or career oriented peripheral employment and its chains of, often low-paid, subcontractors. Direct transplantation would also need an equivalent to the policing of the *nenko* commitment by enterprise-based unions, which ensure workers' voice has some weight. In the UK this would involve a reversal of neo-liberal industrial relations orthodoxy and reforms to establish more pluralistic corporate governance than executives' dirigiste control. As in some Japanese *keiretsu*, policing could require – the governance factor again – a union, or at least worker presence at board level.

2.2 Industrial Districts: Italian Lessons?

Chapter 5 showed that the relative failure of British manufacturing in the 20th century was partly caused by the abandonment of industrial district (ID) organisational forms, in favour of 'economies of scale'. The latter meant that large firms and industrial concentration dominated post-WWII industrial policy thinking. Concurrent merger waves and popularisation of the M-form trends encouraged the supremacy of all-encompassing corporate operations with hierarchical management. IDs in Italy, especially in the so-called 'Third Italy', involved industrial specialisation in sectors like garments and metal engineering, in a high proportion of small and very small enterprises but very few large firms. Regions such as Emilia-Romagna achieved: high employment rates, high average wage levels, hi-tech processes in small firms, key workers with high skills and innovative capabilities, and high export levels. These achievements were attributed to organisational flexibility; but also to trust-sustaining social institutions. Local political cultures motivated local government and representative organisations (such as the artisanal associations) to provide services (for example marketing and finance) for small firms and artisans.

It could be argued that these complexes of small firms could not flourish within economies like that of the UK, which are dominated by ST/EM firms. Yet with a few notable exceptions – mainly in military and aerospace sectors – there is a manufacturing vacuum in the UK which new or revived IDs could start to fill. If industrial policies, based on the often advocated devolution of political powers, could initiate them again, they could fill some of this industrial vacuum and avoid ST/EM dominance. This is because ID clusters are like a company without a constitution. They are significantly socially embedded in local societies, utilising family networks and political ties with, and support from, diverse local institutions. More recent recessions and the migration of manufacturing to lower-wage regions beyond Western Europe have weakened the dynamism of Italian and other IDs. Yet the model has survived and adapted, sometimes into the kinds of service sectors on which the UK economy is supposed to depend (Paniccia 2007, p. 21). It sustains the new ecological industries in countries such as Denmark (Cumbers 2012) and has driven manufacturing growth in south-east China.

2.3 Ownership and Control: Mutual Alternatives

In terms of socially accountable embeddedness, the Mondragon enterprise could be an even more attractive proposition. Mondragon can be considered as an expanded and cooperatively organised industrial district. Based in Spain's Basque country the Mondragon cooperative complex provides an intriguing variant on the Italian ID; one which promises greater durability, internal growth potential and explicitly democratic governance. Mondragon resembles an ethically organised industrial district, which began, like some Italian IDs, in a politically victimised locality. Nourished by the distinctive culture of the Basque region and motivated by the political discrimination against the region under the Franco regime, the Mondragon Cooperative Corporation (MCC) began as a small specialised producer of heaters; spinning off or seeding partner firms in related products.

Mondragon has evolved into a commercial complex with hundreds of federated businesses and tens of thousands of employees – see chapter 7. Like other IDs, Mondragon draws on local institutions such as technical colleges for its social resources. But it has also established its own social security and health care benefits, schools and a university. Unlike the artisanal entrepreneurship in the Italian IDs, its organised evolution has been continuously based on a cooperative democracy of one member (employee) – one vote. Organised through a system of tiered representation from the work-place to the Governing Council, which appoints and oversees managers, Mondragon has avoided dilution or atrophy of employee ownership and control which has debilitated many other cooperatives (Saxena and Craig 1990). There have been problems in Mondragon's expansion into international arenas. Democratic co-ownership has not been extended to the substantial minority of 14,000 non-member workers mainly employed in its foreign subsidiaries. Yet this has not deterred potential imitators amongst trade union activists and officials and local policy makers in the USA (GEO Newsletter 2012).

Policy makers and local agencies in countries like the UK could justifiably promote IDs as supplements and partial alternatives to the dominant corporate economy. However, their growth could take decades to achieve and would not by itself replace entrenched corporate dominance in some sectors. The mutual principle which drives the Mondragon type of ID could be seeded more quickly. In less than three years an alliance between the US Steelworkers union and the MCC has generated a variety of start-up and take-over initiatives (cf Davidson 2012; Clamp 2010). The wider salience of employee-owned mutuals is discussed in the concluding chapter; but the more comprehensive forms of social embedding flourishing in the German business system need to be considered first.

2.4 Germany and Embedded Governance

Socially embedded business in Germany, and variants in different forms in other northern European societies, involves both external institutional supports and internal governance arrangements linked to wider 'stakeholder' interests. This system encourages continuous improvements in products and production processes, thereby favouring technical rather than financial competitiveness. Externally, it is buttressed by the dual system of workplace-college apprenticeships. Firms, employers' associations, regional governments and trade unions help to coordinate the dual system. The much-noted *mittelstand* sector of SMEs, rather than corporate firms per se, provides the system's backbone, with local/regional political authorities and financial institutions affiliated to it and to the larger firms.

In the latter, executive managers' capacity for unilateral action is limited by the system of corporate governance. Managerial appointments and strategic policies depend upon agreement from supervisory boards, which are composed of employee representatives, major shareholders, senior managers from outside, major suppliers and customer firms. Thus embedding is enhanced by the role and presence of these stakeholders which limit the firms' managerial isolation from, and power over the wider society. Stakeholder ties reinforce external forms of network monitoring and favour consensus decision-making.

The German system also gives some protection from hostile, and potentially destructive, take-overs. At plant-level, works councils consisting of elected worker representatives and managers are able to negotiate on working conditions and lay-offs. Pro-market reforms in the last 15 years have loosened the insider role of banks but, paradoxically, increased the influence of trade unions (Jackson and Sorge 2012; Wilks 2013, p. 236–8). So both Japan and Germany have tended to blur their sharp, institutional differences with ST/EM firms. However, institutional persistence suggests that a capacity to compete with neo-liberalised firms and economies derives from the comparative advantages of social embeddedness.

As the wider recession continues, Britain's struggling industrial sectors have been adversely contrasted to the German business system (Groom 2013; Elliot 2014). Certainly UK SMEs and trade unions might have more favourable status if aspects of 'co-determination', and the *mittelstand*'s institutional supports, were introduced. However, there will always be problems with 'cherry picking' some socio-economic traits from one society, because they are often articulated in subtle ways to other social institutions (Maurice et al. 1986; Wilks 2013, p. 235), which are not as easy to transfer. Nevertheless, the German governance system of larger corporations confirms the general advantages of social embedding through institutionalised accountability (Wilks 2013, p. 240) and the kind of institutions needed to achieve this.

Similar configurations in the UK would certainly expand the level of economic democracy, which Korten and others prescribe as stakeholder ownership and participation for ST/EM firms in the USA and for the UK (Korten 2000; Thompson and Driver 2002). However, the financial institutions, other trading businesses and trade union representatives sitting on German firms' supervisory boards might seem a relatively narrow set of socio-economic interests. Balancing of these interests with other, civil society actors is considered in the next, Conclusion chapter. However, as previous debates have shown – see chapter 3 – business interests would vehemently and almost univocally oppose a shift to, say, Germany's two-tier board system. Before prescribing such governance or regulatory recipes for the UK we need to consider the competing policy perspectives from which change is likely to be evaluated and the extent to which the main political actors are independent from, or captives of these perspectives.

3. POLICY PERSPECTIVES FOR REFORMING ACCOUNTABILITY

In neo-liberalised societies like the UK, as earlier chapters have shown, three different perspectives compete for political and policy influence to moderate or reverse corporate over-reach in economic, civil society and political spheres. These perspectives can be grouped within the categories previously used: the neo-liberal, the communitarian, and the radical or transformative approaches.

3.1 Neo-liberal

In the neo-liberal perspective corporations are benevolent machines generating jobs, products/services, innovations and tax revenues for the public good (Micklethwait and Wooldridge 2003). Such alleged benefits, especially the extent of corporate tax contributions, are factually questionable; but neo-liberalism's methods for checking corporate abuses and over-reach at least seem coherent. For both neo-liberal high priest Milton Friedman and more left-of-centre critics, like Bill Clinton's Labor Secretary, Robert Reich, CSR or similar business meddling in social programmes, erodes a necessary distinction between state and private roles. Friedman stresses that companies can remedy society's ills by meeting customers' needs and satisfying shareholders' expectations, thereby maximising profits to fund tax revenues for state programmes. With sufficient competition, if firms fail to meet such demands they will lose customers and investors to rivals and face the ultimate market sanctions of bankruptcy or take-over.

This neo-liberal thesis still frames economic policy making in the Anglo-Saxon world. It has only one distinctive drawback. Empirically it has not worked. As other chapters have shown, governments are loath to let big employers fail because diminished tax revenues and job losses will result. Take-overs rarely benefit the merged entity, or its share-holders, and executives heading any threatened declining firm may see take-overs not as threats but just as another reward (via compensation received) (Mayer 2013, pp. 101–103). Neo-liberal policy also discourages the tighter regulations which might restrain corporate excess: as with the pre-Crash banking sector and the implosion of Enron and some of its peers at the start of this century (Merino et al. 2010). Neo-liberalism's devotion to market forces as the most effective form of regulation also rejects restraint from civil society actors as 'interference'. A riposte would be that this hostility contradicts the very principle of checks and balances which its foundation discourse in classical liberalism saw as vital for curbing political power. Like the prescriptions of pre-modern 'sawbones' for more blood-letting for unresponsive medical conditions, neo-liberalism only recommends more competition and less regulation and outside interference to restrain corporate excess and irresponsibility (Becker 2002; Vidal 2002).

Neo-liberalism stands by the ability of the markets for capital invest-ment and corporate control to promote responsible management and discipline corporate excess. However, the report of the 2012 Kay Review, set up by Vince Cable, Secretary of State for Business, Innovation and Skills, to investigate the role and functions of shareowners, identified severe problems with these mechanisms:

- the critical role of investment intermediaries – interpreting their duties to (shareholding/trading) clients/beneficiaries too narrowly as maximising short-term returns;
- as a consequence setting investment strategies with asset managers based on short-term performance metrics;
- a focus which thus dis-incentivises shareholders' engagement with executive management;
- relatedly, a disregard for long-term factors, such as environmental, social and governance factors, even though these may be relevant to company performance.

Implicitly, Kay is here tapping into the major problem with market 'regulation': the rise of 'financialisation and shareholder value' processes. Chapters 5 and 8 identified this phenomenon as: owners' property rights transcending all other forms of business corporations' social accountability (Dore 2008); with firms' priorities 'financialised' to raise 'shareholder value' (Lazonick and O'Sullivan 2000). Within the neo-liberal belief in market-driven accountability, SV was accentuated by parallel moves to reward executives with shares and share options as a means of overcoming the division of interests inherent in the separation of 'ownership' and control. However, such incentives only intensified executives' focus on a narrow range of indicators of success. Being paid in shares incentivised executives to concentrate primarily on SV.

Neo-liberals see take-overs and mergers as other market sanctions that penalise managers' wayward or inadequate financial performance. But these threats may make things worse. Short-term economic incentives to financial agents (notably those advising companies on take-over activity) led to mergers and acquisitions which have destroyed long-term value for investors; not to mention the destabilisation from the accompanying loss of jobs and community cohesion (cf Jones and Nisbet 2011). Kay's report reflected widespread evidence that some companies place excessive emphasis on acquisitions relative to developing competitive advantage of their existing business operations. More broadly, this pre-occupation with financial goals and interests intensified corporations' disembedding from the rest of society, its institutions and values.

Independent directorships on corporate boards have also come to be cast in the role of agents of market controls. More recently, consistent with communitarian perspectives, they have been accorded the additional role of ethical guardians (Wilson 1994). Independents' presumed omniscience has extended to a capacity for holding executives to their social responsibilities. Their presence actually predates the hegemony of neo-liberalism – they were promoted as a method of securing more corporate accountability during the more interventionist governments of the 1970s. However, they have come to be seen, primarily, as repositories of market experience capable of checking wilful executives. Their duties have also been used as an argument against German-style supervisory boards as they are thought of as monitoring executive directors and therefore avoiding an allegedly divisive separation of powers that two-tier boards might cause. The theory is that 'non-execs' can act in the interests of investors, challenging managements' insularity and self-seeking. Their function is seen as similar to the take-over bid: identifying and pressing for more efficient uses of a firm's resources.

Numbers of independent directors have proliferated and they are required by financial authorities' successive (but largely advisory) codes of conduct (cf Financial Reporting Council 2012). However, they provide only a very minor corrective to corporate excesses and abuses (Froud et al. 2008). For example, they seem to have little or no discernible impact on disproportionate and ever-expanding executive pay levels; even in firms with poor and negative profitability. Various reasons can be adduced for these failings. Independents may not be privy to all the decision-making and machinations of large organisations. They may lack specialised expertise required to monitor and understand areas of potential concern. Often part-time, they may lack the resources, confidence or even inclination to investigate problematic issues closely. But perhaps the most damning possibility is that independents may lack real independence. They are chosen by the very executives they are supposed to monitor and police – 'cronyism' again? (Solomon 2010, chapter 4). The UK's independent directors have had around 50 years to control and restrain executive self-interest. So it seems unlikely that they can, by themselves, fulfil these roles in the way that 'Rhenish' supervisory boards seem to do.

3.2   Corporate Communitarianism and CSR

As Labor Secretary in Clinton's presidency, Robert Reich (later to become more sceptical about corporations) made clear that governments would expect a quid pro quo from business in return for the lowered taxes and de-regulation which it had sought and been granted by Reagan. In future, Reich argued, Corporate America would be expected to take an active responsibility for employees, communities and other stakeholders (Reich 1998). These sentiments meshed with communitarianism's emphasis on citizens' duties, which could translate easily into the concurrent rise of CSR ideas; especially its Corporate Citizenship variant. As corporations had the status of legal subjects it was argued that they had the same reciprocity of rights and duties to the community as, in a communitarian perspective, did human subjects (McIntosh et al. 1998; Thompson 2011).

By equating commercial advantage with social responsibility this perspective effectively countered the neo-liberal claim that CSR would contradict executives' primary duty to provide returns for investors. As chapter 8 showed, this new model CSR was even more welcome in the UK, through a tacit alliance of business groups, NGO pressures and governmental policies from the 1990s onwards. Provoked by MNCs' labour rights and environmental abuses in the global South, CSR was taken up in international forums of IGOs and MNC consultations; and established a partial international consensus on the value of corporate

---

BOX 11.1   REICH ON 'HARD' AND 'SOFT' REGULATION

Corporate officials are bound to two broad sets of laws ... The first, embracing securities and corporate law, requires that they place the interests of their shareholders above all others. The second, comprising all other laws and regulations – covering labour, the environment, and so on – establishes a boundary around the first set of obligations. Board members and executives must place the interests of shareholders above all other interests except as limited by all other laws and regulations. The two sets of laws – the first, establishing their fiduciary responsibility to investors, the second, their responsibility to other stakeholders in the rest of society – form an integrated system of corporate societal responsibility. (Reich 1998, pp. 15–16)

---

citizenship duties. In 2000 UN Secretary-General Kofi Annan established the United Nations Global Compact aimed at rebuilding trust in private sector-led development with a membership of both developed economies' multinationals and developing countries' SMEs. In practice it has been largely ignored by Anglophone MNCs who have seen it, perhaps rightly, as a step towards international regulation (Bremer 2008).

The main operational counterparts of CSR ethical principles are:

- ethical investment policies;
- environmental responsibilities (sustainability);
- acting as corporate citizens – making social and other contributions either financially or in kind;
- 'stakeholder engagement' – consultation/ dialogue with commercial 'partners' or CSO groups;
- transparency of corporate information and communications.

3.3   CSR: Claims and Criticisms

Despite its compatibility with the overall neo-liberal action framework, as we saw in chapter 10, CSR programmes may conflict with investor expectations. Moreover, stakeholder engagement has yet to develop into dialogues that can change corporations' strategic priorities (Browne and Nuttall 2013). In industrial relations parlance there is a need to go beyond 'consultation' to negotiation and, some would argue, participation. CSR practice has not challenged neo-liberalism's primacy of financial aims and market norms. If this judgement is correct then, in its present forms, CSR is of little use in re-integrating corporations with society through accountability. Let us examine this thesis in more detail.

CSR is voluntary. So it reduces 'red tape' and is done out of genuine commitment rather than mere compliance. Executive managers are constrained to act in more responsible ways because of market and reputational pressures from competitors, customers and investors. Thus, if a firm is not seen as responsible, its competitors will be perceived as superior. The latter will attract customers and investors away from irresponsible firms. Defective firms may also be more at risk from take-over by competitors because poorer image will be reflected in lower share prices, making take-overs cheaper for rivals. So CSR maintains the basic, neo-liberal market voluntary framework. In addition this framework is seen as being economically positive: boosting corporate reputations and so contributing to their financial success. On this limited basis it squares off the anti-CSR case of neo-liberal fundamentalists like Milton Friedman, that CSR clouds the corporation's primary focus on profit maximisation.

In the face of neo-liberal opposition to hard regulation and the social consequences of market forces 'regulation' – rising under- and unemployment, income differentials, and general social disintegration – politicians, business leaders and policy makers increasingly turned towards 'soft-regulation'. CSR advocates and communitarians pushed for company-level negotiations, policy 'nudges' and stakeholder pressures to get corporations to package their financial hard-headedness with acts of charity, sponsorship and more responsible business practices to alleviate environmental and community stresses. This CSR version of neo-liberalism's market regulation found its way into company law legislation – the 2006 Companies Act discussed below – via the 2001 Company Law Review, as 'enlightened shareholder value' (Collison et al. 2014, p. 5).

In addition to the limitations highlighted in previous chapters' case studies, the most significant criticisms of CSR concern its selective application, which has legitimating and power enhancing consequences. CSR is selective as firms choose causes that are consistent with their own business goals. These may not be the most significant for society as a whole, or for the communities involved. Businesses may often ignore the more important, or worst problems which do not relate to their business strategy or brand images. As the cases in chapter 10 showed, continuity is problematic: business imperatives may over-ride involvement, so social programmes may be dropped or downgraded because of other, for example financial, corporate priorities. CSR can also add legitimacy to generally irresponsible forms of business because it facilitates 'greenwashing': minor environmental issues are tackled to enhance business reputations while more destructive practices remain intact. Extrapolated, greenwashing now signifies any corporate policies undertaken for image purposes that deliberately or indirectly camouflage the more general or worse practices. Power enhancement accrues because voluntary and self-regulation of CSR is often undertaken not out of genuine commitment but in order to pre-empt legislation or other forms of 'hard regulation'. Effective soft regulation depends on the strength of 'stakeholder'/pressure group influence. Without organised civil society campaigning corporations would often take no action.

Simultaneously, over-reach expands. Stakeholder involvement carries dangers of dependency on, and 'patronage' by corporations rather than equal participation (Jones 2007). Rather than counteracting business 'colonisation' of civil society, CSR can be seen as intensifying this encroachment (Reich 1998; Wilks 2013, p. 210). To exert significant pressure on business behaviour greater parity in business-society relationships is necessary. 'Multi-stakeholder initiatives' involving actors from public sector, civil society as well as business, suggest equality in such 'civil society' regulation of corporate autonomy could provide greater accountability. But such arrangements often involve restricted or selected civil society participants. They depend on contingent factors where corporations surrender a limited degree of autonomy without conceding any of their overall power. CSOs may also become 'captured' or 'co-opted', both politically and ideologically, into corporate and neo-liberal paradigms (Jones 2007; McIntosh et al. 1998; Utting 2005, p. 283). To advance beyond present CSR inadequacies would need supportive and collective institutions/organisations, plus some framework of more effective pressure. The Bangladesh factory disaster of 2013 offers vivid proof of this condition. Despite continuing evasiveness by a few MNCs, a decisive response was made possible because NGOs, unions and other campaigners already had remedial policy prescriptions and had been lobbying with and against firms, in favour of these reforms for years. Unlike the often ineffectual company codes of conduct, the Bangladesh Safety Accord is 'transparent, enforceable and binding' (War on Want 2013; ILO 2014). But such restraints only apply to the most dangerous or shameful aspects of corporate operations. CSR responsiveness does not change the structural traits which generate such types of behaviour.

3.4 Radical/Transformative Perspectives

As described in the previous chapter, at the far pole of Broad and Cavanagh's spectrum are the perspectives proposing changes to corporations' legal and social status as necessary to curb their power and irresponsibility. But, unlike neo-liberal and communitarian paradigms, radical and transformative prescriptions lack an overarching and coherent theoretical framework. Elements of Marxism, libertarianism and social liberalism compete and overlap with the practical campaigns for challenging corporate hegemony. Consequently there are a variety of programmes and proposals concerning ownership, governance and social embedding. The only common theme is that corporations' accumulation of institutionalised powers, managerial systems, and political influence can be changed by making them more widely accountable.

Recipes for achieving these ends include: stricter public regulation; social ownership – nationalised or mutualised (cooperative) arrangements; wider share ownership; democratised governance, and a return to state/ community licensing of corporations' activities via charters or similar devices. With the exception of some CSR proposals for intensifying forms of multi-stakeholder participation, these ideas conflict directly with neo-liberal and communitarian prescriptions. For radicals the re-embedding of business organisations in society requires breaking one or more of the ST/EM corporation's key institutions – such as corporations' status as legal subjects or restricted accountability to investors and their 'limited liability'. Paths towards some of these changes are identified in the concluding chapter. But corporate transformation that depends on systemic economic changes of ownership and finance, as advocated by neo-Marxists such as Schweickart (2002), are deliberately ignored there. The present distribution of political power and opposition makes it highly unlikely that the necessary agents of such transformative change could establish themselves and the degree of influence required.

From the traditional social democratic standpoint there should, in principle, be no problem in retrenching and confining corporate over-reach by means of laws and regulations; but there are two current obstacles to implementation of these. The first, described in chapter 1, is the near-hegemonic position of corporations within the political system. These actors, or their party-political sympathisers and acolytes, can block, dilute or otherwise neutralise proposals for radical new legislation or re-regulation. The second reason is that regulatory institutions alone have proven, at least in the UK, to be ineffective in promoting 'other stakeholders' interests against those of firms and their shareholders. As chapter 4 explained, the UK now has one of the most comprehensive regulatory complexes for dealing with utilities and former nationalised industries – Ofcom, Ofwat, Ofgem, Office of Rail Regulation to name but a few. Yet the paradigm guiding the present regulatory structures means that they prioritise narrower financial objectives over broader social and environmental ones.

3.5 Accountability Implications of the Policy Perspectives

Prescriptions dominated by neo-liberalism advocate intensified or refined market pressures and competitive mechanisms. CSR/communitarianism measures focus, inter-alia, on: 'soft-regulation', consultative forms of negotiation, policy nudges and stakeholder pressure. Radicals of a collectivist stamp favour structural reforms that would transfer the direction of businesses to either sectional or public interest controls: (re)nationalisation, mutualisation, or state control/licensing. Radicals associated with 'new social movements' – campaigning environmental and human rights movements – tend more to favour reforms to widen the social accountability of corporate governance. Most positions within all perspectives see some role for 'hard regulation' of the status quo: legislation, externally enforceable codes of conduct, official regulators, and so on. However, they vary on the degree and scope of such arrangements, from the neo-liberals' minimalist positions to a comprehensive 'web of rules' envisaged by radical campaigners. Table 11.1 summarises the main differences of the perspectives on the key aspects of corporate structure.

Table 11.1   Differences in reform priorities between main perspectives on accountability

| | Paradigms | | |
Area of change	Neo-Liberal	Communitarian/ CSR	Radical
Regulation	Minimise/ replace with competition	'Soft'/'self' regulation	'Hard' regulation
Oversight/ Monitoring	Markets/ investors	Independent directors; regulators	State or stakeholders
Organisational control	Executives	Executives	New governing bodies: two-tier boards, trusts etc
Share ownership	Stock markets	Stock markets	Transfer some/all to states, communities, stakeholders
Accountability	Financial	More information transparency	State/community/ stakeholder powers to hold companies to account
Stakeholder relations	Limit to business counterparts & financial criteria	'Engagement' with range of legitimate stakeholders via consultation/ dialogue	Empower stakeholders to influence or control direction of corporations

One cross-cutting problem complicating each of these modes is their varying and sometimes diverging interpretation of the first pillar of the ST/EM structures identified in chapter 2. That is, the autonomy/independence of executives/managers from financial investors, shareholders and, in some perspectives, 'stakeholders'. These relationships centre on the age-old problem of the separation of ownership (investors, shareholders) from control (executive managers), first highlighted almost a hundred years ago by Berle and Means, and debated voluminously ever since. Despite these debates the exercise of active and legitimate 'ownership' remains the dominant concern. Yet more recent analyses, summarised in the next chapter, challenge this assumption: that financial investment equates to corporate ownership.

4. UK POLITICAL PROGRAMMES FOR 'RESPONSIBLE CAPITALISM'

In view of the mainstream political parties' capacity, albeit constrained, for legislative and regulatory change, their policy recipes need examining to see what they offer towards meaningful accountability. In essence neo-liberal perspectives still dominate party leaderships' responses to the growing crisis of corporate power and legitimacy. Consequently their aspirations are mainly limited to market-based policies and social responsibility through voluntary regulation. They prefer soft regulation and voluntary reform, with hints of political intervention to enforce change only as a last resort. Fundamentals of governance are largely ignored, or regarded as a problem of active vs inactive 'ownership'. The possibility of social accountability to civil society stakeholders is barely recognised.

4.1 Cameron's Caring Conservatism

'The previous government's turbo-capitalism ... turned a blind eye to corporate excess ... we believe in responsible capitalism' (Cameron 2012). In this vision, companies have obligations but within a 'genuinely popular capitalism allowing all to share in success of the market'. Neo-liberal logic is renewed with a pledge to 'make the market work by competition, enterprise, challenging the status quo [to] build a fairer and more worth-while economy'. But shareholders need empowering and the powers of transparency activating (Cameron 2012).

Like Clinton's New Democrat platform in the USA and that tacitly endorsed and pursued by the 1997–2010 New Labour governments in the

UK (Jones 2007), Cameron (2010) talked about a quid quo pro. In 'the Deal', he argued that the Government side of the deal is to 'stand up' for business. By lauding a government committed to 'lower taxes, lighter touch regulation and the most pro-enterprise, business friendly environment that Britain has ever had', Cameron and other Conservatives have invoked basic neo-liberal market freedoms. But in return the PM wanted 'every business committing to responsible business practice', plus business commitment, creativity and innovation to help tackle: worklessness, obesity, break-up of families, break-down of communities, environmental damage, economic dislocation. Corporate responsibility is defined as: '… more than … avoiding doing harm, it's … contributing to a better society'. This trade off consists of a loosely regulated, lightly taxed corporate sphere in return for business cleaning up its own act and applying its resources to socio-environmental problems. This idea is nothing new. Unsurprisingly, for a party committed to neo-liberalism, the mix of status quo CSR and market dependence offers no prospect of structural change.

4.2   Miliband and Labour's Corporate Dualism

As Leader of the Labour Party opposition to the 2010–15 Coalition government, Ed Miliband opined that: 'Growth is built on sand if it comes from our predators and not our producers'. There may be links between business success and corporate responsibility but Miliband's recipe for corporate reform is limited by conflating business's social accountability with 'sustainable' business growth. In various other pronouncements the Labour leader divides big business into responsible 'producers' versus 'predators' and 'vested interests'. He commends Rolls Royce and its (ex) CEO John Rose, for 'creating wealth, keeping jobs in this country', as well as other 'responsible producers, such as Bombardier, BAe systems, and Sheffield Forgemaster'. These firms he contrasts with 'unchallenged energy firms [which] rip off consumers', the failed bank, RBS, and its disgraced CEO, Fred Goodwin. These are classed as 'predators' because they combine low wages and high finance, high levels of executive pay, 'fast bucks' and 'taking what they can out of the business', while 'the vast majority of businesses' have the right values, do the right thing' and 'are rooted in communities, committed to workforces' (Miliband 2011).

This is a reassuring stance for many image-conscious firms: sorting businesses that are responsible because they train and retain, from those that only financialise their business and over-pay their executives. But it hardly gets to the root of the problem. For, as the Cadbury case shows, some firms will do both; or oscillate between the two approaches. Firms that are 'responsible producers' with respect to employment may be deficient in other social/environmental respects. Both BAe Systems and Rolls Royce have, at various times, been arraigned for bribery offences. Miliband does however recognise an underlying structural problem of share ownership and capital markets. The take-over of Cadbury by Kraft (see chapter 10) is described as an outcome of the fact that 'companies in Britain are more easily bought/sold than other countries.' He suggests a 'reform of equity markets' and ending the 'quarterly reporting rule to promote a long term productive view'.

Noting that 'hedge funds and speculators swoop in for quick profit when take-overs begin', he questions whether shareholders' voting rights should 'always be the same from day one of ownership?' (Miliband 2012). In other words, voting rights should vary according to the length of time shares are owned to deter speculative investors from buying into firms solely to promote and benefit from a take-over. To make top pay awards more transparent, Labour recommended employee representation (of a single employee) on 'major companies' remuneration committees' (Umunna, 2012). These are intriguing gestures towards accountability. In the cosy world of UK corporate self-regulation such changes seem revolutionary. But in reality and even if effectively implemented, they are unlikely, by themselves, to do more than, at best, deter the most egregious sharp practices: slowing down predatory take-overs and complicating the award of executive pay hikes. The proposals ignored the possibility of fundamental restructuring of the shareholder-executive governance relationship.

4.3 Liberal Democrats' Soft Regulation of Illegitimate Powers

The Liberal Democrat Vince Cable took government ministerial responsibility for corporate affairs and regulation in the Conservative-Liberal Democrat Coalition. Consequently more detail on his party's ideas and efforts is required, as compared to the other parties. The Liberal Democrats' leader Nick Clegg depicts a wider problem of irresponsible capitalism (Clegg 2012) referring to: 'politicians in the pockets of vested interests, regulators asleep at the wheel, an unrestrained economic elite' as 'symptoms of crony capitalism'. In a critique verging on those of radical-transformationalists, Clegg (2012) argues for a redistribution of power by:

- 'greater transparency': '... force companies to open up their books, so that investors don't need an accountancy degree to decipher them';

- 'rules to stop an executive serving in one company from sitting on the pay board at another, so ... salaries ... are no longer ... decided by their mates';
- 'getting more [shareholders] to be like business owners rather than absentee landlords';
- 'introducing binding shareholder votes to curb executive pay'.

But whether votes are binding or non-binding, a majority of shareholders rarely disapprove of an executive compensation plan. Rather, if they do perceive glaring compensation abuses they exert considerable influence through informal negotiations before either type of vote (Pozen and Hamacher 2013).

In isolating the share ownership and governance problem, this vision is consistent with Miliband's practical reforms. Yet a pathway to change proved more difficult to lay down. Business Secretary Vince Cable did not implement his leader's threats. Instead, he set up the aforementioned Kay Review of 'UK equity markets and long-term decision making' (see p. 210), whose recommendations seem unlikely to achieve Clegg's 're-distribution of power'. For these remain within the voluntaristic, piece-meal, scale of reform. Reiterating conventional wisdom on the nature of the problem, Kay advocated only a wish list for directors/executives to:

- consult shareholders before making major appointments to the board;
- develop long-term trust-based relationships;
- engage in pursuit of sustainable value creation;
- invest as per prevailing ethical standards, recognising beneficiaries' specific wishes; but;
- not use their position to advance political goals or objectives unrelated to [their] beneficiaries' welfare;
- see their duties as being to all of their beneficiaries but not to savers-at-large. (UK Government/Kay 2012)

As to how these worthy behaviours were to be stimulated and overseen, Kay came up only with voluntary 'Investors Forums' for each company. In backing the review, Cable could merely support its emphasis 'on cultural change [not] ... regulation ... by trying to ensure ... the whole complex chain of equity financing ... [is] much more transparent and operates on the basis of trust' (UK Parliament 2013).

A previous Government minister, Lord Myners, told the House of Commons Select Committee on the Review, that Kay's report was based on similar principles to those of his own Report ten years previously. But, like his submission, it 'would have little impact on the sector' and the corporate response would be one 'of considerable comfort' (UK Parliament 2013, pp. 10–11). On the hope that the Kay-Cable changes would constrain executive pay a City expert opined that expectation of:

> a dramatic drop in [executive] pay levels is likely to be disappointed ... the measures should help build public confidence that executive pay decisions are subject to proper scrutiny and transparent ... shareholders will be loath to use the binding vote. (Sean O'Hare, remuneration partner at PWC, cited in Woods 2012)

So a more active share owner role, even on the single issue of executive pay, is not likely to result. In sum, voluntarism and featherweight soft regulation would remain the norm.

There are more general problems with any intensification of shareholder 'activism' in executive management. As Mayer points out, it is often companies with 'good' shareholder governance who play an active role to raise corporations' financial performance, which end up in trouble. Where such pressures have aligned executive rewards with share values, directors have become more short-term and risk-oriented to increase their own wealth. But short cuts and short-termism often, as in the bank crashes of 2007–08, lead to longer-term failure or crisis (Mayer 2012).

Dr Cable's 2013 'Transparency and Trust' paper took aim at opaque company ownership structures and improving directors' accountability. But these changes are not intended to reconnect corporations to societal values and institutions. They aim to create conditions in which: 'honest entrepreneurs and investors can do business more securely ... not be disadvantaged by those who don't play by the rules.' Proposals for banks, for example, aim to strengthen sector regulation and wider company law and to: 'consult on changing the statutory duties of directors of large banks so that they ... prioritise the "safety and stability" of the firm first over the interests of shareholders.' Despite proposing more power for regulators to disqualify directors in specific sectors and rights for courts to consider the social impacts of directors' actions, Cable echoed Miliband's good and bad apple diagnosis 'that the vast majority of companies and directors contribute productively to the economy, abide by the rules and make an enormous contribution to society ... an errant few operate in the shadows, creating complex ownership structures which only serve to deceive' (Cable 2013, pp. 12–13).

The principle here, that legal change and sectoral regulation could be aimed at individuals, might make some corporate leaders more circumspect in the wilder reaches of risk-taking. But these mainstream political remedies essentially endorse the vast majority of top manager roles and the existing functions and structures of governance.

Mainstream politics barely identifies, let alone targets, the structural sources of contemporary corporate power and irresponsibility. The elephant remains undisturbed. To tackle its more fundamental features through social accountability we need to resolve its greatest paradox: the fiction of investors as owners of the corporate business. If the ideas in mainstream politics are inadequate, what specific changes within the prevailing culture and structure of competing interests might open up corporations to stakeholder accountability? The next, and concluding, chapter includes possible change measures that could steer ST/EM firms towards a process of social re-embedding through more focussed accountability of their executive managements.

Conclusion: re-embedding through democratic ownership and governance

> The shareholder primacy theory ... clearly has some major shortcomings ...
> The problem is not so much in finding weaknesses in shareholder primacy, it is
> replacing the theory with something else. Stakeholder theory is the obvious
> answer, but it too has significant shortcomings. There is a desperate need for a
> new approach. (Keay 2010, p. 413)

INTRODUCTION

There are a wide range of ideas for structural change to the share traded/executive managed (STEM) system. They extend from renationalisation of the biggest near-monopolies, through fixed-term state, or local government licensing (cf Bentham et al. 2013) similar to pre-modern charters, and on to employee and stakeholder ownership of firms. In the background there is also the idea of transnational borrowing from more socially embedded systems, such as co-determination and stakeholder-governance in German corporations. Japan's more bureaucratic and 'insider'-oriented system has less direct appeal but its principles are admired (Wilks 2013, p. 246). All of these ideas have their merit but they need to be reality-checked against the amount of institutional and political change and struggle necessary to realise them. There are, for example, rigorously researched proposals, by Karel Williams and Manchester's CRESC centre, for licensing which would claw back economic benefits from state-supported but financialised businesses. But these would also need appraising for their relevance to stakeholder accountability and reduction of corporate over-reach into civil society (cf Bowman et al. 2014). Otherwise, such arrangements carry a risk the business system would settle into a souped-up version of the present utility licensing and regulating system; or the *dirigiste* systems of the old nationalised industries.

This chapter concentrates on the feasibility of stakeholder-owned and democratically controlled businesses as alternatives to the ST/EM model. For these reasons it excludes the communitarian-oriented favourite of 'social enterprises': defined in the UK as businesses in which the prime purpose is meeting social objectives rather than profit maximisation for shareholder gain. Previous analysis has indicated that these types of business are freed from the tyranny of shareholder value. On the other hand, they are small, variable in the extent of their social commitments, lack distinctive governance structures and – though favoured by government policies – find it hard to compete against the ST/EM corporations against whom they often bid for public sector contracts (cf Jones 2007, pp. 162–3).

Despite the claims of the traditional Marxist left, there is little evidence that the biggest economic collapse since the 1930s has generated enough political ferment for structural economic transformation in societies such as the UK. Radical proposals can also be incoherent in terms of the ends and benefits they aim to bring. Much advocacy of a de-financialised system, for example, remains penned within an economistic discourse that looks only for conventional economic gains – higher GDP, stable inflation, productive investment and employment, or a manufacturing renaissance. Such developments are important but they would not necessarily combat the structural power of corporations and the problems of over-reach described throughout this book. The preceding analysis has identified the nexus of share ownership, executive control and socio-legal autonomy of the corporation, as the key to its unaccountable powers: the institutions conventionally covered by the concept of corporate governance.

Even analysts of voluntary and civil society regulation through the ubiquitous 'stakeholder engagement' have recommended the need for 'replacing the three-tiered approach to corporate governance (AGM, board of directors, executive directors) by a structure characterised by stakeholder *participation* in decision-making long-term' (Friedman and Miles 2006, p. 260). The tasks of this concluding chapter are to assess the more significant proposals for corporate reforms, alternatives and transformation in relation to this critical nexus of power and control. This will be done by successive examination of the following structural points:

- the already criticised concept of 'ownership' which frames mainstream debates;
- general options for greater social accountability and integration;
- transformation of both business ownership and accountability including legal status;
- evolutionary change via internal reforms of critical features of conventional governance.

The first, third and fourth of these issues will cover the following: the myth of investor 'ownership', which wrongly tries to privilege a moribund shareholder 'electorate'; transformation by public ownerships and (cooperative) mutualisation; and strategic restructuring of the system of participation in executive (s)election. The second structural point above involves the ways in which ownership and governance changes could contribute to more general aims of greater social accountability and integration. A key criterion for reforms aiming to transform ownership and accountability is how and whether they abolish, redistribute or rationalise conventional ownership rights over the firm's assets. Before tackling all these issues, however, it will be useful to explore relevant meanings of democratic accountability and the ways in which the notionally democratic ST/EM governance system fails to meet these standards.

1. THE STATUS QUO: BUSINESS AS OLIGARCHIC GOVERNANCE

Big business is often compared to political regimes. Such analogical reasoning can usefully explain corporate governance (Gomez and Korine 2008; Wilks 2013, p. 19–20). Perhaps echoing Machiavelli (see p. 43 above), the seminal analyst of the ownership-control disjuncture, Adolf Berle, referred to usurping executives of 'the Modern Corporation' as the 'princes of property' (Berle et al., 1973). Wilks has already drawn an analogy between corporate and parliamentary constitutions to criticise the lack of separation of powers, the narrowness of the franchise and the rudimentary forms of independent accountability of executives (Wilks 2013, p. 220). The comparison can, though, be extended. Shareholders' rights give them roles as voters in deciding the cabinet-as-board. However, in the UK's political system voters have only one vote towards selecting both MPs and, indirectly, the Prime Minister; who, in turn, selects the cabinet. So in principle shareholders have a more direct say in choosing the corporate leaders. Yet, in principle, all members of the national community at least have a right to a vote. Corporate electorates only consist of shareholders, and in some company constitutions not even all shareholders. Yet a corporation has a broader constituency of interests and participants (cf Blair and Stout 1999). Corporate polities have un-enfranchised constituents – the non-share-owning stakeholders – and an unequal electorate as voting power corresponds to the number of shares held. There is inequality because of the likely non-correspondence between an elector's dependence on corporate executive decisions and the number of shares held: the life-savings of a pensioner with a few shares vs the small change of a global investment fund with millions of votes.

The primitive state of corporate democracy has been trenchantly criticised even by City grandees (cf Charkham 1994). Its condition is redolent of the British state of the eighteenth and early nineteenth centuries; or maybe even aspects of today's state. The corporation's many un-enfranchised 'citizens/subjects', its stakeholders, are still involved in, and affected by its rulers' activities. As in the eighteenth century however, the property franchise excludes them. Of course, like their predecessors, today's excluded groups sometimes find ways of making their voices heard, by protest actions. These may include purchasing shares to participate in corporations' AGMs (cf MacKenzie 1993; CORE 2013, p. 13–15); but their votes are rendered irrelevant by the masses of voting shares which major shareowners usually use to preserve the status quo, or their own interests. The chairman/CEO's power is more like that of the Prime Minister's in the quasi-monarchical regimes of the eighteenth century. The latter held immense authority through the fiction 'he' acted for the sovereign. In more nebulous form this principle persists to the present day. Like the top corporate executive the PM can issue instructions down to the lowest function and functionary in the state apparatus. There is a myth of sovereignty in both cases. In monarchical parliamentary regimes the executive minister derives legitimacy from both a limited electorate and from acting as the delegate of an inactive monarch. In ST/EM corporations the legitimacy of the chairman/CEO derives from posing as the representative of the dominant shareholdings; fictionalised as the 'owner'. Disputes between these categories of actor are mainly disagreements within an oligarchy.

However, authentic democracy does embed some political power in civil society. Contemporary western parliamentary democracy has well-publicised limitations (Coggan 2013; Kampfner 2009; Monbiot 2000; Palast 2004). Parliamentary government has failed to make corporate power accountable, or resist its unelected influence and lobbying. Yet there are still more intrinsic checks on the authority of the PM than there are on that of the CEO/chairman. The former can be challenged by her/his own party's MPs, the wider legislature, or even via extra-parliamentary legal initiatives from citizens. Through elections, campaigns and organising, members of civil society can influence political decisions and push for some policy changes or reforms. By contrast, corporate democracy is largely a sham. In practice, the executive of a corporation can remain unaccountable to those constitutionally able to vote it into and out of office. Executives may even affront shareholders' financial interest; for example, by awarding themselves enormous bonuses that could be re-invested into the business or disbursed as dividends. As chapter 10 showed, even then the shareholder voice is largely ineffective. If executives usually pay out generally acceptable financial returns and/or maintain share values, shareholder opposition will usually be isolated or contained.

2. THE OWNERSHIP OXYMORON: WHO OWNS WHAT?

The political analogy highlighted the nebulous status of shareholder-investors. Mainstream politicians have been anxious to turn these passive 'citizens' into responsible activists. Deputy Prime Minister Nick Clegg linked them to the prevailing orthodoxy on corporate deficiencies in his 2012 Mansion House speech: 'First, shareholders. Part of the challenge is getting more of them to behave like business owners rather than absentee landlords'(Clegg 2012). But probing the nature of shareholding more closely we can ask whether any are 'owners', or whether it is more accurate to regard them as merely creditor-lenders?

After the IPO (initial public offer), most ST/EM firms offer new shares only occasionally. So, most share purchases are merely re-circulating old financial assets. Most shareholders are not providing new investment capital but receiving economic 'rents'. New shares issues on New York's stock exchange in 1999 contributed only 7 per cent of the increase in share values. Deducting the value of company buy-backs of shares, which is usually done to increase share prices, leads to a negative value for new share issues (Kelly 2003). In reality share 'owners' are merely claimants on the financial artefacts which represent one dimension of the business. Kay showed tacit understanding of this fact when he suggested directors are stewards of the business whose duties are to the company, not to the markets for the value of its shares (UK Government/Kay 2012, p. 12). But if a company is more than its financial assets and values, why should it be primarily accountable to investors, as maintained by the Kay Review and political orthodoxy described in the previous chapter? Why not aim to embed it socially as well as financially?

Fundamental reform of the present system requires abandonment of such protective myths which conceal the contradictory nature of cor-porate ownership. The multiple shareowners of today's corporations are deemed to have, mostly, taken the place of single entrepreneur-owners, or their families.[1] For that reason convention has it that these are the true – if wayward – owners of a corporate property stewarded, on their behalf, by executive managers. To progress ideas for governance reform towards social integration, the fallacy needs rejecting for two other reasons. Firstly, as Berle and Means argued long ago, the share owners are heterogeneous and rarely act, singly or collectively, like the 'sovereign' owners of other forms of property. Secondly, the limited nature of investors' 'ownership' conveys a relatively narrow set of financial expectations and interests which cannot amount to a stewardship role.

On the first point, most shareholders are investment institutions. As the description of financial deregulation in chapter 5 showed, investors place their funds in corporate shares with similar, though not identical, expectations to those they would hold if the funds were placed in other vehicles: bonds, deposits, government securities. That is, they expect a rate of return and reasonable likelihood that at least the value of capital sum invested can be regained at some future point. Precise expectations differ, between such 'investors' and speculators – who merely seek a quick rise in the selling price via short-term movements in companies' share price, irrespective of the longer-term returns via dividends or share values. Several types of temporary shareholder, such as day trading and short-selling traders, are completely uninterested in practising 'ownership' roles. Kay distinguishes these long-term vs short term as 'investing' vs 'trading' shareholders. However, as even many long-term investors exercise no more interest in their 'property' than its financial returns, should they be regarded as 'owners' at all, or merely as another class of creditor-lenders?[2]

The second problem concerns the status of the 'property', over which shareholding is assumed to confer ownership rights. A variety of authors have pointed out that share-ownership is not equivalent to real ownership of the business represented by the shares (cf Horrigan 2008; Ireland 1999, 2010; Kay 1993; Parkinson, 1993; Thompson 2011; Williamson 2003, p. 514). Businesses are not tangible pieces of property. The shares owned are merely claims on a financial representation of a complex set of physical, cultural and human assets. There is no necessary correspondence between the assets and the shares (Ireland 2010, p. 846). Like a clapped-out car, the component parts of a firm may have second-hand market values but those values are unrelated to their functions in the productive organisation that is the corporation.

Neo-liberal theorists are notorious for reducing firms to bundles of 'transactions' (Jensen and Meckling 1976; Williamson 1990). But within that banality lies a kernel of truth. Businesses, particularly corporate businesses, are complexes of social relationships: transactional, managerial, collective and psychological – relationships, moreover, which extend throughout the organisation and beyond it. They can encompass ties with other organisations – public and private, social groups and communities. Firms cannot function without these relationships; yet these ties have no discrete financial values as commodities. Thus asking how and whether a shareholder or investor 'owns' a corporation is like asking: who owns a family?

In another guise, Kay made a similar point about the 'un-ownability' of a firm (Kay 1993). Perhaps he had that oxymoron in mind when his review concluded that directors are 'stewards of the assets and operations of ... business ... [whose] ... duties ... are to the company, not its share price'. So companies should develop 'relationships with investors', rather than with 'the market' (UK Government/Kay 2012). However, the share-holders' franchise has been largely reduced to symbolic and usually legitimating votes at AGMs – most as carefully stage-managed as any of the party congresses of Stalinist communism. Even the recent UK wave of shareholder unrest, over the litmus test of disproportionate executive salaries and bonuses, has rarely rallied sufficient majorities to prevent company boards securing their pay-outs. Section 439 of the 2008 Com-panies Act provides shareholders with a vote on annual remuneration awards but it is not binding on the board. Section 79 of the Enterprise and Regulatory Reform Act 2013 gave shareholders the right to reject the overall pay policy – but no specific right to determine the amounts awarded. Despite some embarrassing 'shareholder revolts' these have rarely achieved the critical majority needed to prevent the awards. Even after the 2013 Act, the AGMs of 19 companies gave a median level of support for pay proposals of around 97 per cent up to March 2014 (Towers Watson 2014).

The realist depiction of corporations as oligarchic polities makes more sense of these facts than wishful notions of 'stewardship'. Two questions remain:

1.   how could these relationships be governed, institutionalised and constitutionalised?
2.   If a company is more than its financial assets and values why should its stewards be accountable only to financial investors?

The second question raises the bigger requirement posed by Polanyian theory. To what extent will reformed governance structures embed the corporation socially as well as legally and financially?

3.   SOCIAL GOVERNANCE OPTIONS

'Corporate governance' concerns the institutions through which decisions and sovereignty are exercised. Although his focus is on the USA, David

Korten's useful identification of the objectives of a radical transformation of ST/EM-type corporations draws attention to the centrality of governance. His proposals are as follows:

1. curb undue corporate influence in political and legislative systems;
2. reduce privileges in corporations' status as legal persons;
3. balance corporations' international trade and investment with national controls;
4. eliminate the 'corporate welfare' in the manifold subsidies for big business;
5. curb/replace irresponsible investment and speculation by the financial system;
6. external licensing of over-mighty businesses;
7. economic democracy through stakeholder ownership and participation (Korten 2001, p. 266 et seq).

On the first of these points, corporate influence in political and legislative systems should certainly be an urgent priority. Some curbs need not depend on complex regulatory changes to corporate law and regulation of the actual business. Cleansing of political and state governmental procedures – for example, the revolving door between civil service and business appointments and corporate colonisation of the policy making process – could be achieved without a reforming government having to expend too much political capital. A more rigorous register of lobbyists and more transparent disclosure of their communications with ministers and civil servants would be cheap and effective (Cave and Rowell 2014, pp. 276–8; Rowbottom 2010; Unlock Democracy 2014), though other reforms would be needed to make this significantly effective (cf Transparency International 2012). A more structural change would be to resurrect the sectoral business representation which operated under the discredited, but more open, 'tripartite corporatism' of post-WWII social democracy.

Korten's second point, corporate privileges from the status of legal personhood, is a less obvious concern in the UK than in the USA. Legal decisions in both countries have accorded corporations the status of legal personhood. However, in the USA conventions and case law have led to them also being regarded – for legal purposes – as 'natural persons'. Because of the USA's written constitution this status has accrued more pronounced rights to corporations: to engage in political activities and to have constitutional rights such as 'free speech'. In the UK, the absence of such codified rights has left corporate status some way short of equality, although recommendations to restrict corporations' use of Human Rights legislation and increase their liabilities for prosecution over cases like corporate manslaughter should be pursued anyway. Corporate person-hood is broader in the UK than in, say, Germany, in areas such as criminal liability. However curbing corporate 'freedoms' would not necessarily require wholesale revision of the legal status of corporate personhood; as would be required for the reforms urged by radicals for the USA (Sarginger 2011).

National controls over corporations' international trade and investment would require a level of political strength and cross-national support – through the EU for example – that is difficult to envisage at present. However, focussed reforms of corporate accountability via Korten's points 6 and 7, could make it possible to avoid the kinds of irresponsible behaviour which corporate banks practised in, and even since, the financial meltdown of 2008. The complexity of financial processes and regulation would still need dedicated regulation. Despite analogous proposals from the Manchester CRESC group, support for Korten's fourth aim, licensing, is still several moves away from reaching UK political agendas. In addition to the CRESC group ideas (cf Bowman et al. 2014), cited above, oversight by a corporate dispute resolution and monitoring body was proposed by the UK's CORE coalition of NGOs, in the consultation phase of the bill which became the 2006 Companies Act (CORE 2011). If established, such a body would have had powers of sanction over corporations which did not comply with codes of best practice. Otherwise, CORE's campaign was confined to greater accuracy and detailed information transparency – for example via company reports.

Nevertheless, external licensing and the structural changes implicit in Korten's final proposal – stakeholder ownership and participation – could be a means of developing both financial and political responsibility; as well as making corporations more accountable for subsidies, 'welfare' and other advantages received from the public purse. A government committed to changing the criteria by which the privatised utilities are currently regulated could begin to toughen the social conditions under which they are expected to operate in order to sell public goods and services, as shown by the exceptional Glas Cymru case in the next section. As for economic democracy through stakeholder ownership and participation, Korten is unspecific about the precise forms in which these principles should be introduced within organisations:

> to own a share in an enterprise, you should be a worker, a member of the community, a customer, or a supplier of that enterprise so that there is more

than a purely financial connection. Once we have that principle in mind, we can begin to put in place measures that move us in that direction. (Korten 2000)

The next section explores the wider feasibility of some existing ownership forms which embody such principles of stakeholder ownership.

The UK may lack serious attempts at democratising corporate governance, but it already possesses a variety of alternative corporate forms to the ST/EM model, which could move business closer to its social roots. There are traditional Industrial and Provident Societies; the Company Limited by Guarantee; the Company Limited by Shares; and, a more recent innovation, Community Interest Companies. But it would need substantial governmental pressure and incentives, plus intensive battles with a range of domestic and overseas financial investors, to convert existing ST/EM firms to one or more of these models. As far as board governance and ownership are concerned, there are two other potential reform precedents for British-based corporations. One is changes to the shareholder-executive relationship, for which significant adaptations have developed in Sweden – which has the same single-tier board structure as the UK. The other is an extension of the mutual/cooperative model, practised in a handful of British companies, such as the John Lewis Partnership; and in principle – although not as constitutional reality – by the former Welsh Water corporation, described below.

4. STAKEHOLDER OWNERSHIP – RESTRUCTURING AS MUTUALISM?

With the prolongation of the recessionary crisis and a Conservative-Liberal Democrat coalition government in the UK, suddenly mutualism became everybody's favourite panacea. Some advocates of associative self-governance support the creation of community 'mutuals' to run public services instead of privatised firms; see, for example, Mayo and Moore (2001) and the debate in the New Economic Foundation's 'The Mutual State'. From Conservative councils to number 10 policy units, mutuals like the John Lewis Partnership (JLP) are praised and mooted as organisational models to bridge the gulf between 'inefficient' public sector forms and exploitative private sector firms (Clegg 2012). In 2013 the UK Treasury announced tax breaks to encourage more of the much vaunted 'John Lewis model' of employee-owned companies; though sceptics warned that conventional firms could exploit these by using bogus employee share plans (*Telegraph* 2013; Butler 2013). On the other hand, if judged on accountability criteria, social performance, and social embeddedness, the record of the 'Partnership', the enterprise owning John Lewis and Waitrose stores, is as weak as some other cooperatives.

Theoretically 'owned' by its employees or 'partners', the John Lewis group has avoided the volatility of capital and share markets, financing most of its expansion from corporate bonds and retained profits, growing prudently and successfully in the last 20 years. The group rewards and invests well in staff and returns to them up to 60 per cent of profits in 2014 (Yeomans 2014) as pay-related bonuses. Yet it still contracts out some functions, such as cleaning, to low-paid workers with no such rights. Moreover, the distribution of its ownership and internal democratic procedures are more limited than the Mondragon cooperative form described in chapter 7. John Lewis partners do have votes but these votes are not, as in Mondragon, attached to individual employees' shareholdings. Partner/employees are members of the Trust which has the collective, legal ownership of the companies in the Partnership (John Lewis Partnership 2014). As far as governance is concerned, top executives have a fairly free hand to run the company.

The twelve-person Board which runs business affairs, consists of five directors from the employee-elected Partnership Council, and five appointed by the chairman, with automatic Board places for the chairman and deputy chairman. The organisation is effectively controlled by its executives. As one labour lawyer put it:

> … it is very difficult to discern who it is that has responsibility for the appointment and removal of directors of the trustee company. In a sense that is almost … a self-serving oligarchy in that it's the board of directors on the company that appear on the panel that appoint and remove the directors and the shareholders of the trust. (HR Magazine 2010)

Executives are also rewarded with salaries comparable to those of some other executives in the retail sector – albeit without share bonuses, as the Partnership has no shares to trade. JLP's focus on profitability and membership/managerial rewards is reflected in the limited extent of its social embedding. The Partnership has a relatively mediocre record in terms of its environmental, social performance and stakeholder involvement (Ethical Consumer 2011). In 2006, in accordance with practices in other plcs (which is, confusingly, its commercial status) the JLP Board decided to appoint two non-executive directors (Martin 2006). These externals have tended to have directorial backgrounds in other large businesses and quangos (John Lewis Partnership 2014).

Though not without its own governance problems, the largest UK mutual, the Co-operative ('Co-op') Group tends to perform much better on 'ethical' criteria. In theory the Co-op Group has wider stakeholder membership than John Lewis. It is a membership organisation in which customers and local members' groups can elect the representatives who, ultimately, choose the main board. However, size and success risk contamination by the financialisation syndrome of the plc sector. Thus the UK's Co-operative Bank, which had a promising ethical base and close ownership ties to the rest of the co-op movement came to grief in 2013 after failing to digest the debts of the Britannia Building Society, which it had taken over. Lacking a deeper form of social embedding and accountability, its executives became increasingly close to conventional forms of executive performance and financial risk. In 2013 massive debts allowed the hedge fund lenders to force Co-op Bank to convert some of its investor loans into shares and to become a listed London Stock Exchange corporation. In the process it took on ST/EM executives, instead of mutual veterans, to head its board: indicating that its future status will not be different to the shareholder-value orientation of conventional financial corporations (Collinson 2013). At the time of writing there is a serious exercise to convert the whole Co-op Group (which part-owns the Co-operative Bank) to a conventional corporate hierarchy, headed by executive managers. Clearly, entanglement in the strategies and mores of the ST/EM business world – which attends high levels of commercial 'success' – tends to push large-scale mutuals towards ST/EM, rather than cooperative democracy. So, in some respects JLP could be said to have become more viable than the Co-op enterprises. Despite limited internal accountability it has, effectively, quarantined itself from the disruptive effects of financialised ownership and obligations.

However, a more significant example of this principle is the former Welsh Water utility Glas Cymru, which, as a 'company limited by guarantee' has no shareholders. Constitutionally, it is not a mutual but neither is it financed and 'owned' by share holdings. Indeed its operational status and governance is remarkably similar to that of JLP. During a brief period as a share-financed plc, following privatisation of the water industry in 1989, disembedding was intensified by a functional re-organisation (divisionalisation) of its operations, which wrenched its management and user relations further from real local roots (Page 2003). Then in 2000, Welsh Water was converted into Glas Cymru, like many UK charities, a 'company limited by guarantee' without external shareholders. It is officially controlled by a group of 50 members who appoint the executives who manage the business with full operational autonomy.

Members receive no business-related remuneration and since the conversion to a 'not-for profit' enterprise Glas Cymru has turned in financial performances to match JLP. It has reduced the average household water bill in Wales by 6 per cent in real terms, and invested almost £5 billion in plant, facilities and improvements – around £4,000 for every household. It also has the highest credit rating in the water industry, enabling funding requirements to be met from long-term bonds at low cost (Bakker 2003).These more socially rewarding outcomes derive from the 'turn to the local' in the status and governance of the company.

The operating arm, Dyr Cymu, carries out most operations via outsourced contracts. So it is difficult to assess the quality of its employment relations. However, in terms of ownership and strategic control, Glas Cymru is a sort of para-mutual: limited in its internal membership democracy but partially re-embedded, albeit indirectly, in the larger Welsh community. This nesting takes two forms – a notional accountability to the devolved Welsh Assembly government – and the composition of the council of Members, who are the constitutional equivalent of shareholders in a plc (Page and Bakker 2005, p. 53). In practice the Welsh Assembly has no direct powers over the policies of Glas Cymru (Rebecca Television 2014). Members are supposedly drawn from the general population in Wales and the English border areas it serves. The constitution requires that they be 'reflective of the range of customer and other stakeholder interests' (Glas Cymru Cyfyngedic 2009, p. 6). Losing its shareholder financial obligations has meant that Dyr Cymu can focus on consumer and environmental welfare; unlike the financialised priorities of the STEM firms and other privatised utilities, such as the water companies whose shortcomings were analysed in chapter 4. (Every 1 per cent increase in the cost of finance adds 5 per cent to water bills.)

Ofwat the water regulator ruled out the proposed conversion of Kelda, the Yorkshire area water company into a mutual, allegedly because of doubts over the proposed structure's commercial 'efficiency' (Page and Bakker 2005, p. 53); but the Glas Cymru success suggests otherwise. There are no in-principle reasons why the state could not convert failing or delinquent utilities in the regulated sectors into such para-mutuals. Their accountability and embeddedness would, however, need to be taken further than the Glas Cymru model. The latter's executives still seem to have disproportionate powers relative to the Members – they select the 'independent' (that is, external) directors who form the majority of the board and have been criticised for adopting pay award procedures and amounts comparable to ST/EM corporations (Rebecca Television 2014). However, the equivalents to Glas's Members Council could be recruited from and elected by designated stakeholder bodies, such as employees, local government, trade unions and community groups, rather than being individually picked by Glas's existing Council. Care would be needed to ensure new para-mutualised utilities did not reprise some of the accountability problems which plagued the nationalised industries described in chapter 3. Such a conversion would also need significant changes to the existing regulatory bodies, so that they oversaw social and democratic performance, in addition to the present financial ones. With sympathetic presence in national government, such forces might even make it possible to extend such a system to a wider range of FTSE corporations.

A persistent conundrum in the history of British cooperatives is why they, and the broader category of mutual, have been concentrated in general retail; as with the Co-op Group, and services, such as leisure and finance (Mutuo 2013). One reason is the extent of their democratic decision-making compared to Mondragon (MCC) type cooperatives. Specifically, each enterprise within the federal MCC comprises: a General Assembly, in which all members make binding decisions on major policy issues, such as membership rules, production targets, budgets and distribution of profits, and the monthly Governing Council. This body is equivalent to a board of directors. Its members are elected but receive no extra remuneration. The Governing Council reviews and co-ordinates operations. The executive management have full administrative control, but are appointed by the Governing Council, whose meetings they attend but without voting rights. There is also a Social Council which has been described as MCC's trade union equivalent – dealing with wages, conditions and safety – and representing its views on these to the Governing Council. Reasons why this more democratic structure, with its institutional links to the wider Basque community, has been bypassed in UK developments would require a separate study. Plausible reasons include the UK bias to consumer co-ops with passive memberships, the financial failure of industrial worker co-ops in the economic maelstrom of the 1970s and the absence, or break-up, of a coherent egalitarian ideology akin to the radical communitarianism of Mondragon's inspirational founder José María Arizmendiarrieta (Mathews 1999, pp. 36–41, 111–2, 169–70). It is this combination of democratic decision-making with member ownership, *and* community integration that makes MCC a yardstick for the ownership-only or 'democracy-lite' cases that predominate amongst UK mutuals.

5. GOVERNANCE CHANGE THROUGH INTERNAL REFORMS

The above examples show the potential and pitfalls of swapping one cast-iron business model, the ST/EM corporation, for other elaborate mutual ones. If there is only limited embedding and democratic account-ability, plus influence from corporate business practices, mutuals will not escape the gravitational pull of a still-dominant financialised corporate environment. Accountability to civil society interest and stakeholder priority over shareowners will not be achieved without a high-risk political assault on the corporate sector. Such a programme, or one for mutuals organised on similar democratic ownership lines to MCC, would have to be more ambitious than any since the 1940s nationalisation programme. So what of internal changes to corporate governance instead of, or as a complement to, mutualisation?

Wholesale conversion to the German/Rhenish model, of economic stakeholder participation in its governance and the subordination of executive mangers to their oversight, seems improbable. For this to happen there would probably be a need for parallel changes in the industrial relations and financial sectors; and, to complete the replication, in education and training systems too. Simply focussing on Germany's corporate governance system could provide a point of leverage but opposition to the introduction of two-tier boards, with executives under stakeholder direction, would almost certainly provoke tooth-and-nail resistance from the business and financial establishment. The size of the likely opposition is indicated by the failure of the last major attempt at structural reform in this direction described in chapter 3: the 1974–79 Labour Government's proposals for modest forms of industrial democ-racy on corporate boards (Phillips 2011). Moreover, that attempt occurred when big business was in a much weaker political position than it is today when, as chapter 1 showed, business representation has penetrated most of the political establishment.

Any contemporary policy to democratise and re-embed ST/EM corpor-ations must begin with available entry points and chinks in the corporate armour. Specifically: the acknowledged discrepancy between ambiguous shareholder 'ownership' and the power of directors; plus the bridgeheads established by civil society organisations in bringing executives into forms of CSR dialogue and 'stakeholder engagement'. Without some reforms to corporations' governance status, 'external' alternatives – such as mutuals and industrial districts – risk being out-competed or neutral-ised by the sheer financial muscle of the corporate sector, or by cut-price competition from abroad. The 2010–15 Coalition Government initiatives for 'investor forums' referred to in the previous chapter, and the directives on executive pay committees, show recognition of part of the problem. However, these remain largely within the existing structure of executive managers' hegemony and are unlikely to be effective. Nevertheless, these directions of reform do offer a starting point from which to move towards the more socially embedded company structures of countries such as Germany. For example, Colin Mayer has concluded a sophisticated analysis of the failings of corporate governance in the UK's jurisdiction with proposals for a variant on the Rhenish two-tier system. He points out the advantages of separating operational management from strategic guidance by installing boards of trustees as a supervisory organ (Mayer 2013). But who would risk promoting such a transformation and why would executives or investors accept it?

A different point of leverage could come from going beyond the 'investor forums' and widening of membership of executive pay committees that Kay and Cable advocated. As currently proposed, these changes would only be voluntary: clearly a means of avoiding forms of statutory regulation, which business has and will always resist vehemently (cf the Bullock attempts described in chapter 3 and by Phillips 2012). A solution may be to link the idea of investor forums to the influential pressures for corporate reform that CSOs promoted during consultations on the proposals which became the UK 2006 Companies Act: a huge patchwork of pragmatic but timid reforms described as 'the longest piece of legislation ever to have been passed by Parliament' (Collinson et al. 2011, p. 46). Here is another point of political leverage to increase accountability. Under the 2006 Act, for the first time, directors have to consider social and environmental implications of their firms' activities: not only financial outcomes but 'environmental matters' (including corporate impacts on environment), employees, 'social and community issues' and risks throughout company supply chains. Additionally, company reports 'must show how directors are performing in their duties, including ... environmental and social issues' (Chivers 2007, p. 23). There is, however, no external or internal policing apart from shareholders' scrutiny. The lacuna here, as previous chapters have shown, is that shareholders have only limited interest and influence in securing compliance with these duties.

5.1 Borrowing from Sweden?

In one key respect, the Swedish business system is more like the UK's than that of Germany. Companies have single unitary boards rather than the Rhenish two-tier boards. However, unlike the mere guidelines to that effect in the UK, Swedish executives are prohibited from chairing the board – that role is restricted to non-executive directors. In the UK non-executive directors have little independent influence. City codes recommend that they chair boards, but it does not prevent executives from doing so. In any case, as chapter 11 showed, 'independents' are, in effect, chosen by the executives and many are members of the executive 'club', being executive directors at other ST/EM firms.

By contrast, Sweden's non-executive directors are under no obligation to appoint any executives to the board. In 2009 the CEO was not on the board of 55 per cent of Swedish stock exchange companies (Henrekson and Jakobsson 2011, p. 19). In 2005 the Swedish Code of Corporate Governance was further reformed. It prescribed independent appointment committees which deliberately exclude the chair of the board of directors from their deliberations. Representation on the committees is weighted towards size of shareholdings but, increasingly, places are reserved for representatives of small shareholders. The outcomes of these changes have been recognised as providing more transparency in board appointments and limitation of favouritism and nepotism. Despite an apparent bias towards the largest investors in these provisions, in practice members are obliged to act in all shareholders' interests, not only that of a sponsoring owner(s). Thus minorities have a larger say in the direction of the company and the power of a controlling shareholder is restricted (Tomorrow's Company 2010a).

If similar requirements were introduced into UK companies, civil society groups – social and environmental NGOS, for example – could, as some are already advocating, take small shareholdings and press for representation on the nomination committees. This might change little in the short term but it would be difficult for advocates of active investors' ownership to oppose. It could provide a rallying point and arena for 'patient', long-term investors, ethical funds and CSOs to form alliances to change the composition of the board; especially if it could be agreed that candidates should have ethical and social credentials, in addition to their commercial skills. Over time, this influence over selection could increase the number of board appointees sympathetic to paying more heed to social and environmental responsibilities and deepening the participation of CSOs in relevant policy areas. In Sweden it has been recognised that the democratising influence of Swedish nomination committees extends beyond the legal remit of appointments to such wider issues.

5.2   Independent Control with Civil Society Representation

As diverse critics have argued, it is time to restore and expand democratic controls over corporate executives. Firstly, the franchise needs to be widened. If, as has been argued above, the financial investors are: (1) only one stakeholder, and (2) cannot be regarded as owners of the company as a piece of property, then other stakeholders must be given some sort of vote. The industrial democracy proposals for UK business in the 1970s largely foundered because they could be portrayed as ceding influence to a special interest, trade unions, which, at that time, were easily portrayed as too irresponsible. But the stability and economic success of the German system of co-determination shows that workers voting for board representatives does not impede business efficiency and appears actually to enhance it. Moreover, workers are only one category of stakeholder. What I have called 'corporate over-reach' now affects many other sectors of society. If the case for worker franchise and representation rests mainly on their vulnerability to the effects of business decisions, the same principle now applies to other categories such as consumers, local and overseas communities, families and the environment. Clearly these external interests cannot be given direct voting rights, or organise elected representatives in the same manner as the circumscribed numbers of workers. However, there are now multiple civil society organisations that do act for these other types of stakeholder. Properly accredited for their legitimacy and representativeness, these charities, NGOs and campaign groups could, by the purchase or award of shareholdings, secure an electoral voice.

It might be objected that control or influence over executive appointments is a relatively trivial change given the scale of transformation recommended. But a small step can be crucial if it leads in the right direction. Given the array of potential hostile political power and opinion it would be sensible to plan for a long campaign rather than an illusory Big Bang. Adoption of Sweden's shareholder committees system could be a useful initial channel of influence, provided the largest investor-shareholders made space for small investors and stakeholder groups. It would be unrealistic to dictate a road map for such a process. That would be for representatives and committees in each company.

There is no guarantee that shareholder representatives would not try to prioritise their own financial interests ahead of stakeholder groups; but these would have to be debated and decided democratically within the committees, rather than in clandestine or private meetings between executive managers and the most influential shareholders, as presently happens. There would need to be measures to ensure that committed or 'patient' shareholders' views are not displaced by the votes of speculative investors. As Ed Miliband has indicated, there might need to be a qualifying period of up to twelve months before stock ownership gave entitlement to voting rights. Over time the composition of boards could be transformed: improving corporations' strategic priorities and, for example, the presence of under-represented sectors such as women. Potentially wasteful take-overs, mergers and closures could be discouraged. It is difficult to see the symptomatic Kraft-Cadbury tragi-comedy described in chapter 10, being automatically approved under the system proposed here. The same principle that underlies John Lewis/Mondragon mutuals – of directors as stewards of a broader community of interests – ought to be pursued and intensified by a system of non-executive checks on the managements. Such a system would, hopefully, include a wider circle of stakeholders' interests than worker representatives, important though those could be. With control of appointments there could be the opportunity for shareholder/stakeholder representatives to choose suitably experienced figures from CSOs and other NGOs as independent directors, instead of the conventional executives from other companies that are mainly chosen now.

Standard objections to wider stakeholder participation in corporate governance focus on the complications and delays entailed. Opposition could be expected to allege stakeholder involvement would 'prolong and complicate decision making' and face 'agency' problems of ensuring participants' representativeness to the potentially diverse stakeholder groups: 'Turning the modern corporation into a microcosm of national politics would be an extraordinarily inefficient way to achieve "socially responsible" corporate behaviour' (Reich 1998, p. 14). But, as practical experience shows, such objections are superficial and often inaccurate (cf Erdal 2011). Detailed decision-making proposed above, as in the German two-tier system, would remain with the executive board members. The main focus of the shareholder-stakeholder committees would be with selecting executives and determining their remuneration. Further evolution towards de facto, two-tier status might become feasible as executives and representation committees learnt to work together. Reich's other objection has also been superseded in the last decade and a half. Executives in many firms are quite prepared to accept the legitimacy of stakeholder organisations and consult with them. But, faced with opposition on only one front, managers are usually not prepared to follow recommendations from the latter – preferring to follow the business consensus. The oligarchy knows best.

CONCLUSION: REVERSING OVER-REACH

Corporate over-reach is now a critical, perhaps the most critical, social and political, as well as economic problem in societies dominated by the

Anglo-Saxon business corporation. Allied with neo-liberal ideology and globalised economic transactions, it is the principal institutional support for a type of market system that undermines human welfare and destroys the natural environment. It is propelling a culture and practice of consumerism that is both ecologically wasteful and corrosive of human relationships: 'using people and loving things' instead of using things and loving people. Behind a façade of democratic rights – market choices and shareholder democracy – corporate agents are destructive of substantive democracy, subverting society's democratic institutions for their own ends and denying citizenship rights to those subjected to arbitrary corporate and executive powers.

Self-regulation through CSR has improved some specific corporate malpractices but increasingly it has become a means of humanising the face of corporate power and concealing the irresponsible logic of the corporate system. It has begun some re-engagement with civil society but social re-embedding of business power through forms of democratic accountability – expected in the rest of society – is not on its agenda. Mainstream politicians' projections of a 'responsible capitalism' will not be realised by CSR and self-regulation. Instead it has been argued here that social embedding could begin along four lines of policy:

1. seeding of new industrial districts by local government and other relevant agencies;
2. promotion of owner-member democratic mutuals along Mondragon lines;
3. adaptation of some existing regulatory systems, such as those for the privatised utilities to promote and develop para-mutuals, like more socially accountable versions of Glas Cymru;
4. small but strategic reforms to corporations' internal democracy: appointment of executives by combined committees of representatives of long-term shareholders and social stakeholders.

The problem with establishment politicians' nostrums for reform is the adherence to the neo-liberal presumptions of executive autonomy, as accredited agents, from financial and other forms of stakeholding and the myths of ownership by sovereign principals.

Yet the economically significant counter-examples show that this model is not inevitable or superior. Indeed Germany and Japan, and the industrial district and cooperative models in other countries, show how social embedding can be combined with economic efficiency. Worse, the ST/EM model allowed the recklessness of financial corporations to cause the present international recession, and the myopia of the general corporate lobby to prolong it. In its present form this model seems incapable of generating meaningful economic welfare or acting as a basis for social and environmental justice. But the prevailing socio-political conditions in countries like the UK suggest that the corporate juggernaut will not easily be halted or replaced. Not least because the wider the scale of proposed reforms, the easier it would be for business's economic power and political influence to deflect them. The example of the financialisation, destabilisation and incorporation (sic) of the UK Co-operative Bank shows how difficult it would be to establish systemic alternatives to the ST/EM model.

The guiding principle of reform should be that corporations now undertake so many different economic, social and political roles, that they cannot be regarded as simply blocs of financial property. It also follows that, as shareholders are not discrete owners of these organisations, their rights must be redefined in relation to the latent rights of the main stakeholders – a principle which is explicitly if selectively recognised in German corporate governance. Rather than pitting these financial and 'stakeholding' interests against each other, it would be more productive if they were allied together for corporate reform. One way of achieving this redefinition would be to remove disruptive investors altogether from the ownership and control of the business, either through *de facto* or *de jure* cooperative models. The success of the re-organised Welsh Water plc shows that this could be done by buying up shares (or converting them into bonds) for several of the privatised energy and water utilities, with the government appointing stakeholder representatives as directors.

For the majority of stock exchange companies it would be more appropriate to legislate for an application of the principles in the Swedish system of shareholder controls described above. This adaptation should not try to replicate exactly the same institutionally and historically rooted arrangements as in Sweden, but adapt the underlying principles. By so doing non-speculative shareholders as well as stakeholder groups such as unions, local government, community groups and NGOs could, via small shareholdings, agree their representation on the appointments and remuneration committees for the executive managers of their corporations. They could decide the details of their own constitutions with, for example, election procedures and reserved places for specific classes of stakeholder. Gradually, the character of the company boards could reflect more accurately the interests and values of long-term shareholders and stakeholder groups. Many shareholders would, themselves, be corporate funds. As a result, these would also be subject to the same influences on their appointment processes. So over time there would be a general re-embedding of business policies and ethics within those of civil society.

Of course, these reforms would not be uncontested and they would not be realisable without some elaboration in company law. They would not affect powerful 'offshore' multinationals. However many MNCs are registered in London for compelling commercial reasons. Conformity with the above reforms could be seen as a relatively small price to pay for those advantages. Moreover, the changes proposed, or some similar re-enfranchisement of economic and social stakeholders, would have outstanding advantages. They could minimise disruptive changes to the practical management of companies, create a broad coalition for change, and be potentially popular in the electoral arena; as well as making a small step towards bringing democracy and social accountability back to the corporate future.

This book has given numerous instances of the dysfunctional economic, political, social and environmental consequences stemming from the present dominant company model. These are now so serious that academics, policy makers and campaigners cannot afford not to press for reforms in the UK, despite patent and formidable political and international obstacles. Change in current political discourse from the blatant oxymoron of 'responsible capitalism' would be a useful start. Entertaining a wild tiger in a tea shop would be a more productive project than social responsibility under financialised capitalism. '*Accountable capitalism*' should be the theme. The original corporations began life as small, democratic ventures started by ordinary citizens. Uncontrolled, their direction has regressed into a reprise of pre-modern government run by an oligarchy. Capitalism's central contemporary institution, the corporation, must be made more accountable to its employees, customers, supply chain workers, environmental causes and communities. Otherwise it will continue to devour its hosts and helpers ... in responsible ways, of course.

NOTES

1. In fact, as Ireland has shown, multiple-share owner businesses predominated at least as far back as the eighteenth century (Ireland 1999).
2. For detailed analyses of these points, see Ireland (1999, 2010) and Thompson (2011).

References

Abou-Seada, M., Cooper, C., Ghaffari, F., Jones, R., Kyriacou, O. and Simpson, M. (2007), 'The Economic Consequences of Accounting in the English and Welsh Water Industry: a Non-Shareholder Perspective', ECAS CONFERENCE Paper 10. www.st-andrews.ac.uk/business/ecas/7/papers/ECAS-Cooper-et-al.pdf

Ackers, P. (2010), 'Democracy in the Workplace – the Bullock Report Revisited', in *History and Policy*. http://www.historyandpolicy.org/forums/union/meeting_090710.html

Adams, C.A. (2004), 'The Ethical, Social and Environmental Reporting–Performance Portrayal Gap', *Accounting, Auditing & Accountability Journal*, 17 (5), 731–57.

Alchian, A.A. and Demsetz, H. (1972), 'Production, Information Costs, and Economic Organization', *American Economic Review*, 62 (5), 777–795.

Althusser, L. (1990), *For Marx*, London: Verso.

Anderson, G.M. and Tollison, R.D. (1983), 'The Myth of the Corporation as a Creation of the State', *International Review of Law and Economics*, 3, 107–20.

Aoki, M., Jackson, G. and Miyajima, H. (eds) (2008), *Corporate Governance in Japan: Institutional Change and Organizational Diversity*, Oxford and New York: Oxford University Press.

Aranya, T. (2014), 'The Influence of Pressure Groups on Financial Statements in Britain', in T.A. Lee and R.H. Parker (eds), *Evolution of Corporate Financial Reporting* (RLE Accounting), Abingdon: Routledge.

Arjoon, S. (2005), 'A Communitarian Model of Business: A Natural-Law Perspective', *Journal of Markets and Morality*, 8 (2), 455–478.

Armstrong, P., Glynn, P. and Harrison, J. (1984), *Capitalism since World War II*, London: Fontana.

Arnold D. and Bowie, N. (2003), 'Sweatshops and Respect for Persons', *Business Ethics Quarterly*, 13 (2), 221– 42.

Arnold, P.J. and Cheng, R.H. (2000), 'The Economic Consequences of Regulatory Accounting in the Nuclear Power Industry: Market Reaction to Plant Abandonments', *Journal of Accounting and Public Policy*, 19 (2), 161–87.

Arrighi, G. (2007), *Adam Smith in Beijing: Lineages of the Twenty-First Century*, London: Verso.

Arrighi, G. (2009), 'The Winding Paths of Capital', Interview by David Harvey, *New Left Review*, 56, March–April.

Arts, B. (2002), '"Green Alliances" of Business and NGOs. New Styles of Self-regulation or "Dead-End Roads"?', *Corporate Social Responsibility and Environmental Management*, 9 (1), 26–36.

Bagnasco, A. (1977), *Tre Italie: la problematica territoriale dello sviluppo italiano*, Bologna: Il Mulino.

Bakan, J. (2004), *The Corporation: the Pathological Pursuit of Profit and Power*, New York: Free Press.

Bakker, K.J. (2003), 'From Public to Private to … Mutual? Restructuring Water Supply Governance in England and Wales', *Geoforum*, 34 (3), 359–74.

Banerjee, S.B. (2007), *Corporate Social Responsibility: The Good, the Bad and the Ugly*, Cheltenham: Edward Elgar.

Banerjee, S.B. (2009), *Corporate Social Responsibility: The Good, the Bad and the Ugly*, Cheltenham, UK and Northampton, MA, USA: Edward Elgar (paperback).

Barber, W.J. (1967), *A History of Economic Thought*, Harmondsworth: Penguin.

Barclay's Entertainment Sponsorships (2014). http://group.barclays.com/about-barclays/sponsorship/our-entertainment-sponsorships

Barnes, R. (2012), 'Super PAC Mania', *Columbia Law School Magazine*. http://www.law.columbia.edu/magazine/621141/super-pac-mania

Bartle, I. (ed.) (2003), *The UK Model of Utility Regulation*, CRI Proceedings 31, University of Bath, September.

Bartle, I. and Vass, P. (2007), 'Independent Economic Regulation: A Reassessment of its Role in Sustainable Development', *Utilities Policy*, 15 (4), 261–9.

Batstone, E. and Davies, P. (1976), *Industrial Democracy: European Experience*, London: HMSO.

BBC News (2010), 'Ex-BP boss Lord Browne to Lead Whitehall Reform', 30 June. http://www.bbc.co.uk/news/10467532

BBC News (2014), 'Former BP Executive Manzoni Gets Top Whitehall Job', 3 October. http://www.bbc.co.uk/news/uk-politics-29472921

Beacham, A. (1950), 'Nationalization in Theory and Practice', *Quarterly Journal of Economics*, 64 (4), 550–58.

Beattie, A. (2002), 'Change of attitude needed on corporate crime says Lindsey', *Financial Times*, London Edition, 15 July.

Beccatini, G. (1979), 'Dal settore industriale al distretto industriale', *Rivista de economia e politica industriale*, 5 (1), 7–21.

Becker, G.S. (2002), 'Enron Was Mostly Right about One Thing: Deregulation', *Business Week*, 18 March, 3774, 26.

Beckert, J. (2008), 'The Road Not Taken: The Moral Dimension and the New Economic Sociology', Discussion Forum, *Socio-Economic Review*, 6 (1), 135–173.

Bell, D. (1961), *The End of Ideology: On the Exhaustion of Political Ideas in the Fifties*, New York: Collier-Macmillan.

Bellandi, M. and Di Tommaso, M.R. (2005), 'The Case of Specialized Towns in Guangdong, China', *European Planning Studies*, 13 (5), 707– 29.

Bello, W. (n.d.), 'Building an Iron Cage. The Bretton Woods Institutions, the WTO, and the South'. http://www.thirdworldtraveler.com/Globalization/Building_Iron_Cage_VFTS.html

Bendell, J. (2004), *Barricades and Boardrooms. A Contemporary History of the Corporate Accountability Movement*, Technology, Business and Society Programme Paper Number 13, Geneva: United Nations Research Institute for Social Development.

Bentham, J., Bowman, A., de la Cuesta, M., Engelen, E., Erturk, I., Folkman, P., Froud, J., Johal, S., Law, J., Leaver, A., Moran, M. and Williams, K. (2013), 'Manifesto for the Foundational Economy', *CRESC Working Paper* 131, Manchester: Centre for Research on Socio-Cultural Change.

Berger, P. (1988), 'An East Asian Development Model', in P. Berger and M. Hsiao Hsin-huang (eds), *In Search of an East Asian Development Model*, New Brunswick, NJ: Transaction Books, pp. 3–11.

Berggren, C. and Nomura, M. (1997), *The Resilience of Corporate Japan: New Competitive Strategies and Personnel Practices*, London: Paul Chapman.

Berle, A.A. and Means, G.C. (1932/1968), *The Modern Corporation and Private Property*, New York: Harcourt, Brace & World.

Berle, A.A., Ascoli, M., Jacobs, T.B. and Berle, B.B. (1973), *Navigating the Rapids, 1918–1971: From the Papers of Adolf A. Berle*, New York: Harcourt Brace Jovanovich.

BITC (Business in the Community) (2007), *Who We Are*, available at: http://www.bitc.org.uk/who_we_are/index.html (accessed 11 April 2007).

BITC (2014), *Annual Report 2013*. http://www.bitc.org.uk/our-resources/report/annual-report-and-accounts-2013

Bjuggren, P.-O. and Mueller, D.C. (eds) (2009), *The Modern Firm, Corporate Governance and Investment (New Perspectives on the Modern Corporation)*, Cheltenham, UK and Northampton, MA, USA: Edward Elgar.

Black Triangle Campaign (2011), 'New Evidence of Corporate Giant's Influence on Welfare Reform'. http://blacktrianglecampaign.org/2011/11/23/new-evidence-of-corporate-giant%E2%80%99s-influence-on-welfare-reform/

Blaiklock, T.M.(2013), 'The Thames Tideway Tunnel; an Engineer's "Pipe-Dream"? The Case for an Alternative'. http://cleanthames.org/wp-content/uploads/2013/09/The-Thames-Tideway-Tunnel-an-Engineer%E2%80%99s-%E2%80%9CPipe-Dream%E2%80%9D.pdf

Blair, M.M. and Stout, L.A. (1999), 'A Team Production Theory of Corporate Law', *Virginia Law Review*, 85 (2), 248–328.

Block, F. (2003), 'Karl Polanyi and the writing of "The Great Transformation"', *Theory and Society*, 32 (3), 275–306.

Block, F. and Evans, P. (2005), 'The State and the Economy', in N. Smelser and R. Swedberg (eds), *The Handbook of Economic Sociology*, 2nd edition, Princeton: Russell Sage, pp. 505–26.

Bondy K., Matten, D. and Moon, J. (2004),'The Adoption of Voluntary Codes of Conduct in MNCs: A Three-Country Comparative Study', *Business and Society Review*, 109 (4), 449–77.

Boseley, S. (2013), 'Sugar Intake Must Come Down, says WHO – But UK Likely to Resist', *Guardian*, 7 September.

Bowman, A., Froud, J., Johal, S., Moran, M. and Williams, K. (2013), 'Business Elites and Undemocracy in Britain: A Work in Progress', *CRESC Working Paper* 125, University of Manchester: Centre for Research in Socio-Cultural Change.

Bowman, A., Froud, J., Johal, S., Law, J., Leaver, A., Moran, M. and Williams, K. (2014), *The End of the Experiment? From Competition to the Foundational Economy*, Manchester Capitalism, Manchester: Manchester University Press.

Boyd, R. (1987), 'Government-industry Relations in Japan: Access, Communication, and Competitive Collaboration', in S. Wilks and M. Wright, *Comparative Government-Industry Relations*, Oxford: Clarendon Press; New York: Oxford University Press.

Brammer, S. and Millington, A. (2003),'The Evolution of Corporate Charitable Contributions in the UK between 1989 and 1999: Industry Structure and Stakeholder Influences', *Business Ethics: A European Review*, 12 (3), 216–28.

Brammer, S. and Pavelin, S. (2005), 'Corporate Community Giving in the UK and USA', *Journal of Business Ethics*, 56 (4), 15–26.

Bräuninger, D. (2013), 'Privatisation in the Euro Area: Differing Attitudes towards Public Assets', *DB Research Briefing*, Deutsche Bank. http://www.dbresearch.com/PROD/DBR_INTERNET_EN-PROD/PROD0000000000318583/Privatisation+in+the+euro+area%3A++Differing+attitudes+towards+public+assets.pdf

Brejning, J. (2012), *Corporate Social Responsibility and the Welfare State: The Historical and Contemporary Role of CSR in the Mixed Economy of Welfare*, Farnham: Ashgate.

Brittan, S. (1975), 'Towards a Corporate State?', *Encounter*, June, 58–63.

Broad, R. and J. Cavanagh (1999), 'The Corporate Accountability Movement: Lessons and Opportunities', *The Fletcher Forum of World Affairs*, 23 (2), 151–69.

Brooke, S. (1991), 'Atlantic Crossing? American Views of Capitalism and British Socialist Thought 1932–1962', *Twentieth Century British History*, 2 (2), 107–36.

Browne, J. and Nuttall, R. (2013), 'Beyond Corporate Social Responsibility: Integrated External Engagement', McKinsey & Co. http://www.mckinsey.com/insights/strategy/beyond_corporate_social_responsibility_integrated_external_engagement

Brusco, S. (1982), 'The Emilian Model: Productive Decentralisation and Social Integration', *Cambridge Journal of Economics*, 6 (2), 167–84.

Bulmer, M. (1978), *Mining and Social Change: Durham County in the Twentieth Century*, London: Croom Helm.

Burge, A. (2012), *Co-operation. A Post-war Opportunity Missed? A Welsh Perspective*, Bevan Foundation. http://www.cooperatives-wales.coop/wp-content/uploads/2013/08/bevan-fdn-co-operatives-a-post-war-opportunity-missed.pdf

Burgess, C. (2013), 'Dividends – a sacred cow for UK utilities?'. http://www.premierfunds.co.uk/media/7986/dividends-fund-insight-2013-march.pdf

Burnham, J. (1941), *The Managerial Revolution*, Harmondsworth: Penguin.

Butler, S. (2013), 'Treasury Keen to Boost John Lewis-style Ownership', *The Guardian*, Wednesday 3 July.

Butler, D.E. and Kavanagh, D. (1988), *The British General Election of 1987*, London: MacMillan.

Byoir et al. (1970), *Industry-Wide Program for Recycling Glass Containers: Summary and Supplemental Report*, Glass Containers Manufacturers Institute and Carl Byoir & Associates, Inc.

Cable, V. (2013), 'Transparency & Trust', Discussion Paper, Responsible Capitalism conference, London: Reform.

Calder, G. (2004), 'Communitarianism and New Labour', *Social Issues*, 2 (1), Special Issue: 'Futures of Community'.

Calder, F. and Culverwell, M. (2005), *Following up the World Summit on Sustainable Development Commitments on Corporate Social Responsibility: Options for Action by Governments*, Final Report, London: Sustainable Development Programme, Chatham House.

Callaghan, J. (2000), 'Rise and Fall of the Alternative Economic Strategy: From Internationalisation of Capital to Globalisation', *Contemporary British History*, 14 (30), 105–30.

Callon, M. (1998) 'Introduction: The Embeddedness of Economic Markets in Economics', in M. Callon (ed.), *The Laws of the Markets*, Oxford and Keele: Blackwell and the Sociological Review, pp. 1–57.

Cameron, D. (2010), Speech to the Business in the Community Leadership Summit, London, 2 December. https://www.gov.uk/government/speeches/business-in-the-community-speech

Cameron, D. (2012), Speech on Moral Capitalism, New Zealand House, London, 19 January. http://www.newstatesman.com/uk-politics/2012/01/economy-capitalism-market

Campbell, D., Moore, G. and Metzger, M. (2002), 'Corporate Philanthropy in the UK 1985–2000: Some Empirical Findings', *Journal of Business Ethics*, 39 (1), 29–41.

Cannon, T. (1992), *Corporate Responsibility*, London: Pitman.

Carroll, A. (1999), 'Corporate Social Responsibility, Evolution of a Concept', *Business and Society*, 38 (3).

Cassis, Y. (2007), 'Big Business', in G. Jones and J. Zeitlin (eds), *The Oxford Handbook of Business History*, Oxford: Oxford University Press, pp. 171–93.

Cave, T. and Rowell, A. (2014), *A Quiet Word: Lobbying, Crony Capitalism and Broken Politics in Britain*, London: Bodley Head.

CECP (2013), *Giving in Numbers*, 2013 edition. http://cecp.co/research/benchmarking-reports/giving-in-numbers.html

CERES (Coalition for Environmentally Responsible Economies) (1991), *Valdez Principles* (7 September 1989), reprinted in 'The Text of the Valdez Principles', *National Law Journal*, 2 September.

Chandler, A.D. (1977), *The Visible Hand*, Cambridge, MA: Harvard University Press.

Chandler, A.D. (1990), *Strategy and Structure*, Cambridge, MA: MIT Press.

Channon, D.F. (1973), *The Strategy and Structure of British Enterprise*, London: Macmillan.

Charkham, J.P. (1990), 'Are Shares Just Commodities?', in *Creative Tension*, London: National Association of Pension Funds, pp. 34–42.

Charkham, J.P. (1994), 'A Larger Role for Institutional Investors', in Dimsdale, N. and Prevezer, M. (eds), *Capital Markets and Corporate Governance*, Oxford: Clarendon Press.

Charkham, J. (1995), *Keeping Good Company: A Study of Corporate Governance in Five Countries*, Oxford: Oxford University Press.

Chennells, L. (1997), *Labour's Windfall Levy*, London: Institute for Fiscal Studies.

Chicago Tribune (1988), 'Philip Morris Offers $11 Billion for Kraft October 18'. http://articles.chicagotribune.com/1988-10-18/news/8802 080264_1_hamish-maxwell-kraft-philip-morris-cos

Chivers, D. (2007), *The Companies Act 2006: Directors' Duties Guidance*, Corporate Responsibility (CORE) Coalition. http://corporate-responsibility.org/wp-content/uploads/2013/11/directors_guidance_final.pdf

Chopra, S. and Meindl, P. (2007), *Supply Chain Management: Strategy, Planning and Operation* (3rd edn), New Jersey: Pearson Prentice Hall.

Christerson, B. (1997), 'The Third China? Emerging Industrial Districts in Rural China', *International Journal of Urban and Regional Research*, 21 (4), 569–88.

Clamp, C.A. (2010), 'Social Entrepreneurship in the Mondragon Co-operative Corporation and the Challenges of Successful Replication', *Journal of Entrepreneurship*, 19 (2), 149–177.

Clapp, J. and Dauvergne, P. (2005), *Paths to a Green World: The Political Economy of the Global Environment*, Cambridge: MIT Press.

Clarke, T. and Pitelis, C. (1993), *Political Economy of Privatization*, London: Routledge.

Clegg, N. (2012), Deputy Prime Minister's Speech at Mansion House. https://www.gov.uk/government/speeches/deputy-prime-ministers-speech-at-mansion-house

Clement, M. (2010), 'Local Notables and the City Council Revisited, the Use of Partnerships in the Regeneration of Bristol', *Social and Public Policy Review*, 4 (1), 34–49.

Clifton, R. and Maughan, E. (1999), *The Future of Brands: Twenty-Five Visions*, London: Macmillan.

Clifton, J., Comin, F. and Díaz-Fuentes, D. (2004), 'Nationalisation, Denationalisation and European Integration: Changing Contexts, Unfinished Debates', *Enterprises et Histoire*, N° 37.

Coase, R.H. (1937), 'The Nature of the Firm', *Economica*, November, 4 (16), 386–405.

Coates, K. and Topham, T. (eds) (1970), *Workers' Control*, London: Panther (previously published as *Industrial Democracy in Great Britain*, MacGibbon and Kee, 1968).

Coates, A., Farnsworth, K. and Zulauf, M. (2000), 'Social Exclusion and Inclusion: Partnerships for Neighbourhood Regeneration in London', *South Bank University Occasional Paper*, London.

Coen, D. (2005), 'Business–Regulatory Relations: Learning to Play Regulatory Games in European Utility Markets', *Governance*, 18 (3), 375–98.

Coen, D. (2009), 'Business Lobbying in the European Union', in David Coen and Jeremy Richardson, *Lobbying the European Union: Institutions, Actors, and Issues*, Oxford: Oxford University Press.

Coen, D. and Thatcher, M. (2005), 'The New Governance of Markets and Non-Majoritarian Regulators', *Governance*, 18 (3), 329–46.

Coggan, P. (2013), *The Last Vote: The Threats to Western Democracy*, London: Penguin.

Colgan, J. (2005), *The Promise and Peril of International Trade*, Peterborough, Ontario: Broadview Press.

Collinson, P. (2013), 'Co-ops Blow to Mutuality', *Guardian*, 22 June.

Collison, D., Cobb, G., Power, D. and Stevenson, L. (2009), 'FTSE4Good: Exploring Its Implications for Corporate Conduct', *Accounting, Auditing & Accountability Journal*, 22 (1), 35–58.

Collison, D., Cross, S., Ferguson, J., Power, D. and Stevenson, L. (2011), *Shareholder Primacy in UK Corporate Law: An Exploration of the Rationale and Evidence*, ACCA, vol. 125.

Collison, D., Cross, S., Ferguson, J., Power, D. and Stevenson, L. (2014), 'Financialization and Company Law: A Study of the UK Company Law Review', *Critical Perspectives on Accounting*, 25 (1), 5–16.

Commission of the European Community (1992), *Report of the Committee of Independent Tax Experts on Company Taxation*, Brussels: Office for Official Publications of the European Communities.

Conley, J.G. (2006), *Environmentalism Contained: A History of Corporate Responses to the New Environmentalism*, PhD thesis, Princeton University.

Consalvo, M. (2003), 'Cyber-Slaying Media Fans: Code, Digital Poaching, and Corporate Control of the Internet', *Journal of Communication Inquiry*, 27 (1), 67–86.

Conyon, M.J. and Peck, S.I. (1998), 'Board Control Remuneration Committees, and Top-management Compensation', *Academy of Management Journal*, 41, 146–57.

Cooper, A. (2003), 'The Changing Sponsorship Scene', *Admap*, November, issue 444.

CORE and the Trade Justice Movement (2013), *Act Now! A Campaigner's Guide to the Companies Act* http://corporate-responsibility.org/wp-content/uploads/2013/11/campaigners_guide_final.pdf

CORE (2014), 'About CORE'. http://corporate-responsibility.org/about-core/

Cornforth, C. (1995), 'Patterns of Cooperative Management: Beyond the Degeneration Thesis', *Economic and Industrial Democracy*, 16, 487–523.

Corporate Watch (n.d.). http://www.corporatewatch.org.uk/?lid=2695

Corporate Watch (2010), 'Corporate Penetration of Government', in *Corporate Influence on Government: An Introduction*. http://corporate-rule.co.uk/drupal/node/44

Coulson, A. (1997), 'Business Partnerships and Regional Government', *Policy and Politics*, 25 (1), 31–9.

Crompton, G. (2009), 'Lines of Division: Railway Unions and Labour 1900–1939', in M. Worley (ed.), *Foundations of the British Labour Party*, Farnham: Ashgate.

Crooks, E. (2010), 'National Grid Shares Fall 7% after Rights Issue', *Financial Times*, 20 May. http://www.ft.com/cms/s/0/88c5ef0a-63d7-11df-ad7c-00144feab49a.html#axzz2mdLT3YI7

Crosland, C.A.R. (1956), *The Future of Socialism*, London: Jonathan Cape.

Crouch, C. (2008), 'What Will Follow the Demise of Privatised Keynesianism?', *Political Quarterly*, 79 (4), 476–87.

Cumbers, A. (2012), *Reclaiming Public Ownership: Making Space for Economic Democracy*, London: Zed.

Cumbers, A. and McMaster, R. (2012), 'Revisiting Public Ownership: Knowledge, Democracy and Participation in Economic Decision Making', *Review of Radical Political Economics,* 44 (3), 358–373.

Cuthbert, J. (2012), *Excessive Profits and Overcharging, Multiple Errors in the UK's Model for Setting Utility Prices*, Biggar, Scotland: The Jimmy Reid Foundation. http://reidfoundation.org/wp-content/uploads/2012/08/Excessive-Profits-and-Overcharging.pdf

Cuthbert, J.R. and Cuthbert, M. (2007), 'Fundamental Flaws in the Current Cost Regulatory Capital Value Method of Utility Pricing', *Fraser of Allander Institute Quarterly Economic Commentary*, 31 (3).

Cutler, A.C. (2006), 'Transnational Business Civilization, Corporations, and the Privatization of Global Governance', in May, C.T. (ed.), *Global Corporate Power*, *International Political Economy Yearbook* Boulder, Colorado: Lynne Reinner.

Cutler, A., Hindess, B., Hirst, P.Q. and Hussain, A. (1978), *Marx's Capital and Capitalism Today: Volume 2*, London: Routledge Kegan Paul.

Dahlberg, L. (2004), 'Cyber-Publics and the Corporate Control of Online Communication', *New Perspectives on Critical Communication Studies*, 11 (3), 77–92.

Dahler-Larsen, P. (1994), 'Corporate Culture and Morality: Durkheim-Inspired Reflections on the Limits of Corporate Culture', *Journal of Management Studies*, 31 (1), 1–18.

Daily Mail (2012), 4 March. 'The firm that hijacked the NHS: MoS investigation reveals extraordinary extent of international management consultant's role in Lansley's health reforms', http://www.dailymail.

co.uk/news/article-2099940/NHS-health-reforms-Extent-McKinsey–
Companys-role-Andrew-Lansleys-proposals.html#ixzz2b5yzMrdo

Dan, S., Jilke, S., Pollitt, S., van Delft, R., Van de Walle, S. and van
Thiel, S. (2012), *Effects of Privatization and Agencification on Citizens
and Citizenship: an International Comparison*, Coordinating for Cohesion in the Public Sector of the Future Project. http://www.eerste
kamer.nl/id/vj45ispjadtf/document_extern/effects_of_privatization_and/
f=/vj45it0u3itp.pdf

Davey, E. (2013), 'Opening up the Energy Markets', Speech to Energy
UK, UK Government: Department of Energy and Climate Change.
https://www.gov.uk/government/speeches/opening-up-the-energy-markets-
speech-to-energy-uk

Davidson, C. (2012), 'USW Report: A "Union Model" Plans to Bring
Worker Coops to the Ohio Valley', Thursday 26 April. http://
carldavidson.blogspot.co.uk/2012/04/usw-report-union-model-plans-to-
bring.html

Davies, P. (1978), 'Bullock Report and Employee Participation in Corporate Planning in the UK', *Journal of International Law*, 1 (3), Art. 3.

Davies, G. and Wilkinson, S. (2014), 'Shareholder Activism in the UK',
ICLG, *Mergers and Acquisitions*, pp. 7–11. http://www.herbertsmith
freehills.com/-/media/Files/PDFs/2014/ICLG%202014%20-%20Share
holder%20Activism%20in%20the%20UK.PDF

Davis, K. (1967), 'Understanding the Social Responsibility Puzzle',
Business Horizons, 10 (4), 45–50.

Day, G. (2006), *Community and Everyday Life*, London: Routledge.

de Roover, R. (1946), 'The Decline of the Medici Bank', *Journal of
Economic History*, 7 (1), 69–82.

De Tocqueville, A. (1946), *Democracy in America*, Vol. II, New York:
Alfred A. Knopf.

Deakin, S. and Slinger, G. (1997), 'Hostile Takeovers, Corporate Law,
and the Theory of the Firm', *Journal of Law and Society*, 24, 124–51.

Democracy Unlimited (2014), *The Hidden History of Corporate Rule*.
http://www.duhc.org/page/the-hidden-history-of

Democratic Underground (2009), *Ending Corporate Governance*. http://
www.democraticunderground.com/discuss/duboard.php?az=view_all&
address=104x773912.

Demos (2012), *Election Spending 2012: Post-Election Analysis of Federal
Election Committee Data*. http://www.demos.org/publication/election-
spending-2012-post-election-analysis-federal-election-commission-data

Demsetz, H. (1988), 'The Theory of the Firm Revisited', *Journal of Law,
Economics and Organization*, 4 (1), 141–61.

Dennis, N., Henriques, F. and Slaughter, C. (1969), *Coal is Our Life: An Analysis of a Yorkshire Mining Community*, London: Tavistock Publications.

Deorn, B. and Wilks, S. (2007), 'Accountability and Multi-level Governance in UK Regulation', in P. Vass (ed.), *Regulatory Review 2006/ 2007*, 10th Anniversary Edition, School of Management, University of Bath.

Department of Energy and Climate Change (2013), 12 November. https://www.gov.uk/government/speeches/opening-up-the-energy-markets-speech-to-energy-uk

Department of the Environment (1980), *Anglo-American Conference on Community Involvement*, AT81/162, Kew: The National Archives.

Devall, B. (1988), *Simple in Means, Rich in Ends: Practicing Deep Ecology*, Layton, Utah: Peregrine Smith.

Dhir, A.A. (2012), 'Shareholder Engagement in the Embedded Business Corporation: Investment Activism, Human Rights, and TWAIL Discourse', *Business Ethics Quarterly*, 22 (1), 99–118.

DNV-GL (2007), *Taking Care of the Environment Takes Care of Business (Kraft, ISO 14001)*. http://www.dnvba.com/UK/information-resources/meet-our-customers/Pages/Taking-care-of-the-environment.aspx

Doane, D. (2005), 'Beyond Corporate Social Responsibility: Minnows, Mammoths and Markets', *Futures*, 37, 215–229.

Doherty, B. (1999), 'Paving the Way: The Rise of Direct Action against Road-building and the Changing Character of British Environmentalism', *Political Studies*, 47(2), 275–91.

Doig, A. and Wilson, J. (1998), 'The Effectiveness of Codes of Conduct', *Business Ethics: A European Review*, 7 (3), 140–9.

Domhoff, G.W. (1990), *The Power Elite and the State: How Policy Is Made in America*, Hawthorne, NY: Aldine de Gruyter.

Dore, R. (2006), 'Japan's Shareholder Revolution', *CentrePiece Magazine*, 11 (3), 22–24.

Dore, R. (2008), 'Financialization of the Global Economy', *Industrial and Corporate Change*, 17 (6), 1097 –1112.

Doyle, T. and McEachern, D. (2001), *Environment and Politics*, London: Routledge.

Driver, S. and Martell, L. (1997), 'New Labour: Culture and Community', in L. Ray and A. Sayer (eds), *Culture and Economy after the Cultural Turn*, London: Sage.

Drucker, P.F. (1993/2002), *The Ecological Vision: Reflections on the American Condition*, New Brunswick, NJ: Transaction Publishers.

Dunkley, J. (2009), 'Utilities Face Rights Issues and Cuts', *The Telegraph*, November. http://www.telegraph.co.uk/finance/newsbysector/utilities/6630912/Utilities-face-rights-issues-and-cuts.html

Dunning, J.H. and Archer, H. (1987), 'The Eclectic Paradigm and the Growth of UK Multinational Enterprise 1870–1983', *Business and Economic History*, 16.

Dyson, K. (1983), 'The Cultural, Ideological and Structural Context', in K. Dyson and S. Wilks (eds), *Industrial Crisis: A Comparative Study of the State and Industry*, New York: St. Martin's Press.

The Economist (2005), Special Report: 'The Good Company. The movement for corporate social responsibility has won the battle of ideas. That is a pity, argues Clive Crook', 20 January.

Economist (2011), 'Defending Jobs', 12 September.

Eichengreen, B. (1994), 'The British Economy between the Wars 1', in R. Floud and P. Johnson (eds), *The Economic History of Britain Since 1700, vol. 2*, Cambridge: CUP.

Elbaum, W. and Lazonick, B. (1986), 'An Institutional Perspective on British Decline', in W. Elbaum and B. Lazonick, *The Decline of the British Economy*, Oxford: Oxford University Press.

Elkington, J. (1997), *Cannibals with Forks: The Triple Bottom Line of Twenty-First Century Business*, Oxford: Capstone.

Elliot, L. (2014), 'Andy Haldane questions British model of corporate governance', *Guardian*, 29 May.

Epstein, K. (2005), 'How Today's Corporate Donors Want Their Gifts to Help the Bottom-line', *Stanford Social Innovation Review*, 3 (2), 20–27.

Erdal, D. (2011), *Beyond the Corporation, Humanity Working*, London: The Bodley Head.

Ernst and Young (2014), 'OECD Releases Common Reporting Standard', *Global Tax Alert*, 20 February. http://www.ey.com/GL/en/Services/Tax/International-Tax/Alert–OECD-releases-Common-Reporting-Standard

Erturk, I., Froud, J., Johal, S. and Williams, K. (2005), 'Pay for Performance or Pay as Social Division', *Competition and Change*, 9 (1), 49–74.

Erturk, I., Froud, J., Johal, S., Leaver, A. and Williams, K. (2006), 'Agency, the Romance of Management Pay and an Alternative Explanation', CRESC, University of Manchester.

Ethical Consumer (2011), 'Ethical Product Guide to Supermarkets, from Ethical Consumer'. http://www.ethicalconsumer.org/buyersguides/food/supermarkets.aspx

Etzioni, A. (1988), *The Moral Dimension, Toward a New Economics*, New York: The Free Press.

Etzioni, A. (1993), *The Spirit of Community*, New York: Crown.

Etzioni, A. (2001), 'Enron Type Scandals Will End When Penalties Fit Crimes', *USA Today*, 26 March, p. 16A, reproduced at: http://www.gwu.edu/~ccps/etzioni/B383.html

Etzioni, A. (2008), 'The Moral Dimension Revisited', *Socio-Economic Review*, 6(1), 168–173.

Etzioni, A. (2014), 'The Corporation as a Community: Stakeholder Theory', in M. Boylan (ed.), *Business Ethics*, Wiley-Blackwell.

Evans, R. (2013a), 'Experts Warn of Threat to Utility Shares Income', *Telegraph*, 4 May.

Evans, S. (2013b), 'German Call to "Undo" Energy Privatisation amid Berlin Vote', BBC News. http://www.bbc.co.uk/news/world-europe-24763311

Fama, E. (1980), 'Agency Problems and the Theory of the Firm', *Journal of Political Economy*, 88, 288–307.

Fama, E. and Jensen, M. (1983), 'Separation of Ownership and Control', *Journal of Law and Economics*, 26, 301–25.

Farnsworth, K. and Holden, C. (2006), 'The Business-Social Policy Nexus: Corporate Power and Corporate Inputs into Social Policy', *Journal of Social Policy*, 35 (3), 473–94.

Feigenbaum, H., Henig, J.R. and Hamnett, C. (1998), *Shrinking the State: The Political Underpinnings of Privatization*, Cambridge: Cambridge University Press.

Ferner, A. (1988), *Governments, Managers and Industrial Relations*, Oxford: Basil Blackwell.

Financial Reporting Council (2012), *The UK Corporate Governance Code*, London: FRC. https://frc.org.uk/Our-Work/Publications/Corporate-Governance/UK-Corporate-Governance-Code-September-2012.pdf

Financial Times/Rahul Jacob (2012), 'HK Tycoon Sees Land of Opportunity in Hong Kong', 10 August.

Fleischer, A., Hazard, G.C. Jr. and Klipper, M.Z. (2002) *Board Games: The Changing Shape of Corporate Power*, Washington: Beard Books.

Fligstein, N. (1990), *The Transformation of Corporate Control*, Cambridge, MA: Harvard University Press.

Fligstein, N. (1993), *The Transformation of Corporate Control*, Cambridge: Harvard University Press.

Florio, M. (2004), *The Great Divestiture. The Welfare Impact of British Privatizations 1979–1997*, Cambridge, MA: MIT Press.

Floud, R. and McCloskey, D.N. (1992), *The Economic History of Britain Since 1700: 1939–1992*, Cambridge: Cambridge University Press.

FoEI (Friends of the Earth International) (2002), *Towards Binding Corporate Accountability*, FoEI position paper for the WSSD, London: Friends of the Earth International. www.foe.co.uk/pubsinfo/briefings/html/20020730133722

Forbes (2013), 'United Health Exec to Run Embattled British National Health Service', 20 April. http://www.forbes.com/sites/brucejapsen/2013/10/24/unitedhealth-exec-to-run-embattled-british-national-health-service/

Forester, T. (1979), 'Neutralising the Industrial Strategy', in Coates, K. (ed.), *What Went Wrong? Explaining the Fall of the Labour Government*, London: Spokesman.

Forrester, S. (1990), *Business and Environmental Groups: A Natural Partnership?*, London: Directory of Social Change.

Forum for the Future and PIRC (2002), *Sustainability Pays*, Manchester: Co-operative Insurance Society.

Frankental, P. (2006), 'Why Socially Responsible Investment Requires More Risk for Companies Rather Than More Engagement', in R. Sullivan and C. Mackenzie (eds), *Responsible Investment*, Sheffield: Greenleaf.

Franks, J. and C. Mayer (1997), 'Corporate Ownership and Control in the UK, Germany, and France', in D.H. Chew (ed.), *Studies in International Corporate Finance and Governance Systems: A Comparison of the U.S., Japan, and Europe*, New York: Oxford University Press.

Fraser, N. (2013), 'A Triple Movement? Parsing the Politics of Crisis after Polanyi', *New Left Review*, 81, May–June.

Freeman, E. (1984/2010), *Strategic Management: A Stakeholder Approach*, Cambridge: Cambridge University Press.

Freeman, R.E. and Reed, D.L. (1983), 'Stockholders and Stakeholders: A New Perspective on Corporate Governance', *California Management Review*, 25 (3), 88–106.

Friedman, M. (1970), 'The Social Responsibility of Business is to Increase its Profits', *The New York Times Magazine*, 13 September.

Friedman, A.L. and Miles, S. (2006), *Stakeholders: Theory and Practice*, Oxford: Oxford University Press.

Froud, J., Haslam, C., Johal, S. and Williams, K. (2000a), 'Shareholder Value and Financialization: Consultancy Promises, Management Moves', *Economy and Society*, 29 (1), 80–110.

Froud, J., Haslam, C., Johal, S. and Williams, K. (2000b), 'Restructuring for Shareholder Value and its Implications for Labour', *Cambridge Journal of Economics*, 24 (6), 771–97.

Froud, J., Johal, S., Leaver, A. and Williams, K. (2006), *Financialization and Strategy. Narrative and Numbers*, London: Routledge.

Froud, J., Leaver, A., Tampubolon, G. and Williams, K. (2008), 'Everything for Sale: How Non-Executive Directors Make a Difference', in M. Savage and K. Williams (eds), *Remembering Elites*, Oxford: Blackwell.

Fuchs, D. (2007), *Business Power in Global Governance*, London: Lynne Rienner.

Fukuyama, F. (1995), *Trust: The Social Virtues and the Creation of Prosperity*, New York: Simon and Schuster/Free Press.

Galaskiewicz, J. (1991), 'Making Corporate Actors Accountable: Institution-Building in Minneapolis-St. Paul', in W.W. Powell and P.J. DiMaggio (eds), *The New Institutionalism in Organizational Analysis*, Chicago: University of Chicago Press.

Garside, W.R. (2002), *British Unemployment 1919–1939: A Study in Public Policy*, Cambridge: CUP.

Garside, J. (2014), 'Europe Gears Up to Fight Back against Giant US Beasts of the Internet', *Guardian*, 12 September.

Gedajlovic, E. and Shapiro, D. (2002), 'Ownership and Firm Profitability in Japan', *Academy of Management Journal*, 45 (3), 575–585.

Gedajlovic, E., Yoshikawa, T. and Hashimoto, M. (2004), 'Ownership Structure, Investment Behaviour and Firm Performance in Japanese Manufacturing Industries', *Organization Studies*, 25 (8), 1363–92.

GEO (2012), 'Mondragon and the US Steelworkers Partnership: an Update. Grassroots Economic Organizing', *GEO Newsletter*, II (6). http://geo.coop/node/584; USW 2012: http://www.usw.org/media_center/releases_advisories?id=0523

Gillies, C.S. (1992), *Beyond Charitable Giving: Board Policy and Community Involvement*, London: Business in the Community.

Glas Cymru Cyfyngedic (2009), *Policy and Procedure for the Selection and Appointment of the Members of Glas Cymru Cyfyngedig*. http://www.dwrcymru.com/_library/leaflets_publications_english/application_forms/glas_cymru_membership/Policy_Procedures_Members_Appointment_2009.pdf

Glasbergen, P. and Groenenberg, R. (2001), 'Environmental Partnerships in Sustainable Energy', *European Environment*, 11, 1–13.

Global Policy (n.d), 'Comparison of Corporations with GDP of Countries'. https://www.globalpolicy.org/component/content/article/150-general/50950-comparison-of-the-worlds-25-largest-corporations-with-the-gdp-of-selected-countries.html

Global Water Intelligence (2010), 'Water Companies Count the Cost of the FD', 11 (2), February.

Gold, M. (2010), 'From Prisons to Palaces: New Forms of Work Organization in the UK in the 1970s', Paper to the International Labour Process Conference, Rutgers, New York.

Goldfarb, Z.A. (2006), 'Once a Friend and Ally, Now a Distant Memory', *The Washington Post*, 26 May. http://www.washingtonpost.com/wpdyn/content/article/2006/05/25/AR2006052501958.html

Goldstein, A. (2012), 'Revenge of the Managers, Labor Cost-Cutting and the Paradoxical Resurgence of Managerialism in the Shareholder Value Era, 1984 to 2001', *American Sociological Review*, 77 (2), 268–294.

Gomez, P.-Y. and Korine, H. (2008), *Entrepreneurs and Democracy: A Political Theory of Corporate Governance*, Cambridge: Cambridge University Press.

Goodpaster, K.E. and Matthews, J.B. Jr. (1982), 'Can a Corporation Have a Conscience?', *Harvard Business Review*, January.

Gordon, D.M. (1996), 'Conflict and Cooperation: An Empirical Glimpse of the Imperatives of Efficiency and Redistribution', *Politics and Society*, 24 (4), 433–56.

Gosling, P. (2008), *The Rise of the 'Public Services Industry'*, report for UNISON. http://psigeneralsecretary.typepad.com/files/rise-of-the-public-services-industry.pdf

Gospel, H., Pendleton, A., and Vitols, S. (eds) (2014), *Financialization, New Investment Funds, and Labour: An International Comparison*, Oxford: Oxford University Press.

Graeber, D. (2011), *Debt: The First 5,000 Years*, New York: Melville House Publishing.

Granovetter, M. (1985), 'Economic Action and Social Structure: The Problem of Embeddedness', *American Journal of Sociology*, 91 (3), 481–510.

Gray, R., Kouhy, R. and Lavers, S. (1995), 'Corporate Social and Environmental Reporting: A Review of the Literature and a Longitudinal Study of UK Disclosure', *Accounting, Auditing & Accountability Journal*, 8 (2), 47–77.

Greenleaf, W.H. (2003), *The British Political Tradition: The Rise of Collectivism*, London: Routledge.

Greider, W. (1996) '"Citizen" GE', in J. Mander and E. Goldsmith (eds), *The Case Against the Global Economy and for a Turn Toward the Local*, San Francisco: Sierra Club.

Groom, B. (2013), 'They all want to be German now', *Financial Times*, 15 April.

Groves, J. (2014), 'Harnessing the Private Sector Makes Sense for UK's Education System', *British Politics and Policy*, London School of Economics Blogs. http://blogs.lse.ac.uk/politicsandpolicy/archives/21014

Guardian (2011), 'UK Broadband Market Share. Who is Dominating on the Broadband Market, and Who is Providing the Fastest Connections', Thursday 28 July.

Guardian (2012), 'Datablog, Autumn statement 2012, Government spending by department, 2011–12'. http://www.theguardian.com/news/datablog/2012/dec/04/government-spending-department-2011–12

Guardian (2012a), 'Hands Poised for £820 Million Swoop on UK's Biggest Care Homes Business', 30 April.

Guardian (2012b), 'Apple's Investment Manager Wrestles with $120bn Problem', 26 October.

Guardian (2013), 'Doggone? Shareholder Urges Greyhound Sale', 12 December.

Guardian (2013a), 'How Private Care Firms Have Got Away with Breaking the Law on Pay', 13 June.

Guardian (2013b), 'CBI Boss: Business Must Rebuild Reputation', 1 November.

Guardian (2014), 'Manchester United to Announce Record Revenues of around £420m', 9 September.

Guglielmo, C. (2013), 'Apple's Supplier Labor Practices In China Scrutinized After Foxconn, Pegatron Reviews', *Forbes*, 12 December. http://www.forbes.com/sites/connieguglielmo/2013/12/12/apples-labor-practices-in-china-scrutinized-after-foxconn-pegatron-reviewed/

Habermas J. (1981), New Social Movements, *Telos*. 49, 33-7.

Haigh, M. and J. Hazelton (2004), 'Financial markets: a tool for social responsibility?', *Journal of Business Ethics*, 52 (1), 59–71.

Hale, A. and Wills, J. (2007), 'Women Working Worldwide: Transnational Networks, Corporate Social Responsibility and Action Research', *Global Networks*, 7 (4), 453–76.

Hall, J. and O'Malley, T. (2009), *Corporate Governance and the Effectiveness of Shareholder Engagement*, JCA Group for the Financial Reporting Council. http://www.jcagroup.net/perch/resources/publications/corporate-governance-shareholder-engagement.pdf

Hall P.A. and Soskice, D. (2001), *Varieties of Capitalism: The Institutional Foundations of Comparative Advantage*, Oxford: Oxford University Press.

Hamann, R., and Acutt, N. (2003), 'How Should Civil Society (and the Government) Respond to "Corporate Social Responsibility"?, A Critique of Business Motivations and the Potential for Partnerships', *Development Southern Africa*, 20 (2), 255–70.

Hancher, L. (2007), 'Regulation in the European Union – Regulating the Regulators', in Vass, P. (ed.), *Regulatory Review 2006/2007*, 10th Anniversary Edition, School of Management, University of Bath.

Hannah, L. (1983), *The Rise of the Corporate Economy*, 2nd edition, London: Methuen.

Hansmann, H. and Kraakman, R. (2001), 'The End of History for Corporate Law', *Georgetown Law Journal*, 89 (2), 439–68.

Harris, J. (2013), 'Serco, the Cost-cutting Company That's Running Britain', *Guardian G2*, 30 July.

Hart, O. (1995), *Firms, Contracts, and Financial Structures*, Oxford: Oxford University Press.

Hartman, L.P. and Wokutch, R.E. (2003), 'Nike, Inc.: Corporate Social Responsibility and Workplace Standard Initiatives in Vietnam', in L.P. Hartman, D.G. Arnold and R.E. Wokutch (eds).

Hartman L.P., Arnold, D.G. and Wokutch, R.E. (eds) (2003), *Rising Above Sweatshops: Innovative Approaches to Global Labour Challenges*, London: Praeger.

Harvey, B., Wilkinson, B. and Smith, S. (1984), *Managers and Corporate Social Policy*, London: Macmillan.

Hatfield, M. (1978), *The House the Left Built*, London: Victor Gollancz.

Haufler, V. (2006), 'International Governance and the Private Sector', in C. T. May (ed.).

Hawley, E.W. (1995), *The New Deal and the Problem of Monopoly: A Study in Economic Ambivalence*, Fordham University Press.

Heald, M. (1970), *The Social Responsibilities of Business: Company and Community, 1900–1960*, Cleveland, Ohio: Case Western Reserve.

Health Service Journal (2014), 'NHS Contracts "Going to Private Firms"', 16 January.

Heath, J. (2004), 'Stakeholder Theory, Corporate Governance and Public Management: What Can the History of State-Run Enterprises Teach Us in the Post-Enron Era?', *Journal of Business Ethics*, 53, 247–65.

Heath, A. and Fournier, E. (2013), 'The CBI Boss on Why Political Risk is Now the Biggest Threat to Business', 1 November, City AM. http://www.cityam.com/article/1383266253/cbi-boss-why-political-risk-now-biggest-threat-business

Helm, D. (2013), *Labour's Energy Policies*, University of Oxford. http://www.dieterhelm.co.uk/sites/default/files/Labour%E2%80%99s%20energy%20policies%20FINAL.pdf

Henrekson, M. and Jakobsson, U. (2011), 'The Swedish Corporate Control Model: Convergence, Persistence or Decline?', *IFN Working Paper 857*, Stockholm: Research Institute of Industrial Economics.

Hertz, N. (2001), *The Silent Takeover*, London: Heinemann.

Hessen, D. (1989), 'Do Economic Historians Understand Corporations?', Stanford: Hoover Institute, *Working Papers in Economics* E-89-14.

Higgs, R. (2013), 'Fagor Enters Bankruptcy After Crisis Talks Fail', *European Plastics News*, 20 November. http://www.europeanplasticsnews.com/subscriber/headlines2.html?id=3802

High Pay Centre (2013), *One Law for Them: How Big Companies Flout Rules on Executive Pay*. http://highpaycentre.org/files/one_law_for_them_report.pdf

Hildyard, N. and M. Mansley (2001), *The Campaigners' Guide to Financial Markets: Effective Lobbying of Companies and Financial Institutions*, Sturminster Newton: Corner House.

Hindess, B. (1984), 'Rational Choice Theory and the Analysis of Political Action', *Economy and Society*, 13 (3).

Hirschman, A. (1970), *Exit, Voice and Loyalty: Responses to Declines in Firms, Organizations, and States*, Cambridge, MA: Harvard University Press.

History and Policy (2010), 'Democracy in the Workplace – the Bullock Report Revisited'. http://www.histpol.hist.cam.ac.uk/forums/union/meeting_090710.html

Hoang, D. and Jones, B. (2012), 'Why Do Corporate Codes of Conduct Fail? Women Workers and Clothing Supply Chains in Vietnam', *Global Social Policy*, 12 (1), 67–85.

Hobbes, T. (n.d.), *Leviathan, Or the Matter, Forme and Power of a Commonwealth, Ecclesiastical and Civil*, Oxford: Basil Blackwell.

Hodge, M./Public Accounts Committee (2013), 'Continuing Weakness of HMRC in Its Efforts to Deal with Tax Avoidance'. http://www.parliament.uk/business/committees/committees-a-z/commons-select/public-accounts-committee/news/tax-avoidance-the-role-of-large-accountancy-firms/

Hodgson, G. (2012), 'On the Limits of Rational Choice Theory', *Economic Thought*, 1 (1), 94–108.

Holland, S. (1972), 'State Entrepreneurship and State Intervention', in S. Holland (ed.), *The State as Entrepreneur. New Dimensions for Public Enterprise: The IRI State Shareholding Formula*, London: Weidenfeld & Nicolson.

Hollstein, B. (2008), '"The Moral Dimension" and Its Meaning for Economic Ethics', Discussion Forum, *Socio-Economic Review*, 6 (1), 142–53.

Holzer, B. (2010), *Moralizing the Corporation: Transnational Activism and Corporate Accountability*, Cheltenham, UK and Northampton, MA, USA: Edward Elgar.

Horrigan, B. (2008), *Corporate Social Responsibility in the 21st Century: Debates, Models and Practices across Government, Law and Business*, Cheltenham, UK and Northampton, MA, USA: Edward Elgar.

House of Commons (2013), *Committee of Public Accounts, HMRC Tax Collection: Annual Report & Accounts*, 2012–13, Thirty-fourth Report of Session 2013–14. http://www.publications.parliament.uk/pa/cm201314/cmselect/cmpubacc/666/666.pdf

House of Lords (2007), *UK Economic Regulators*, Select Committee on Regulation, First Report, Session 2006–2007, HL 189-I, 189–II.

HR Magazine (2010), 'Employee Share Ownership: John Lewis Partner-ship "not what it purports to be"', 25 November. http://www. hrmagazine.co.uk/hro/news/1018756/employee-share-ownership-john-lewis-partnership-purports#sthash.FWbN5QdE.dpuf

Huitson, O. (2012), 'How the BBC Betrayed the NHS: An Exclusive Report on Two Years of Censorship and Distortion', *Open Democracy*, 27 September. http://www.opendemocracy.net/ourbeeb/oliver-huitson/how-bbc-betrayed-nhs-exclusive-report-on-two-years-of-censorship-and-distortion

Hunt, G.C. (1992), 'Division of Labour, Life Cycle and Democracy in Worker Co-operatives', *Economic and Industrial Democracy*, 13 (1), 19–43.

Hutton, W. (2012), 'Thames Water – A Private Equity Plaything That Takes Us For Fools', *Observer*, 11 November.

IBLF (International Business Leaders Forum) (2002), *Food for Thought – Corporate Social Responsibility for Food and Beverage Manufacturers*. http://commdev.org/files/1329_file_Food_for_Thought.pdf

IEG (1999), Sponsorship Report, cited in Klein (2000).

ILO (International Labour Organization) (2014), 'The ILO's response to the Rana Plaza tragedy'. http://www.ilo.org/global/about-the-ilo/activities/all/WCMS_240343/lang–en/index.htm

Independent (2014), 'Secret Memo Shows Michael Gove's Plan for Privatisation of Academies', Thursday 15 May.

Insight Investment (2004), *Building Your Way into Trouble: The Challenge of Supply Chain Management*, London: Acona Limited.

Institute for Global Labour and Human Rights (2012), 17 December. http://www.globallabourrights.org/alerts?id=0403

Institute of Directors (2014), 'Barclays' Results: Banks Must be Run for Shareholders, not Executives, Says IoD', Institute of Directors. http://www.iod.com/influencing/press-office/press-releases/barclays-results-banks-must-be-run-for-shareholders-not-executives-says-iod

Investment Week (2011), 'Apple Has More Cash on Balance Sheet than US Government', *Investment Week*, 1 August. http://www.investment week.co.uk/investment-week/news/2098197/apple-cash-balance-sheet-government

IPPR (2001), 'Building Better Partnerships: Business and Industry, Economy, Employment, Finance, Jobs, Taxation, Trade', *Commission on Public Private Partnerships*, 25 June. http://www.ippr.org/images/media/files/publication/2011/05/cppp_1234.pdf

Ireland, P. (1999), 'Company Law and the Myth of Shareholder Owner-ship', *The Modern Law Review*, 62 (1), 32–57.

Ireland, P. (2010), 'Limited Liability, Shareholder Rights and the Problem of Corporate Irresponsibility', *Cambridge Journal of Economics*, 34, 837– 856.

Ireland, P. (2011), 'Shareholder Primacy and the Distribution of Wealth, *Modern Law Review*, 68 (1), 49–81.

IRTK (International Right to Know Campaign) (2003), *International Right to Know: Empowering Communities through Corporate Transparency.* http://www.eldis.org/vfile/upload/1/document/0708/DOC11 739.pdf

Jackall, R. (2010), *Moral Mazes: The World of Corporate Managers*, Oxford: Oxford University Press.

Jackson, B. (2012), 'Socialism and the New Liberalism', in B. Jackson and M. Stears (eds), *Liberalism as Ideology: Essays in Honour of Michael Freeden*, Oxford: Oxford University Press.

Jackson, G. and Sorge, A. (2012), 'The trajectory of institutional change in Germany, 1979–2009', *Journal of European Public Policy*, 19 (8), 1146–67.

Jacoby, S.M. (2007), *Management and the Varieties of Capitalism, from the Embedded Corporation: Corporate Governance and Employment Relations in Japan and the United States*, Princeton: Princeton University Press.

Jacques, P.J., Riley E., Dunlap B. and Freeman, M. (2008), 'The Organisation of Denial: Conservative Think Tanks and Environmental Scepticism', *Environmental Politics*, 17 (3), 349–385.

Jenkins, S. (1995), *Accountable to None: The Tory Nationalization of Britain*, London: Hamish Hamilton.

Jenkins, R. (2001), 'Corporate Codes of Conduct: Self-Regulation in a Global Economy', UNRISD, *Technology, Business and Society Programme Paper*, 2, April.

Jensen, M.C. and Meckling, W.H. (1976), 'Theory of the Firm: Managerial Behaviour, Agency Costs and Ownership Structure', *Journal of Financial Economics*, 3, 305–60.

Jepperson, R.L. (1991), 'Institutions, Institutional Effects and Institutionalism', in W.W. Powell and P.J. Di Maggio (eds), *The New Institutionalism in Organizational Analysis*, Chicago: University of Chicago Press.

Jessop, B. (2001), 'Regulationist and Autopoieticist Reflections on Polanyi's Account of Market Economies and the Market Society', *New Political Economy*, 6 (2), 213–32.

John Lewis Partnership (n.d.), Partnership Board. http://www.johnlewis partnership.co.uk/about/the-partnership/governing-authorities/partnership-board/non-executive.html#KeithWilliamsnameId (accessed 28 August 2014).

John Lewis Partnership (2014), *Constitution of the John Lewis Partnership, Introduction, Principles and Rules*. http://www.john lewispartner ship.co.uk/content/dam/cws/pdfs/about%20us/our%20constitution/john-lewis-partnership.constitution.pdf

Jones, B. (1997), *Forcing the Factory of the Future: Cybernation and Societal Institutions*, Cambridge: Cambridge University Press.

Jones, B. (2005), 'The Corporate Patronage of Public Welfare? Interpretations and Developments in the UK and USA', Paper to the Annual Conference of the Social Policy Association, University of Bath, 27 June.

Jones, B. (2007), 'Citizens, Partners or Patrons? Corporate Power and Patronage Capitalism', *Journal of Civil Society*, 3 (2), 159–77.

Jones, B. and Cento Bull, A. (2006), 'Governance through Civil Society? An Anglo-Italian Comparison of Democratic Renewal and Local Regeneration', *Journal of Civil Society*, 2 (2), 89–110.

Jones, B. and Nisbet, P. (2011), 'A Better Model for Socio-economic Governance?', *Revue de la Régulation*, 9, Spring.

Jones, B. and O'Donnell, M. (2014), '2011 and 1968: Transnational Crisis – Transnational Social Movements?', Paper to Joint Session of RC02 Economy and Society and RC07 Futures Research, XVIII ISA World Congress of Sociology, *Facing an Unequal World: Challenges for Global Sociology*, Yokohama, Japan.

Jones, K.A. (2004), *Who's Afraid of the WTO?*, Oxford: Oxford University Press.

Julius, D. (2008), *Public Services Industry Review*. http://www.bis.gov.uk/files/file46965.pdf

Kahn, H. (1979), *World Economic Development: 1979 and Beyond*, Boulder, CO: Westview Press.

Kampfner, J. (2009), *Freedom for Sale: Why the World Is Trading Democracy for Security*, London: Simon & Schuster.

Kantarelis, D. (2010), *Theories of the Firm*, Olney, Bucks: Inderscience.

Kay, J. (1993), *Foundations of Corporate Success: How Business Strategies Add Value*, Oxford: OUP.

Kaysen, C. (1957), 'The Social Significance of the Modern Corporation', *The American Economic Review*, 47 (2), 311–319.

Keay, A. (2010), 'Shareholder Primacy in Corporate Law: Can it Survive? Should it Survive?', *European Company and Financial Law Review*, 7 (3), 369–413.

Kelly, M. (2003), *The Divine Right of Capital*, San Francisco, California: Berrett-Koehler.

Kemp, J. (2013), 'Britain's Energy Utilities Must Embrace Glasnost', Reuters. http://uk.reuters.com/article/2013/10/29/britain-utilities-idUK L5N0IJ1N220131029

Keynes, J.M. (1926), *The End of Laissez-faire*, Volume 9 (*Essays in Persuasion*), in Elizabeth Johnson and Donald Moggridge (eds), *The Collected Writings of John Maynard Keynes*, Cambridge: Royal Economic Society. http://universitypublishingonline.org/royaleconomic society/chapter.jsf?bid=CBO9781139524162&cid=CBO978113952416 2A037

Khor, M. (n.d.), *A Disappointing Summit*, Third World Network. http://www.twnside.org.sg/title/twr145a.htm

Kinderman, D. (2010), 'The Political Economy of (Institutional) Ambiguity and Ambivalence: The Rise of Corporate Responsibility and Market Liberalism, 1977–2009', paper to the Regular Session on Economic Regulation, *2010 American Sociological Association Convention*. citation.allacademic.com//meta/p_mla_apa_research_citation/ 4/1/0/6/3/pages410634/p410634-1.php

Kinderman, D. (2012), '"Free Us Up So We Can Be Responsible!" The Co-evolution of Corporate Social Responsibility and Neo-liberalism in the UK, 1977–2010', *Socio-Economic Review*, 10 (1), 29–57.

King, D. and Narlikar, A. (2003), 'The New Risk Regulators? International Organisations and Globalisation', *The Political Quarterly*, 74 (3), 337–348.

Klein, N. (2000), *No Logo*, London: Flamingo.

Knowlton, B. and Grynbaum, M.M. (2008), 'Greenspan "Shocked" that Free Markets Are Flawed', *New York Times*, 23 October.

Knudsen, T. (1993), *Den danske stat i Europa, Denmark*: Jurist- og Økonomforbundets Forlag.

Kolk, A. and Pinkse, J. (2007), 'Multinationals' Political Activities on Climate Change', *Business and Society*, 46 (2), 201–28.

Korten, D. (1995), *When Corporations Rule the World*, London: Earthscan; Bloomfield, Connecticut: Berrett-Koehler.

Korten, D. (2000), *Creating a Post-Corporate World*, Twentieth Annual E.F. Schumacher Lecture, edited by Hildegarde Hannum, Salisbury, CT: New Economics Institute. http://neweconomy.net/publications/ lectures/korten/david/creating-a-post-corporate-world

Korten, D. (2001), *When Corporations Rule the World*, San Francisco: Berrett-Koehler.

Kristensen, P.H. (1992), 'Strategies against Structure: Institutions and Economic Organization in Denmark', in R. Whitley (ed.), *European Business Systems: Firms and Markets in Their National Context*, London: Sage, pp. 117–136.

Kumazawa, M. and Matsui, Y. (n.d.), *Dialogue with Men*. http://www. ajwrc.org/english/sub/voice/8-1-2.pdf

Kushida, K. (2005), *The Politics of Restructuring NTT – Historically Rooted Trajectories from the Actors, Institutions and Interests*, Stanford University.

Kushimoto, K. (2007), 'Stakeholder Management of Japanese Big Corporations: Unethical Structure of Japanese Stakeholder Relations and Its Current Changes for the Worse', University of Geneva: Advanced Studies programme dissertation.

Labour Party (1918), *Labour and the New Social Order, A Report on Reconstruction*, London: The Labour Party.

Labour Party (1934), *For Socialism and Peace*, London: The Labour Party.

Labour Party (1973) *Labour's Programme*, London: The Labour Party.

Labour Party (1974), *Labour Party Manifesto. Let Us Work Together – Labour's Way Out of the Crisis*, London: The Labour Party. http://www.labourarchive.com/322/

Labour Party (1979), *The Labour Way is the Better Way. The Labour Party Manifesto*, London: Labour Party.

Layzer, J.A. (2007), 'Deep Freeze: How Business Has Shaped the Global Warming Debate in Congress', in Michael E. Kraft and Sheldon Kamieniecki (eds), *Business and Environmental Policy: Corporate Interests in the American Political System*, Cambridge: MIT Press, 93–125.

Lazonick, W. (1990), *Competitive Advantage on the Shop Floor*, Cambridge, MA: Harvard University Press.

Lazonick, W. (2012), 'Big Payouts to Shareholders Are Holding Back Prosperity', *Guardian*, 27 August.

Lazonick, W. and O'Sullivan, M. (2000), 'Maximizing Shareholder Value: A New Ideology for Corporate Governance', *Economy and Society*, 29 (1), 13–35.

Leighton, M, Roht-Arriaza, N. and Zarsky, L. (2002), *Beyond Good Deeds: Case Studies and a New Policy Agenda for Corporate Accountability*, Report for the California Corporate Accountability Project, Berkeley, CA: Nautilus Institute for Security and Sustainable Development.

Leone, V. and Philp, B. (2010), 'Surplus-Value and Aggregate Concentration in the UK Economy, 1987–2009', *Discussion Papers in Economics*, No. 2010/10, Nottingham: Nottingham Trent University.

Levy, D.L. and Egan, D. (1998), 'Capital Contests: National and Transnational Channels of Corporate Influence on the Climate Change Negotiations', *Politics and Society*, 26 (3), 335–59.

Lewchuck, W. and Wells, D (2008), 'Workplace Cohesion and the Fragmentation of Society: The Magna Model in Canada', in R.

O'Brien (ed.), *Solidarity First: Canadian Workers and Social Cohesion*, Vancouver: UBC Press.

Lewis, C. (1993), 'Distorted Democracy: NAFTA, Revolving Doors and Deep Lobbying'. http://multinationalmonitor.org/hyper/issues/1993/10/mm1093_06.html

Lewis, A. and Mackenzie, C. (2000), 'Support for Investor Activism among UK Ethical Investors', *Journal of Business Ethics*, 24, 215–222.

Leys, C., and Player, S. (2011), 'The Plot against the NHS', *Renewal*, 19 (2).

Littlechild, S.C. (1983), 'The Regulation of British Telecommunications' Profitability', London: Department of Industry, para 4.11. Reprinted in Bartle, I. (ed.), *The UK Model of Utility Regulation*, CRI Proceedings 31, University of Bath, September 2003.

Littlechild, S. (2003), 'The Birth of RPI-X and Other Observations', in Bartle, I. (ed.), *The UK Model of Utility Regulation*, CRI Proceedings 31, University of Bath, September..

Loveridge, R. (1982), 'Business Strategy and Community Culture: Policy as a Structured Accommodation to Conflict', in D. Dunkerley and G. Salaman (eds), *International Yearbook of Organization Studies*, London: RKP.

Loveridge, R. (1983), 'Centralism versus Federalism: Corporate Models in Industrial Relations', in K. Thurley and S. Wood (eds), *Industrial Relations and Management Strategy*, Cambridge, pp. 170–93.

Luzarraga, J.M. (2008), *Mondragon Multilocalisation Strategy: Innovating a Human Centred Globalisation*, PhD thesis, Mondragon University and MIK Research Centre.

Mackenzie, C. (1993), *Shareholder Action Handbook*, Newcastle upon Tyne: New Consumer.

Mackenzie, C. (1997), *Ethical Investment and the Challenge of Corporate Reform. A Critical Assessment of the Procedures and Purposes of UK Ethical Unit Trusts*, PhD thesis, University of Bath.

MacKenzie, D., Muniesa F. and Siu L. (2007), *Do Economists Make Markets? On the Performativity of Economics*, Princeton: Princeton University Press.

Maclagan, P. (1998), *Management and Morality. A Developmental Perspective*, London: Sage.

MacLeod, M.R. (2007), 'Financial Actors and Instruments in the Construction of Global Corporate Social Responsibility', in A. Ebrahim and E. Weisband (eds), *Global Accountabilities: Participation, Pluralism and Public Ethics,* Cambridge: Cambridge University Press.

Mangold, W. Glynn and Faulds, D.J. (2009), 'Social Media: The New Hybrid Element of the Promotion Mix', *Business Horizons*, 52 (4), 357–365.

Malament, B.C. (1978), 'British Labour and Roosevelt's New Deal: The Response of the Left and the Unions', *Journal of British Studies*, 17 (2), 136–67.

Manifest (2010), http://blog.manifest.co.uk/2010/01/2944.html#sthash. mGBessRw.dpbs

Marens, R. (2012), 'We Don't Need You Anymore: Corporate Social Responsibilities, Executive Class Interests, and Solving Mizruchi and Hirschman's Paradox', *Seattle University Law Review*, 35 (4).

Marinetto, M. (1998), *Corporate Social Involvement: Social, Political and Environmental Issues in Britain and Italy*, Aldershot: Ashgate.

Marinetto, M. (2003), 'Governing beyond the Centre: A Critique of the Anglo-Governance School', *Political Studies*, 51 (3), 592–608.

Markham, J.W. (2002), *A Financial History of the United States: From Christopher Columbus to the Robber Barons*, New York: M.E. Sharpe.

Marshall, A. (1920), *Principles of Economics* (revised edition), London: Macmillan, reprinted by Prometheus Books.

Martin, D. (2006), 'John Lewis Breaks with Tradition over Non-execs', *Accounting Web*. http://www.accountingweb.co.uk/topic/business/john-lewis-breaks-tradition-over-non-execs-dan-martin).

Martin, S. and Parker, D. (1997), *The Impact of Privatisation: Ownership and Corporate Performance in the UK*, London: Routledge.

Martinelli, F. and Schoenberger, E. (1991), 'Oligopoly Is Alive and Well: Notes for a Broader Discussion of Flexible Accumulation', in G. Benko and M. Dunford (eds), *Industrial Change and Regional Development*, New York: Belhaven Press, pp. 117–133.

Marx, K. (1875), 'Critique of the Gotha Programme', *Marx/Engels Selected Works, Volume Three*, Moscow: Progress Publishers, 1970, p. 13–30. http://www.marxists.org/archive/marx/works/1875/gotha/index. htm

Marx, K. and Engels, F. [1848] (1976), *Manifesto of the Communist Party*, in K. Marx and F. Engels, *Collected Works*, vol. 6, Moscow: Progress.

Mason, C.M. (1987), 'Job Creation Initiatives in the UK: The Large Company Role', *Industrial Relations Journal*, 18, 298–311.

Mathews, R. (1999), *Jobs of Our Own: Building a Stakeholder Society*, Sydney: Pluto Press (Australia), and West Wickham, UK: Comerford and Miller.

Mattli, W. and Büthe, T. (2005), 'Accountability in Accounting? The Politics of Private Rule-Making in the Public Interest', *Governance*, 18 (3), 399–429.

Maurice, M., Sellier, F. and Silvestre, J.-J. (1986), *The Social Foundations of Industrial Power: A Comparison of France and Germany*, Cambridge: MIT Press.

May, C.T. (ed.) (2006), *Global Corporate Power, International Political Economy Yearbook*, Boulder, Colorado: Lynne Reinner.

Mayer, C. (2012), 'Restraining Influence', *RSA Fellowship*, Digital Journal, Summer 2012. http://neweconomy.net/publications/lectures/korten/david/creating-a-post-corporate-world

Mayer, C. (2013), *Firm Commitment: Why the Corporation is Failing Us and How to Restore Trust in It*, Oxford: Oxford University Press.

Mayo, M. and Moore, H. (2001), *The Mutual State*, London: New Economics Foundation.

McFadyean, M. and Rowland, D. (2002), S*elling off the Twilight Years: The Transfer of Birmingham's Homes for Older People*, London: Menard Press.

McIntosh, M., Leipziger, D., Jones, K. and Coleman, G. (1998), *Corporate Citizenship, Successful Strategies for Responsible Companies*, London: Pitman/Financial Times.

McKendrick, N. and Outhwaite, R.B. (1986), *Business Life and Public Policy: Essays in Honour of D.C. Coleman*, Cambridge: CUP.

McLaren, D. (2004), 'Global Stakeholders: Corporate Accountability and Investor Engagement', *Corporate Governance: An International Review*, 12 (2), 191–201.

Merino, B.D., Mayper, A.G. and Tolleson, T.D. (2010), 'Neoliberalism, Deregulation and Sarbanes-Oxley: The Legitimation of a Failed Corporate Governance Model', *Accounting, Auditing & Accountability Journal*, 23 (6), 774 – 792.

Micklethwait, J. and Wooldridge, A. (2003), *The Company: A Short History Of A Revolutionary Idea*, London: Weidenfeld.

Milbank, D. (2001), 'Needed: Catchword For Bush Ideology; "Communitarianism" Finds Favor', *The Washington Post*, 1 February.

Miliband, E. (2011), Labour Leader's speech, Liverpool. http://www.britishpoliticalspeech.org/speech-archive.htm?speech=312

Miliband, E. (2012), Speech to Labour Party Annual Conference, 2 October. http://www.labour.org.uk/ed-miliband-speech-conf-2012

Miller, D. (2008), 'I Hear "Reason", I See Lies', *New Scientist*, issue 2666, 23 July.

Miller, D. and Dinan, W. (2003), *A Century of Spin: How Public Relations Became the Cutting Edge of Corporate Power*, London: Pluto Press.

Mindful Money (2012), 'Executive Pay across the World', 11 January. http://www.mindfulmoney.co.uk/economy/economic-impact/executive-pay-across-the-world/

Monbiot, G. (2000), *Captive State: The Corporate Takeover of Britain*, London: MacMillan.

Monbiot, G. (2014a), 'How Have These Corporations Colonised Our Public Life?', *Guardian*, 8 April.

Monbiot, G. (2014b), *Loved to Death*, 8 April. http://www.monbiot.com/2014/04/08/loved-to-death/

Mondragon (n.d.). http://www.mondragon-corporation.com/eng/

Monks, R. (2007), *Corpocracy*, New York: Wiley.

Moon, J. (2002), 'The Social Responsibility of Business and New Governance', *Government and Opposition*, 37 (3), 385–408.

Morana, C. and Sawkins, J. (2002), 'Stock Market Reaction to Regulatory Price Review in the English and Welsh Water Industry', *Journal of Regulatory Economics*, 22 (2), 185–204.

Morgan, K.O. (1997) *Callaghan: A Life*, Oxford: Oxford University Press.

Mueller, D.C. (2003), *The Corporation: Investment, Mergers and Growth*, London: Routledge.

Mullerat, R. (2010), *International Corporate Social Responsibility: The Role of Corporations in the Economic Order of the 21st Century*, Netherlands: Kluwer Law International.

Munck, R. (2002), 'Globalisation and Democracy: a New "Great Transformation"', *Annals of the American Academy of Political and Social Science*, 581, 10–21.

Murphy, R. (n.d.), *The Missing Billions: The UK Tax Gap*, TUC Touchstone Pamphlet, # 1. http://www.tuc.org.uk/sites/default/files/documents/1missingbillions.pdf

Murray, J. (2004), *Corporate Social Responsibility: An Overview of Principles and Practices*, Geneva: Policy Integration Department World Commission on the Social Dimension of Globalization, International Labour Organisation.

Mutuo (2013), *Mutuals Yearbook 2013*. http://www.mutuo.co.uk/wp-content/uploads/2013/12/Yearbook-13-final.pdf

NAO (National Audit Office) (2014), *The Privatisation of Royal Mail. Report by the Comptroller and Auditor General, Department for Business, Innovation & Skills*, London: UK Parliament.

National Property Office (2013), *The Japanese National Property System and Current Conditions*, Tokyo: Financial Bureau, Ministry of Finance. http://www.mof.go.jp/english/national_property/2013.pdf

New Economic Foundation (2009), *The Mutual State*. http://edmayo.wordpress.com/2009/12/15/the-mutual-state/

New Scientist (1975), 'Alternative Technology Fails the Lucas Test', November, 472.

Newell, P.J. and Levy, D. L. (2006), 'The Political Economy of the Firm in Global Environmental Governance', in C. May (ed.), *Global Corporate Power*, Boulder, CO: Lynne Rienner.

Newswise (2007), 'Corporate Contributions Rise Again', 17 January. http://www.newswise.com/articles/corporate-contributions-rise-again

North, D.C. (1990), *Institutions, Institutional Change and Economic Performance*, Cambridge: Cambridge University Press.

O'Hara, G. (2009), 'What the Electorate Can Be Expected to Swallow. Nationalism, Transnationalism and the Shifting Boundaries of the State in Post War Britain', *Business History*, 51 (4).

O'Sullivan, M. (2003), 'The Political Economy of Comparative Corporate Governance', *Review of International Political Economy*, 10 (1), 23–72.

OECD (2001), 'Codes of Corporate Conduct: Expanded Review of their Contents', OECD Directorate for Financial, Fiscal and Enterprise Affairs, *Working Papers on International Investment*, no. 2001/6. http://www.oecd.org/industry/inv/corporateresponsibility/1922656.pdf

OECD (2002), *OECD Economic Surveys 2001–2002: United Kingdom*, Paris: OECD.

OECD (2008), 'Around One-third of UK 2007 Economic Activity Derives from "Foreign" MNCs'. http://stats.oecd.org/

OECD (2013), *Action Plan on Base Erosion and Profit Shifting*, OECD Publishing. http://dx.doi.org/10.1787/9789264202719-en

OECD (2013), Secretary-General Report to the G20 Leaders, St Petersburg, Russia, 5–6 September. http://www.oecd.org/tax/SG-report-G20-Leaders-StPetersburg.pdf

OECD (2014), *Economic Surveys: Germany*, OECD, May. http://www.oecd.org/eco/Germany-Overview-2014.pdf

Ofgem (2008), *Energy Supply Probe – Initial Findings Report*. https://www.ofgem.gov.uk/ofgem-publications/38437/energy-supply-probe-initial-findings-report.pdf

Ofwat (2011), 'Financeability and Financing the Asset Base', Discussion Paper. http://www.ofwat.gov.uk/future/monopolies/fpl/prs_inf1103fpl_financeability.pdf

Oliver, A.L. (1850), *A Brief Inquiry into the Origin of Corporate Privileges and Individual Responsibilities of the Members of Trading Corporations at Common Law*, Cincinatti: Lawyer and Dumas Partners.

ONS (Office of National Statistics), *HM Revenue and Customs, KAI Data Policy and Coordination*, HMRC TAX & NIC RECEIPTS, Monthly and annual historical record. http://www.hm-treasury.gov.uk/national_statistics.htm

ONS (Office of National Statistics) (2006), *Economic Trends*, 635, October.

Ortiz, I. and Cummins, M. (2013), *The Age of Austerity: A Review of Public Expenditures and Adjustment Measures in 181 Countries*, New

York/Geneva: Initiative for Policy Dialogue and the South Centre, Working Paper.

Page, B. (2003), 'Has Widening Stakeholder Participation in Decision-making Produced Sustainable and Innovative Water Policy in the UK?', *Water Policy*, (5), 313–329.

Page, B. and Bakker, K. (2005), 'Water governance and water users in a privatised water industry: participation in policy-making and in water services provision: a case study of England and Wales', *International Journal of Water*, 3 (1), 38–60.

Palast, G. (2004), *The Best Democracy Money Can Buy: An Investigative Reporter Exposes the Truth About Globalization, Corporate Cons and High Finance Fraudsters*, London: Penguin.

Palast G., Oppenheim, J. and MacGregor, T. (2003), *Democracy and Regulation: How The Public Can Govern Essential Services*, Pluto Press.

Palpacuer, F. and Tozanli, S. (2008), 'Changing Governance Patterns in European Food Chains: the Rise of a New Divide between Global Players and Regional Producers', *Transnational Corporations*, 17, 1.

Paniccia, I. (2007), 'The Recent Evolution of Italian Industrial Districts and Clusters: Analytical Issues and Policy Implications', Paper to Regional Studies Association International Conference, Regions in Focus? Lisbon, April 2–5.

Parker, D. (2004), 'The UK's Privatisation Experiment: The Passage of Time Permits a Sober Assessment', *CESIFO Working Paper* No. 1126, Category 9: Industrial Organisation.

Parkinson, J.E. (1993), *Corporate Power and Responsibility: Issues in the Theory of Company Law*, Oxford: Clarendon Press.

Paskov, M. and Dewilde, M. (2012), *Income Inequality and Solidarity in Europe*, Discussion Paper 33, GINI Project (European Commission), Amsterdam: AIAS.

Pattberg, P. (2006), 'The Influence of Global Business Regulation: Beyond Good Corporate Conduct', *Business and Society Review*, 111 (3), 241–268.

Patten, D.M. (1992), 'Intra-industry Environmental Disclosures in Response to the Alaskan Oil Spill: a Note on Legitimacy Theory', *Accounting, Organizations and Society*, 17 (5), 471–5.

Paun, A. and Atkinson, D. (2011), *Balancing Act: The Right Role for Parliament in Public Appointments*, Institute of Government. http://www.instituteforgovernment.org.uk/sites/default/files/publications/Balancing%20Act.pdf

Pearce, G. and Martin, S. (1996), 'The Measurement of Additionality: Grasping the Slippery Eel', *Local Government Studies*, 22 (1), 78–92.

Pearson, R., and Seyfang, G. (2001), 'New Hope or False Dawn? Voluntary Codes of Conduct, Labour Regulation and Social Policy in a Globalizing World', *Global Social Policy*, 1 (1), 49–78.

Peetz, D. and Murray, G. (2012), 'Finance Capital and Global Corporate Ownership', in G. Murray, G. and J.G. Scott (eds), *Financial Elites and Transnational Business: Who Rules the World?*, Cheltenham, UK and Northampton, MA, USA: Edward Elgar, pp. 38–69.

Pendleton, A. (2004), *Behind the Mask: The Real Face of Corporate Social Responsibility.* http://www.christian-aid.org/indepth/0401csr/index.htm

Pendleton, A. (2005), 'How Far Does the United Kingdom Have a Market-based System of Corporate Governance? A Review and Evaluation of Recent Developments in the United Kingdom', *Competition and Change*, 9 (1), 107–126.

Perrow, C. (1991), 'A Society of Organizations', *Theory and Society*, 20 (6), 725–62.

Perrow, C. (2002), *Organizing America: Wealth, Power, and the Origins of Corporate Capitalism*, Princeton: Princeton University Press.

Peston, R. (2007), 'Cadbury's Reorganisation', *BBC News*. http://www.bbc.co.uk/blogs/legacy/thereporters/robertpeston/2007/06/cadburys_reorganisation.html

Phillips, J. (2011), 'UK Business Power and Opposition to the Bullock Committee's 1977 Proposals on Worker Directors', *Historical Studies in Industrial Relations*, 31/32, 1–30.

Piketty, T. (2014), *Capital in the Twenty-First Century*, Cambridge MA/London: Belknap Press.

Pingeot, L. (2014), *Corporate Influence in the Post-2015 Process*, Bonn, Germany: Global Policy Forum.

Piore, M.J. and Sabel, C.F. (1984), *The Second Industrial Divide: Possibilities for Prosperity*, New York: Basic Books.

Polanyi, M. (1944), *The Great Transformation: The Social and Political Origins of Our Time*, Boston: Beacon Press (1968 edition).

Political Economy of Football (n.d.). http://www.footballeconomy.com/statistics2.htm

Pollard, S. (1965), *The Genesis of Modern Management: A Study of the Industrial Revolution in Great Britain*, Cambridge: Harvard University Press.

Porter, M.E. (1990), *The Competitive Advantage of Nations*, New York: The Free Press.

Pozen, R. and Hamacher, T. (2013), 'The (Advisory) Ties that Bind Executive Pay', *Financial Times*, 3 November. http://www.ft.com/cms/s/0/eabb294e-4170-11e3-b064-00144feabdc0.html#axzz2yxETpTBq

Pratley, N. (2013), 'The Hard Road Ahead Is Where Firstgroup Should Be Going', *Guardian*, 12 December.

Prowse, S.D. (1995), 'Corporate Governance in an International Perspective', *Financial Markets, Institutions and Instruments*, 4, 1–63.

Purdy, D. (n.d.), *The Wages of Militancy: Incomes Policy, Hegemony and the Decline of the British Left*. http://hegemonics.co.uk/docs/Incomes-Policy-Hegemony-1970s.pdf

Pyke, F., and Sengenberger, W. (eds) (1992), *Industrial Districts and Local Economic Regeneration*, Geneva: International Institute for Labour Studies.

Rand, A. (1964), *The Virtue of Selfishness: A New Concept of Egoism*, New York: The American Library.

Rand, A. (1967), 'Theory and Practice', in A. Rand (ed.), *Capitalism: The Unknown Ideal*, New York: New American Library.

Rangan, V.K. and Rajan, R. (2007), 'Unilever in India: Hindustan Lever's Project, Shakti – Marketing FMCG to the Rural Consumer', *Harvard Business School Review*, 9-505-056 June 27.

Raworth, K. and Coryndon, A. (2004), *Trading Away Our Rights: Women Working in Global Supply Chains*, London: Oxfam International.

Rebecca Television (2014), *The Great Welsh Water Robbery*. http://paddyfrench1.wordpress.com/tag/glas-cymru/ (accessed 1 July 2014).

Reeves, C.B. (1970), 'Ecology Adds a New PR Dimension', *Public Relations Journal*, June, 7–9.

Reich, R. (1998), 'The New Meaning of Corporate Citizenship', *California Management Review*, 40 (2), 8–17.

Reisman, D. (2003), 'Alfred Marshall on Social Capital', in Richard Arena and Michel Quéré (eds), *The Economics of Alfred Marshall: Revisiting Marshall's Legacy*, New York: Palgrave MacMillan.

Reporters Committee for Freedom of the Press (2007). http://www.rcfp.org/privatization-v-publics-right-know

Responsive Philanthropy (1996), 'Republicans Persist in Believing Charities Will Fill Budget Gaps', Winter. http://www.ncrp.org/articles/dap/7.htm (accessed 12 November 2004).

Reuschke, D. (2004), *Public Private Partnerships in Urban Development in the United States*, NERUS Programme, Irvine: University of California.

Richardson, J. (1983), 'The Development of Corporate Responsibility in the UK', *Strathclyde Papers on Government and Politics*, 1, 1–39.

Richter, J. (2001), *Holding Corporations Accountable: Corporate Conduct, International Codes and Citizen Action*, London: Zed Books.

Rinaldi, R. (2005), 'The Emilian Model Revisited: Twenty Years After', *Business History*, 47 (2), 244–66.

Roberts, I. (1993), *Craft, Class and Control: The Sociology of a Shipbuilding Community*, Edinburgh: Edinburgh University Press.

Robertson, M. (2009), 'A Union of Forces Marching in the Same Direction? Relationship between the Cooperative and Labour Parties 1900–1939', in M. Worley (ed.), *The Foundations of the British Labour Party*, Farnham: Ashgate.

Rootes, C. (ed.) (2003), *Environmental Protest in Western Europe*, Oxford: Oxford University Press.

Rowbottom, J. (2010), *Democracy Distorted: Wealth, Influence and Democratic Politics*, Cambridge: Cambridge University Press.

Rowell, A. (2001a), 'Green Activists and Multi-Nationals "Get Engaged" at Controversial Rendezvous', *Big Issue*, 2–8 July.

Rowell, A. (2001b), 'Corporations "Get Engaged" to the Environmental Movement', PR Watch Archives, 8/3 (2001). http://www.prwatch.org/prwissues/2001Q3/engaged.html

Rowell, A., Marriott, J. and Stockman, L. (2005), *The Next Gulf – London, Washington and Oil Conflict in Nigeria*, London: Constable.

Rowley, T.J. (1997), 'Moving Beyond Dyadic Ties: A Network Theory of Stakeholder Influences', *Academy of Management Review*, 22 (4), 887–910.

Rowlingson, K. (2011), *Does Income Inequality Cause Health and Social Problems?*, Joseph Rowntree Foundation. http://www.jrf.org.uk/publications/income-inequality-health-social-problems

Ruggie, J.G. (2003), 'Taking Embedded Liberalism Global: The Corporate Connection', in D. Held and M. Koenig-Archibugi (eds), *Taming Globalization*, Cambridge: Polity Press.

Santisteban, M.A. (2006), 'Industrial Clusters in Spain and Denmark: Contextualized Institutional Strategies for Endogeneous Development', European Urban and Regional Studies Conference, September, Roskilde, Denmark.

Sarginger, B.R. (2011), 'The Artificial Becoming Natural – A Study of Corporate Personhood as it has Developed within the United States and European Union', MA thesis, West Virginia University, Morgantown, West Virginia.

Saunders, P. and Harris, C. (1994), *Privatization and Popular Capitalism*, Buckingham: Open University Press.

Savage, M. and Williams, K. (2008), 'Elites: Remembered in Capitalism and Forgotten by Social Sciences', in M. Savage and K. Williams (eds), *Remembering Elites*, Oxford: Blackwell, pp. 1–24.

Saxena, S.K. and Craig, J.G. (1990), 'Consumer Cooperatives in a Changing World, A Research Review', *Annals of Public and Cooperative Economics*, 61 (4), 489–518.

Scanlon, H. (1968), *The Way Forward for Workers' Control*, Institute for Workers' Control.

Schmitoff, C.M. (1951), 'The Nationalization of Basic Industries in Great Britain', *Law and Contemporary Problems*, 16.

Schumacher, E.F. (1973), *Small Is Beautiful, A Study of Economics as if People Mattered*, London: Blond and Briggs.

Schweickart, D. (2002), *After Capitalism,* Lanham, Maryland: Rowman and Littlefield.

Scott, C. (2000), 'Accountability in the Regulatory State', *Journal of Law and Society*, 27, 38–60.

Sell, S.K. (1999), 'Multinational Corporations as Agents of Change: The Globalization of Intellectual Property Rights', in A. C. Cutler, V. Haufler and T. Porter (eds), *Private Authority and International Affairs*, Albany, New York: SUNY Press.

Sethi, P.S. (1999), 'Codes of Conduct for Multinational Corporations: An Idea Whose Time Has Come', *Business and Society Review*, 104 (3), 225–241.

Sethi, P.S. (2003), *Setting Global Standards: Guidelines for Creating Codes of Conduct in Multinational Corporations*, New Jersey: John Wiley & Sons.

Shah, A. (2009), 'Media Conglomerates, Mergers, Concentration of Ownership: The Quest for the Internet?', *Global Issues*, January 02. http://www.globalissues.org/article/159/media-conglomerates-mergers-concentration-of-ownership

Shannon, H.A. (1933), 'The Limited Companies of 1866–1883', *The Economic History Review*, 4 (3), 290–316.

Shaoul, J. (1997), 'The power of accounting: reflecting on water privatization?', *Accounting, Auditing & Accountability Journal*, 10 (3), 382–405.

Share the World's Resources (2007). http://www.stwr.org/multinational-corporations/key-facts.html 2013

Shin, T. (2012), 'CEO Compensation and Shareholder Value Orientation among Large US firms', *The Economic and Social Review*, 43 (4), 535–59.

Sklair, L. (2002), 'The Transnational Capitalist Class and Global Politics: Deconstructing the Corporate-State Connection', *International Political Science Review*, 23 (2), 159–174.

Skonicki, A. (2008), 'Karl Polanyi, the Market and Socialism', *La vie des idees.* http://www.booksandideas.net/IMG/pdf/20090915_polanyiENG.pdf

Slideshare (n.d.). http://www.slideshare.net/keshavcrashk/kraft-cadbury-merger

Smith, C. (1996), *New Questions for Socialism*, London: Fabian Society.

Smith, D. (1993), *Business and the Environment*, London: Paul Chapman.

Smith, K.E., Fooks, G., Collin, J., Weishaar, H., Mandal, S. et al. (2010), '"Working the System"– British American Tobacco's Influence on the European Union Treaty and Its Implications for Policy: An Analysis of Internal Tobacco Industry Documents', *PLoS Med*, 7 (1) e1000202.

Solomon, J. (2010), *Corporate Governance and Accountability*, Chichester: John Wiley.

Sparkes, R. (2003), *A Pragmatic Approach to Corporate Social Responsibility*, address to the School of Management, London School of Economics, 19 May. http://cep.lse.ac.uk/seminarpapers/19-05-03-SPA.pdf

Sparkes, R., and Cowton, C. (2004), 'The Maturing of Socially Responsible Investment: A Review of the Developing Link with Corporate Social Responsibility', *Journal of Business Ethics*, 52 (1), 45–57.

Spencer, B. (1991), 'Trade Unionism, Workplace, and Politics in Post-War Britain: And Inferences for Canada', *Labour / Le Travail*, 28, 187–217.

STEPS (2014), *The Lucas Plan and Socially Useful Production*, University of Sussex.http://steps-centre.org/2014/blog/new-paper-lucas-plan-socially-useful-production/

Sullivan, R. and Mackenzie, C. (eds) (2006), *Responsible Investment*, Sheffield, UK: Greenleaf.

Suzuki, A. (2006), 'History of Labour in Japan in the Twentieth Century, Cycles of Activism and Acceptance', in J. Lucassen (ed.), *Global Labour History: A State of the Art*, Bern: Peter Lang.

Swank, D. (2002), *Global Capital, Political Institutions, and Policy Change in Developed Welfare States*, New York: Cambridge University Press.

Takano, Yoshiro (2002), 'Nippon Telegraph and Telephone Privatization Study: Experience of Japan and Lessons for Developing Countries', Volume 1, *World Bank Discussion Papers*, no. WDP 179, 2002/09/17.

Talbot, L.E. (2012), 'Polanyi's Embeddedness and Shareholder Stewardship: A Contextual Analysis of Current Anglo-American Perspectives on Corporate Governance', NILQ, 18 November, 62 (4), 451–68; Symposium paper, Oxford, April 2010; Warwick School of Law Research Paper No. 2012/20. Available at SSRN: http://ssrn.com/abstract=2177645

Talking Retail (2008), *Cadbury Evaluates its Green Initiatives*, 22 September. http://www.talkingretail.com/category-news/supermarket/cadbury-evaluates-its-green-initiatives/

Teeple, G. (2000), *Globalization and the Decline of Social Reform*, Aurora, Ontario: Garamond Press.

Telegraph (2012), Barclays' $453m fine for energy market manipulation upheld by FERC. http://www.telegraph.co.uk/finance/newsbysector/banksandfinance/10184178/Barclays-453m-fine-for-energy-market-manipulation-upheld-by-FERC.html

Telegraph (2013), 'John Lewis-style Businesses Receive Extra £25m Boost', 5 December. http://www.telegraph.co.uk/finance/economics/10498538/John-Lewis-style-businesses-receive-extra-25m-boost.html

Telegraph (2014), 'Energy Companies Face Break-up Threat over High Profits and Prices', 12 June. http://www.telegraph.co.uk/finance/newsbysector/energy/10726037/Energy-companies-face-break-up-threat-over-high-profits-and-prices.html

Thatcher, M. (n.d.), *Independent Regulatory Agencies in Europe*. http://www.hec.fr/var/corporate/storage/original/application/2a458a2d758a981892128ec02ee7e178.pdf

Thatcher, M. (2005), 'The Third Force? Independent Regulatory Agencies and Elected Politicians in Europe', *Governance*, 18 (3), 347–73.

Thelen, K. (n.d.), *Varieties of Labor Politics in the Developed Democracies*. http://www.people.fas.harvard.edu/~iversen/PDFfiles/Thelen.pdf

Thelen, K. and Kume, I. (1999), 'The Effects of Globalization on Labor Revisited: Lessons from Germany and Japan', *Politics and Society*, 1999 (27) 477–505.

Thompson, G.F. (2003), 'Globalisation as the Total Commercialisation of Politics?', *New Political Economy*, 8 (3).

Thompson, G.F. (2011), 'Companies as "Cyborgs"? The Political Implications of Limited Liability, Legal Personality and Citizenship', *Working Paper* 75, Copenhagen Business School, Department of Business and Politics.

Thompson, G.F. (2013), *The Constitutionalization of the Global Corporate Sphere?*, Oxford: Oxford University Press.

Thompson, G.F. (2013), 'Should We Worry about Global Quasi-constitutionalization?', *Open Economy*, 23 January. https://www.opendemocracy.net/openeconomy/grahame-thompson/should-we-worry-about-global-quasi-constitutionalization

Thompson, G.F. and Driver, C. (2002) 'Corporate Governance and Democracy: The Stakeholder Debate Revisited', *Journal of Management and Governance*, 6 (4), 111–30.

Thompson, N.W. (2006), *Political Economy and the Labour Party: The Economics of Democratic Socialism, 1884–2005*, Oxford: Routledge.

Thompson, S. (2005), 'The Impact of Corporate Governance Reforms on the Remuneration of Executives in the UK', *Corporate Governance: An International Review*, 13 (1), 19–25.

Tokatli, N. (2008), 'Global Sourcing Insights from the Clothing Industry: The Case of Zara, a Fast Fashion Retailer', *Journal of Economic Geography*, 8, 21–38.

Tomlinson, J. (2002), 'The Limits of Tawney's Ethical Socialism: A Historical Perspective on the Labour Party and the Market', *Contemporary British History*, 16 (4), 1–16.

Tomorrow's Company (2010a), *Tomorrow's Corporate Governance: Bridging the UK Engagement Gap Through Swedish-style Nomination Committees*, London: Tomorrow's Company.

Tomorrow's Company (2010b), *Tomorrow's Corporate Governance*. http://www.forceforgood.com/Uploaded_Content/tool/2432010114858 75.pdf

Toms, S. and Wilson, J. (2003), 'Scale, Scope and Accountability: Towards a New Paradigm of British Business History', *Business History*, 45 (4), 1–23.

Towers Watson (2013), *Executive Compensation Market Watch – August 2013*. http://www.towerswatson.com/en-GB/Insights/Newsletters/Europe/ executive-compensation-market-watch/2013/08/Executive-Compensation-Market-Watch-August-2013

Towers Watson (2014), *Executive Compensation Market Watch*, 27 March. http://www.towerswatson.com/en-GB/Insights/Newsletters/Europe/ executive-compensation-market-watch/2014/03/executive-compensation-market-watch-late-march-2014

Transparency International UK (2012), *Cabs for Hire: Fixing the Revolving Door between Government and Business?*, London: Transparency International UK.

Treanor, J. (2012), 'Barclays £500m Tax Loophole Closed by Treasury in Rare Retrospective Action', *Guardian*, Tuesday 28 February.

Treanor, J. (2014), 'The Long View', *Guardian*, 4 July.

Tuckman, A. (2011), 'Workers' Control and the Politics of Factory Occupation, Britain, 1970s', in Immanuel Ness and Dario Azzellini (eds), *Ours to Master and to Own, Workers' Councils from the Commune to the Present*, Chicago: Haymarket Books, pp. 281–384.

Tugenhadt, C. (1973), *The Multinationals*, Harmondsworth: Pelican.

UK Government (n.d.), Companies Act 2006. http://www. legislation.gov.uk/ukpga/2006/46/contents

UK Government/N. Clegg (2012), Deputy Prime Minister's Speech at Mansion House https://www.gov.uk/government/speeches/deputy-prime-ministers-speech-at-mansion-house

UK Government/Kay, J. (2012), *The Kay Review of UK Equity Markets and Long-term Decision Making, Final Report*. https://www.gov.uk/ government/uploads/system/uploads/attachment_data/file/253454/bis-12-917-kay-review-of-equity-markets-final-report.pdf

UK Government (2013), Department for Work and Pensions, *Work Programme: Contract Package Area and Prime Providers*, updated 30 October. https://www.gov.uk/government/uploads/system/uploads/attachment_data/file/253680/cpa-preferred-bidders.pdf

UK Parliament (2002a), House of Lords, Select Committee on Economic Affairs, *Minutes of Evidence*. http://www.publications.parliament.uk/pa/ld200102/ldselect/ldeconaf/143/2020502.htm

UK Parliament (2002b), House of Lords Select Committee on Economic Affairs, *First Report*.

UK Parliament (2007), *Select Committee on Regulators First Report*, chapter 3. http://www.publications.parliament.uk/pa/ld200607/ldselect/ldrgltrs/189/18906.htm).

UK Parliament (2012), *HM Revenue and Customs: Annual Report and Accounts*, House of Commons: Public Accounts Committee. http://www.publications.parliament.uk/pa/cm201213/cmselect/cmpubacc/716/71605.htm]

UK Parliament (2013), *The Kay Review of Equity Markets and Long-Term Decision Making*, Department of Business, Innovation and Skills: Third Report of Session 2013–14, London: Stationery Office.

UK White Paper (1978), *Industrial Democracy*, Cmnd. 7231, HMSO, May.

Umunna, C. (2012), Speech to the High Pay Commission and Institute for Public Policy Research, 12 January. http://www.totalpolitics.com/print/speeches/288962/chuka-umunna-on-executive-pay.thtml

United Nations (2002), *A/CONF.199/20 Report of the World Summit on Sustainable Development*, Johannesburg, South Africa, 26 August– 4 September, New York: United Nations.

Unlock Democracy (2014). http://www.unlockdemocracy.org.uk/projects/open-up-lobbying

US Treasury (2012), *The President's Framework for Business Tax Reform*, Joint Report by the White House and the Department of the Treasury, February. http://www.treasury.gov/resource-center/tax-policy/Documents/The-Presidents-Framework-for-Business-Tax-Reform-02-22-2012.pdf

Useem, M. (1982), 'Classwide Rationality in the Politics of Managers and Directors of Large Corporations in the United States and Great Britain', *Administrative Science Quarterly*, 27 (2), 199–226.

USGAO (United States General Accounting Office) (1993), 'Competitiveness Issues: The Business Environment in the US, Germany and Japan', *Report to Congressional Requesters*, Washington: USGAO.

Utility Week (2013), 'Ofgem to Force "Transparent" Reporting of Energy Company Profits'. http://www.utilityweek.co.uk/news/ofgem-to-force-%

E2%80%98transparent%E2%80%99-reporting-of-energy-company-profits/
931042#.UqCFa3dQLtE 14/10/2013

Utting, P. (2005), 'Corporate Responsibility and the Movement of Business', *Development in Practice*, 15 (3–4), 375–388.

van der Schot, J. and van de Veen, H. (1997), 'De nieuwe macht van NGO's', in Houdbare Duurzaam Nederland, K. Waagmeester (eds), *Platform von Duurzame Ontwikkeling*/Uitgeverij Jan Mets, 197–209.

Van Tulder, R. and Kolk, A. (2001), 'Multinationality and Corporate Ethics: Codes of Conduct in the Sporting Goods Industry', *Journal of International Business Studies*, 32 (2), 267–83.

Vernon, R. (1971), *Sovereignty at Bay: The Multinational Spread of US Enterprises*, London: Longman.

Vernon (1977), *Storm over the Multinationals: The Real Issues*, Cambridge, MA: Harvard University Press.

Vidal, M. (2002), 'The corporate ethics red herring', *Counterpunch*, 12 July, available at: www.counterpunch.org/vidal0712.html

Visser, W. (2006), 'Revisiting Carroll's CSR Pyramid: An African Perspective', in M. Huniche and E.R. Pedersen (eds), *Corporate Citizenship in Developing Countries: New Partnership Perspectives*, Copenhagen Business School Press.

Vitali, S., Glattfelder, J.B. and Battiston, S. (2011), 'The Network of Global Corporate Control', PLoS ONE, 6 (10). http://www.plosone.org/article/info%3Adoi%2F10.1371%2Fjournal.pone.0025995#s3

Vitols, S. (2005), 'Changes in Germany's Bank-based Financial System: Implications for Corporate Governance', *Corporate Governance: An International Review. Special Issue on Germany and Japan*, 13 (2), 386–96.

Vogel, S.K. (1996), *Freer Markets, More Rules: Regulatory Reform in Advanced Industrial Countries*, Ithaca, New York: Cornell University Press.

Vogel, D. (2005), *The Market for Virtue: The Potential and Limits of Corporate Social Responsibility*, Washington, DC: Brookings Institute.

Wachman, R. (2011), 'Southern Cross's Incurably Flawed Business Model Let Down the Vulnerable', *Guardian*, 16 July.

Waddock, S.A., Bodwell, C. and Graves, S.B. (2002), 'Responsibility: The New Business Imperative', *Academy of Management Executive*, 16 (2).

War On Want (2008), *Fashion Victims II: How UK Clothing Retailers Are Keeping Workers in Poverty*, London: War On Want.

War on Want (2013), 'Six Months After the Rana Plaza Disaster, Gap and Asda Still Risking Workers' Lives'. http://www.waronwant.org/campaigns/love-fashion-hate-sweatshops/18013-6-months-on-from-the-rana-plaza-disaster

Warwick, D. and Littlejohn, G. (1992), *Coal, Capital, and Culture: A Sociological Analysis of Mining Communities in West Yorkshire*, London: Taylor and Francis.

Watkins, M. and Passow, S. (2002), *Sunk Costs: The Plan to Dump the Brent Spar*, Harvard Business School Paper N9-903-010, Cambridge, MA.

Webb, B. (n.d.), *Diary of Beatrice Webb*, volumes 13–16. London: London School of Economics. http://digital.library.lse.ac.uk/objects/lse:wip502kaf/read#page/368/mode/2up

Westergaard, J. (1977), 'Class, Inequality and Corporatism', in A. Hunt (ed.), *Class and Class Structure*, London: Lawrence and Wishart.

Whitefield, W. (2009), 'Shareholders, Stakeholders and Resolutions: A Study of CSR-related Shareholder Resolutions Proposed at UK Companies by NGOs and Other Stakeholder-Representative Groups', MSc Dissertation, University of Bath.

Whitfield, D. (2001), *Public Services or Corporate Welfare: The Future of the Nation State in the Global Economy*, London: Pluto Press.

Wilks, S. (1988), *Industrial Policy and the Motor Industry*, Manchester: Manchester University Press.

Wilks, S. (1997), 'The Amoral Corporation and British Utility Regulation', *New Political Economy*, 2 (2), 279–298.

Wilks, S. (2013), *The Political Power Of The Business Corporation*, Cheltenham, UK and Northampton, MA, USA: Edward Elgar.

Wilks, S. and Doern, B. (2007), 'Accountability and Multi-Level Governance in UK', in P. Vass (ed.), *Regulation, Regulatory Review 2006/ 2007*, 10th Anniversary Edition, University of Bath: Centre for the Study of Regulated Industries.

Williams, K. (2000), 'From Shareholder Value to Present-day Capitalism', *Economy and Society*, 29 (1), 1–12.

Williamson, J. (2003), 'A Trade Union Congress Perspective on the Company Law Review and Corporate Governance Reform since 1997', *British Journal of Industrial Relations*, 41 (3), 511–30.

Williamson, O.E. (1981), 'The Modern Corporation: Origins, Evolution, Attributes', *Journal of Economic Literature*, 19, 4.

Williamson, O.E. (1990), *The Firm as a Nexus of Treaties: An Introduction*, London: Sage.

Wilson, A. (1994), 'Business Ethics and the Role of Non-Executive Directors', in *Proceedings of the Fifth Annual Meeting of the International Association for Business and Society*.

Wilson, H. (2012), 'Barclays Hit with £290m Fine over Libor Fixing', *Telegraph*, 27 June.

Wilson, H. (2013), 'Barclays' $453m Fine for Energy Market Manipulation Upheld by FERC', *Telegraph*, 17 July.

Witt, M.A. (2014), 'Japan: Coordinated Capitalism between Institutional Change and Structural Inertia', in M.A. Witt and G. Redding, *The Oxford Handbook of Asian Business Systems*, Oxford: Oxford University Press.

Wolf, M. (2012), 'Seven Ways to Fix the System's Flaws', *Financial Times*, 22 January.

Woods, D. (2012), 'Vince Cable Pledges to Curb Executive Pay', *HR Magazine*, 24 January. http://www.hrmagazine.co.uk/hro/news/1020744/vince-cable-pledges-curb-executive-pay

Wright, S., Mason, R., and Miles, D. (2003), *A Study into Certain Aspects of the Cost of Capital for Regulated Utilities in the UK*, 13 February, London: Smithers & Co Ltd.

WSSD (2002), *Report of the World Summit on Sustainable Development*, Johannesburg, South Africa, 26 August–4 September. http://www.un.org/jsummit/html/documents/summit_docs/131302_wssd_report_reissued.pdf

Yeomans, J. (2014), 'Waitrose Staff Get 15% Bonus as Sales and Profits Grow', *The Grocer*, 6 March. http://www.thegrocer.co.uk/channels/supermarkets/waitrose/waitrose-staff-get-15-bonus-as-sales-and-profits-grow/355179.article

Yoshikawa, T. and Gedajlovic, E.R. (2002), 'The Impact of Global Capital Market Exposure and Stable Ownership on Investor Relations, Practices and Performance of Japanese Firms', *Asia Pacific Journal of Management*, 19, 525–540.

Index

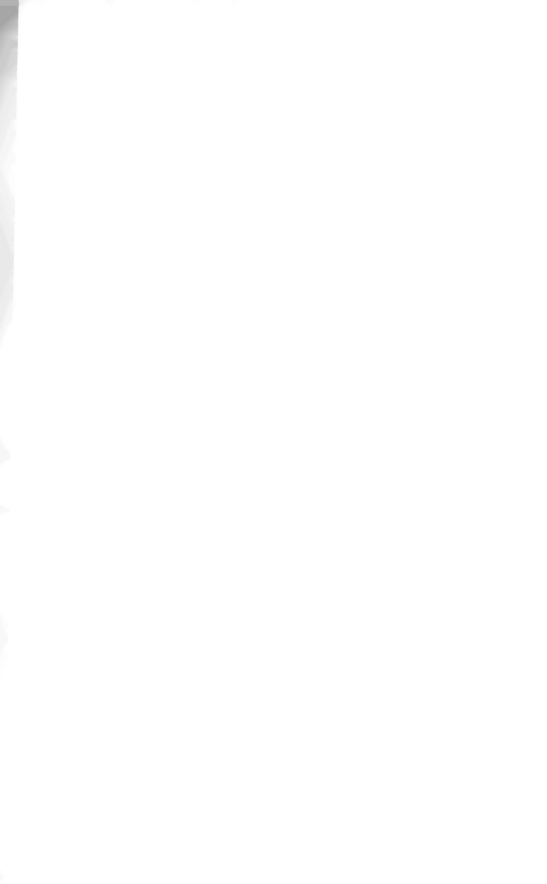